The HOUSE OF INTELLECT

Other Books by Jacques Barzun

jacques barzun

The **HOUSE OF INTELLECT**

PERENNIAL ◼ CLASSICS

A hardcover edition of this book was published in 1959 by Harper & Brothers.

THE HOUSE OF INTELLECT. Copyright © 1959 by Jacques Barzun. Preface to the Perennial Classics edition copyright © 2002 by Jacques Barzun. All rights reserved. Printed in the United States of America. No part of this book may be used or reproduced in any manner whatsoever without written permission except in the case of brief quotations embodied in critical articles and reviews. For information address HarperCollins Publishers Inc., 10 East 53rd Street, New York, NY 10022.

HarperCollins books may be purchased for educational, business, or sales promotional use. For information please write: Special Markets Department, HarperCollins Publishers Inc., 10 East 53rd Street, New York, NY 10022.

First Harper Torchbook edition published 1961.

First Perennial Classics edition published 2002.
Perennial Classics are published by Perennial, an imprint of HarperCollins Publishers.

Library of Congress Cataloging-in-Publication Data

Barzun, Jacques.
    The house of intellect / Jacques Barzun.—1st Perennial
    Classics ed.
        p. cm.
    Originally published: New York : Harper & Brothers, 1959.
    Includes bibliographical references.
    ISBN 0-06-010230-6
    1. Learning and scholarship.   I. Title.

AZ221 .B3 2002
001.2—dc21
                                            2002074924

02 03 04 05 06 WB/RRD 10 9 8 7 6 5 4 3 2 1

Contents

Preface to the Perennial Classics Edition

◆◈◆

The reception of The House of Intellect *some 40 years ago is col-*ored in my memory by a string of incidents that have a bearing on its reissue, and that contain as well an element of comedy not apparent at first. From the start the reviewers and the public found that the thesis I set forth was persuasive, though naturally not all agreed on all points.

But closer to home—so to speak—in the academic world and its moneyed supporters, the response to the discussion of philanthropy—no other topic seemed to matter—was oddly mixed. I was at the time dean of faculties and provost of Columbia University and as such responsible for the budget and the programs of all its schools and departments. I gave the president, Grayson Kirk, a copy of my book, and he was appalled: 'If our alumni and donors—and the faculty—read you, it will be a disaster for us.' His tone was mild, but his panic showed through. He saw the stream of gifts drying up, which it was his responsibility to keep flowing.

I tried to comfort him by saying that 'family members' never read one's book. We were both wrong. The contingent in the humanities departments on the whole agreed with my ideas, but in the social and physical sciences I had but few supporters; the rest frowned and 'didn't know what I was getting at.' As for the chief alumni and donors, their silence was complete and dubiously reassuring.

Soon, word came from the foundations. Its executives and trustees formed a sizable club that met for luncheon once a month. I was invited to speak to them, presumably to defend what I had said about the adverse effects of their philanthropic work. I knew no more than three or four of the group and these not at all well. When the coffee was served I was introduced in a cool impartial way and I improvised in 25 minutes a summary of the points made in the book about what I called 'The Three Enemies of Intellect.' Then, with intentional ambiguity, I added that I was 'questionable.' But no questions came. Instead and to my surprise, a standing ovation.

Some time later, further expressions of opinion trickled in, from a couple of university trustees and one or two of our influential donors. They were not shocked or hostile to my account of the place and peril of Intellect in contemporary culture. It was, they said 'a new perspective.' I concluded that despite this see-sawing of judgments there was still, among these closely interested parties, and certainly in the public at large, an awareness of what Intellect was, and was for. The argument was only about its being or not being in danger, and if in danger, what the hostile forces could be said to be.

The situation today is greatly changed, as everybody will acknowledge. And I owe it solely to my thoughtful Harper editor, Hugh Van Dusen, that he saw the continuing relevance of what I had diagnosed half a century ago. It was he who called for the book's reissue. The truth is that Intellect has been pushed out of public view and public esteem; the House that shelters its many-sided action now stands all but abandoned, in a dilapidated neighborhood.

If this is so, the nature and role of Intellect need re-affirmation and the new shapes of the old aggressors need signalizing. For the first part of this double purpose, the opening chapters of this book suffice. For the second, it is enough to point here to a few states of mind and modes of action prominent in society today. Instances and events, vogues and turns of speech that show the temper of our time, the reader will easily think of without further detail.

The most obvious feature of the phase of civilization we are in is the flattening of the merit curve. It is almost level—a wobbly line. The demand for competence is weak. This is acknowledged in the cliché 'decline of standards,' which applies to every institution, from schooling to the professions and from manners to language. Error, often born of indifference, is accepted, indeed saluted, as a proof of 'being human.' The word 'elitism' has arisen to condemn any expression of desire for what is in any way high. All these attitudes are validated to the possessors by the conviction that to display and act upon them is 'democratic.'

Clearly, every impulse behind this general surrender is inimical to Intellect, since it is mind disciplined in specified ways to overcome Difficulty. This discipline implies things now abhorred—rigor, power, authority, superiority.

Now, in what ways can art, science, and philanthropy, which I named as Intellect's three enemies, have brought about the widespread self-assurance of 'Not to worry—anything goes' so complacently accepted? Obviously, the three influences cited as menaces carried within them no such intention, nor did they act on Intellect directly, but through side effects.

Literature and the arts ever since the First World War may be said to have specialized in pastiche, parody, and destruction by caricature. Making fun of everything on the one hand, and depicting man and nature in endless distortions (horror, cruelty in the novel) inevitably undermined the will to control and achieve. The double lesson taught to the spirit has been: 'Nothing is worth the effort' and 'viciousness is all.' In the visual arts—in anti-art, found art, disposable art, minimalist art; in museum 'installations' and other varieties of exhibited work—the dominant purpose is bare design, absence of idea. In such a world, Intellect is stuffy, passé—'out of sync.'

The work of science has remained, thanks to its rigid ways and

tests, serious and productive. Its findings have been useful in pro-
longing life and creating conveniences to ease daily tasks. At the
same time, it has taught the world to judge by numbers and think
of human beings and behavior as mechanical. Whether the aim
is to test achievement in school and college or to choose the
announcers of television news, the numbers decide—often dubious
numbers, like those used to gauge every few weeks the business
health of corporations or the will of the people about political candidates and foreign policy. Contrary to the verdict of Intellect,
which may include numbers when they are of things truly counted,
the voice of the bottom line marks the low point of human responsibility.

On some minds too, the theoretical reports of science tend in
the same direction as the offerings of art: not only has physics ceased
to be graspable by the educated, but the ultimate account of the
universe of matter raises doubt about the very notion of reality. And
in any case, the meaning of the equations has reached a state that
defies translation into human speech. Intellect can but shrink back
discomfited.

Lastly, philanthropy or good will, has run in parallel with the
'democratic' relaxation—necessarily so, since charity by definition
goes out to all without regard to merit, station, origin or any other
criterion. Nobody can quarrel with the relief thus brought to suffering human beings by the numberless private charities and the welfare state or with the positive help given to the striving young by the
same agencies. But this desirable result does not alter the fact that it,
too, has side effects. It makes for less attention to quality, weaker
expectations from mind and will, habitual resistance to judgment—
and a flood of half-talents disgruntled by half success.

These traits have been most conspicuous in the school, now
acknowledged as an institution in decay. The wish not to humiliate
the child that prevents the teacher from correcting or punishing; the
practice of promoting both passing and failing pupils to the next
grade; and the giving to those who have attended but do not finish

high school a 'certificate of achievement' have been philanthropic gestures productive of an ever greater number of illiterates.

A similar negation of learning has afflicted higher education. A surfeit of courses but no curriculum, inflated grades, and the offering of subjects from 'the real world': 'programming for television,' jewelry, photography, or the ins-and-outs of current social rights and wrongs—these subjects possibly enhance the attraction of four years in college, but the product of so much time, effort, and money is at best a half-education. Intellect or the power to build one is not in sight.

To conclude from these observations about the fate of the House would be as premature now as it would have been at the time these pages were first written. It is no part of the cultural critic's role to prophesy. But it is part of his duty at any time to remind the world of the valuable things that are at risk. Even if the warning evokes no alteration in the present, it can happen that such a reminder in an easy-drifting age stands out as a marker a later age will use for the return voyage.

May 1, 2002

Note to the Reader

❦

It is deliberately that I have given this book the comprehensive title of *The House of Intellect* and omitted any modifier such as "in America." For the description I have undertaken applies not solely to America but to the entire Western world, and indeed to any nation that adopts egalitarian democracy, mass education and journalism, the cult of art and philanthropy, and the manners coincident with these. If, therefore, the examples in this book are chiefly drawn from the life of the United States, the reason is not alone convenience or unity of tone; it is rather that in this country the first, or the most massive, illustrations of certain generalities are to be found. Foreign readers of these examples and American readers of the foreign press will readily supply parallels from other countries, and convince themselves of the sameness I discern in the conditions now governing Intellect.

I would also ask the reader to remember that in a critical description of this sort only examples of the best have any probative value. And by the best I mean the most developed, the most serious, the most highly regarded efforts in any relevant kind. The worst, and even the mediocre, must be taken for granted as a cultural constant.

It is waste of time to belabor shady schools, corrupt journals, stupid government officials, and unscrupulous exploiters of the eternally gullible. The ignorance of the unlettered takes no scrutiny to establish. What we need to plumb is the ignorance of the educated and the anti-intellectualism of the intellectual. What matters to a nation is whether the best product, or in certain cases the high average, which prides itself on excellence, deserves its reputation. In these pages, then, all descriptions and criticism are of the best examples that would define a category: the institutions examined are worthy of remark and, in some ways, of esteem; and all references to groups have in view the educated, or at least the college-bred, whose words and acts imply a claim or a duty related to Intellect.

J. B.

The HOUSE OF INTELLECT

I

◈

The Three Enemies
of Intellect

As we use them today, the words 'intellectual' and 'anti-intellectual'
are scarcely more than sixty years old. Their continual use, in praise
and blame, goes back to the Dreyfus Affair* and points to the coming of age of the first generation taught under the free-education
acts and penny press of the seventies. Men who are thirty today
belong to the third generation so brought up, and, if intellectual,
bemoan their fate. Misfortune—they feel—degradation, has overtaken the mind in western civilization. They blame capitalism, liberalism, the machine, the masses—everything outside themselves, and
thus attain the desired status of victim. The beleaguered intellectual—it is a badge and a position in life.

---

*The modern English usage is derived form, or at least strongly influenced
by, the French. In English, 'intellectual' as a singular or plural noun originally meant the mind—'crazed [i.e., cracked] in his intellectuals.' In the
meaning of 'an intellectual being' the Oxford dictionary gives no instance
between 1652 and 1813, when Byron used it in his diary, and again none
until 1884. It becomes current in that sense in the late nineties, usually with
a derogatory intent: 'the so-called intellectuals of Constantinople, who were
engaged in discussion while the Turks were taking the city.' *Daily News*,
London, November 30, 1898.

The position is unexpectedly comfortable because, contradicting all the charges of anti-intellectualism and neglect of 'intellectual values' by a 'materialistic society,' is the plain fact of the intellectual's unprecedented share of public trust. The expert, the Ph.D. or his equivalent, is everywhere—in government, industry, labor unions, banking, philanthropy, city planning, written and spoken journalism, espionage, national leadership and international councils—as well as in the hobby that makes the whole world kin, preparing for war.

To understand our situation, this paradox must be kept whole. Both halves are true. Intellect is despised and neglected. Intellectuals are well paid and riding high. We may be able to reconcile the conflicting pair of truths when we notice the slippage from 'Intellect' to 'intellectuals' and look into the source of the complaints. Who makes these complaints? Intellectuals, naturally. What are their grievances directed against? Institutions manned or led by intellectuals. Though it is assumed that some giant abstraction causes the particular evils—'commercialism' or 'power politics' or 'mass culture'—the recrimination begins and ends with the intellectuals themselves. It is they who find one another corrupt and unsatisfactory. The name 'intellectual' itself they use with pride or derision, depending on the extent to which their ideas are 'advanced.' Thus *Partisan Review* is 'intellectual' and *Life* magazine is not, though both designations manage to give comfort to each side.*

By the detached observer the two periodicals must indeed be called intellectual products, from which it follows that the intellectuals' chief cause of anguish are one another's works. The intellectuals do not attack bars and bowling alleys, or Tammany Hall and the chemical trust; they attack the philosophy of John Dewey and the State Department's policy on modern art. The humanists inveigh against science, and the scientists decry 'vague inspirational subjects.' The intelligent intellectuals who read or write for *The New*

---

*In army camps during the last war *Life* was considered a highbrow magazine by the majority, for whom the principal reading matter apart from newspapers was the so-called comic books.

Yorker and are strong on civil liberties weekly ridicule 'the legal mind at work'; while everywhere that ironic form of reference, 'the professor,' is heard not among farmers and workingmen, but among intellectuals who profess something else than learning.

Nor does this war of words betray only the ordinary struggle for prestige. The complaints are in part disinterested; the criticism is just; the contempt is hard to resist. There *is* a degradation of Intellect. It is in the moment of success that it feels its powers failing.

This paradox is not resolved by pointing to the split between some ideal of Intellect and the sordid reality of aching intellectual groups. The groups and their relations must be described, the causes and effects of their divisions ascertained, and further paradoxes disclosed. But first we need a clear idea of what is properly meant by Intellect.

What most people think of when Intellect is discussed as a social force seems to be an echo of conventional history (Athens, the thirteenth century, the Renaissance), eked out with notions drawn from religion or science, or from reactionary and revolutionary utopias. To remove these images and replace them with more tenable ones is difficult, because the clichés have for so long served the contemporary intellect as a quite satisfactory means of attack or defense.* The attempt to do without them must seem perverse and the appeal to common experience trivial. Yet personal testimony and illustrations from the unregarded in life are in fact the only evidences relevant to fresh inquiry.

That part of the world I call the House of Intellect embraces at least three groups of subjects: the persons who consciously and methodically employ the mind; the forms and habits governing the activities

---

*In order to make clear the ideas and words that seem to me disputable or false or empty, though generally they seem legitimate and respectable, I shall use—and perhaps abuse—the privilege of putting them repeatedly in quotation marks, though to lessen the possible irritation that this might cause I shall follow the English practice of using single marks as the principal ones and double ones within.

in which the mind is so employed; and the conditions under which these people and activities exist. There is an important reason for not calling this domain more simply the House of Mind. Mind is properly equated with intelligence, and by Intellect I most emphatically do not mean intelligence. Intellect is at once more and less than Mind. The House of Mind may turn out to be as large as the universe; to treat of it would require dealing with the mental prowess of apes and bees and, for all I know, of fishes and flowers. Mind or intelligence is widely distributed and serves an infinity of purposes.

We ought, parenthetically, to remember this when the United States is assailed, from within or without, as a nation lacking in Mind and hostile to it. We have in fact intelligence in plenty and we use it perhaps more widely than other nations, for we apply it with praiseworthy innocence to parts of life elsewhere ruled by custom or routine.* We like ideas, new ideas especially, and we drive a brisk trade in them: the quickest way to get three Americans to travel a thousand miles is to propose an exchange of ideas. And there is reason to believe that this restless searching is becoming a habit the world over.

The modern educated democrat, then, is not anti-intellectual in the sense of shunning novelty or undervaluing intelligence. The truer and more serious charge is that he neglects or resists or shies away from one form of intelligence, which is Intellect. And this we see with peculiar vividness in the United States where, precisely, customs and routines do not mask the defect: it is for lack of Intellect that we have such a hard time judging persons and ideas; it is absence of Intellect that makes us so frightened of criticism and so inept at conversation; it is disregard of Intellect that has brought our school system to its present ridiculous paralysis. In any large collective enterprise, such as the production of rockets and satellites, it is dearth of Intellect—not of intelligence—that aggravates the normal causes of friction and slows down accomplishment.

What then is this rare lubricant and propellant that we lack? Intellect is the capitalized and communal form of live intelligence; it

---

*For instance, in the refined organization of all forms of work and play.

is intelligence stored up and made into habits of discipline, signs and symbols of meaning, chains of reasoning and spurs to emotion—a shorthand and a wireless by which the mind can skip connectives, recognize ability, and communicate truth. Intellect is at once a body of common knowledge and the channels through which the right particle of it can be brought to bear quickly, without the effort of redemonstration, on the matter in hand.

Intellect is community property and can be handed down. We all know what we mean by an intellectual tradition, localized here or there; but we do not speak of a 'tradition of intelligence,' for intelligence sprouts where it will and is spent day by day like income for incessant needs. Intelligence is the native ability of the creature to achieve its ends by varying the use of its powers—living, as we say, by its wits. Accordingly, we can distinguish the intelligent from the stupid throughout the scale of sentient beings: an intelligent, but not intellectual, dog or child; an intellectual, but not intelligent, bluestocking or university professor. Intelligence is by definition the protean faculty. We find it in a political move or in a work of art, in the performance of a football team or in a piece of repartee, none of which are specifically intellectual. And though Intellect neither implies nor precludes intelligence, two of its uses are—to make up for the lack of intelligence and to amplify the force of it by giving it quick recognition and apt embodiment.

For intelligence wherever found is an individual and private possession; it dies with the owner unless he embodies it in more or less lasting form. Intellect is on the contrary a product of social effort and an acquirement. A man cannot help being intelligent, but he can easily help becoming intellectual. Intellect is an institution; it stands up as it were by itself, apart from the possessors of intelligence, even though they alone could rebuild it if it should be destroyed.

That is why I have used the image of a house. I would speak of the *realm* of mind—limitless and untamed—but I say the House of Intellect, because it is an establishment, requiring appurtenances and prescribing conventions. The distinction becomes unmistakable if one thinks of the alphabet—a product of successive acts of intelligence which, when completed, turned into one of the indispensable furnishings of the House of Intellect. To learn the alphabet calls for no great intelligence: millions learn it who could never have invented it; just as millions of intelligent people have lived and died without learning it—for example, Charlemagne.

The alphabet is a fundamental form to bear in mind while discussing the decay of Intellect, because intellectual work as here defined presupposes the concentration and continuity, the self-awareness and articulate precision, which can only be achieved through some firm record of fluent thought; that is, Intellect presupposes Literacy.

But it soon needs more. Being by definition self-aware, Intellect creates linguistic and other conventions, it multiplies places and means of communication, it seeks relief from other duties, such as fighting and tilling the soil—in short, it needs a house, with house rules and an income for its upkeep.

The need for rules is a point of difficulty for those who, wrongly equating Intellect with intelligence, balk at the mere mention of forms and constraints—fetters, as they think, on the 'free mind' for whose sake they are quick to feel indignant, while they associate everything dull and retrograde with the word 'convention.' Here again the alphabet is suggestive: it is a device of limitless and therefore 'free' application. You can combine its elements in millions of ways to refer to an infinity of things in hundreds of tongues, including the mathematical. But its order and its shapes are rigid. You cannot look up the simplest word in any dictionary, you cannot work with books or in a laboratory, you cannot find your friend's telephone number, unless you know the letters in their arbitrary forms and conventional order.

From the image of a house and its economy, one can see what an inquiry into the institution of Intellect must include. The main topics are: the state of the language, the system of schooling, the means and objects of communication, the supplies of money for thought and learning, and the code of feeling and conduct that goes with them. When the general tendency of these arrangements makes for order, logic, clarity, and speed of communication, one may say that a tradition of Intellect exists.

Now, let us for a moment call this whole apparatus Literacy, and remember that it rests upon the alphabet, or literacy with a small 'l.' The striking fact then breaks in on us that in the history of the West there was no 'problem of Intellect' so long as literacy was scarce. Before the promise of universal free schooling that was given by the French Revolution, there was no talk of anti-intellectualism and cultural crisis, of 'disinherited minds' and alienation from 'materialistic society.' Everybody had known since Saint Augustine, if not since Hammurabi, that materialistic was what society inevitably is. 'Intellectual' remained a quiet, undemonstrative adjective, used with democratic impartiality and without pride or derision.*

Today, the 'plight of the intellectual' is, throughout the West, an accepted truth like the rotation of the earth. Except in new nations where intellectuals engage, freely or not, in politics and state service, the chief subject of intellectual discussion is the futility of Intellect. Yet literacy spreads, and it is a swelling number of intellectuals that bewails the decline of Intellect. The falling off is said to result ultimately from democracy and industry, which are accordingly denounced, with not a murmur from demos or the industrialists. On the contrary, the shortest way to popularity is to keep up a verbal war against the social order, an order which is in fact the result of intellectual emancipation through extended literacy.†

If you ask an intellectual how modern society causes his distress,

*Since we saw that the modern use of the term to describe a person or social class has French origins, it is interesting to note that Littré does not list it either in his *Dictionnaire* of 1885 or in his *Supplément* of 1886.
†To gauge the extent of the emancipation, compare the testimony of Francis Place in 1835: '[Formerly] the prejudice against a man having a book was very great. In my own case, even in 1812, I lost as many customers as paid me for the goods they had to the amount of £500 a year, on a gentleman discovering that I had a room full of books.' *Parliamentary Papers*, Select Committee on Education, 1835, VII, 69:796.

he will probably cite as a self-evident truth the anti-intellectualism of a commercial civilization. He is not likely to explain why older commercial societies, from Greece onward, seem to him more favorable to Intellect, or how he is able to conceive of civilization without trade. The truth is that commercialism is not per se the enemy of intellect, but something much deeper. The hostility of the common man toward the intellectual is of all times and places.* It is an understandable animus related to the herd instinct and probably latent in every man. The great symbol of martyred Intellect, Socrates, was a victim of the same spontaneous resentment which makes the majority at school gang up on the bookish boy—or at least pretend that regular fellows despise study and prove their mettle by any means except the systematic use of mind.

This sentiment is so universal that anyone who sets himself against it soon knows that he is trying to resist a force of nature. Yet although this natural opposition to intellectual beings has dealt them injuries, it has never by itself kept down Intellect. Indeed, if we look further into this primal anti-intellectualism, we find that it enshrines a true perception and an impulse of respect. The perception is that, like all artifacts, Intellect is the enemy of life. This may be what the schoolboy has an inkling of: spontaneity is checked, strength tamed, where Intellect rules. It is enough that intellectual work enforces sedentary habits—that Intellect shuns the outdoors to coop itself up in a house—to suggest an antagonism between it and the free exercise of the body that seems to typify life. Nor is this equation a denial of *intelligence,* for as we saw, intelligence is compatible with every kind of life: with athletic or martial skill, with adventure, fantasy, and art, with wresting a livelihood directly from nature. These very images make Intellect look by contrast like the unfailing damper of animal spirits—a wet blanket as wide as the sky.

But animal energy is only one threat. Intellect is also hated

---

*Scholars believe they see signs of it in ancient Egypt about 2000 B.C. See T. Eric Peet, *Comparative Study of the Literatures of Egypt, Palestine and Mesopotamia*, London, 1931, 101.

because it is envied, and envied because it is felt as a sign or pretense of social superiority. From below, on sketchy evidence, Intellect is readily associated with aristocracy and power. We should therefore expect that in an age of egalitarian democracy anti-intellectualism would increase, for everyone now has the right to resent whatever looks like privilege and eminence.

And it turns out at the same time that Intellect has lost the great secret of its power, which was literacy. Nearly everyone can read and write or feels on the verge of doing so; everyone has access to the treasures of the Intellect hoarded in libraries and museums; everyone is urged to pass into the House of Intellect through the pathway of education, which has been smoothed and greased till it resembles the *facilis descensus Averno*. The feeling of mystery and awe having departed from learning, the feeling of resentment redoubles and strikes at anyone who asserts that Intellect retains inherent power, or who is even suspected—from his speech, his bearing, or the look on his face—of harboring such a thought.

The old, fitful, embarrassed anti-intellectualism, though made worse by 'equality,' is not, then, the true cause of the misery avowed by modern intellectuals; nor are the sporadic manifestations of hostility toward them the most important effect of changed social relations under an industrial democracy. For if naïve anti-intellectualism cannot be abolished, it can be fought, and the fight can be invigorating. The truth is that Intellect can be diminished in its own eyes only with its own consent; its troubles become obsessions, its presence a canker, only from within: the real disaster haunting the intellectual today is that the alienation, the disinheriting, the loss of authority have occurred, not between the intellectuals and the rest—the commercial rump—of society, but among the intellectuals themselves and as a result of their own acts. As will appear again and again, they have abdicated but live on, self-exiled. Hence the mutual recriminations, the contempt for life, and the search for scapegoats. Intellectuals speak of alienation because it suggests a casting out by the people; but the intellectual class of Western civilization had never been close to the untutored mass, and at worst the mass remains as indifferent as before. Intellectuals speak of their lost prestige and authority, but they had rarely been more than servants to those in power. We have only to consult tables of precedence to discover their place in a preindustrial society:

'One hundred and ninety-thirdly [and lastly] Professional Gentlemen, as: solicitors, attorneys, proctors, engineers, architects, medical practitioners, artists, literary men, merchants, master manufacturers, scientific professors, and others not engaged in manual labour, farming of land, or retail trade, are considered to possess some station in society, although the law takes no cognizance of their ranks *inter se.*'[1]*

Even when the Church supplied Intellect with a house and a prestige of its own, it lived there under the continual threat of the temporal power, which was wielded, inevitably, by illiterates and Philistines.† The painful loss newly felt by men of intellect in the last third of the nineteenth century, which artists took up as a theme in the first third of ours, and which promises to remain a lucrative cliché for an indefinite future, is thus no loss of an outward strength once granted as a due: it is an internal loss, the loss of one another and of a common idea. Externally, as I need hardly point out again, the status of the intellectual has risen well above the one-hundred-and-ninety-third place.

Divided against itself, the House of Intellect has lost the sense of being a company apart, associated perhaps fitfully with authority, yet comforted by a freemasonry of manners and speech; envied or scorned from above and below, yet justifying the envy and helped to

---

*Superior numbers refer to notes, which will be found in a group beginning on page 279.

†Exceptions were—exceptional: 'The Emperor Frederick II, for instance, was wont to sneer at King René of Sicily for his addiction to the arts, obliging that monarch to indulge his gift for painting in the privacy of his own closet. Learning was derided as a practice fit only for clerks and bearing no relation at all to knightly duties and accomplishments. Chaucer's squire was exceptional in knowing how to read and write.' Harold Nicolson, *Good Behaviour*, 1956, 113.

forget the scorn by qualities and powers it had earned and felt free to enjoy. When literacy drew a dividing line across society, all the initiates found more in common with one another than with any other group. Besides the diverse professional bonds, there existed a more inclusive one based on the two fundamental habits of reading books and being articulate. Priests, poets, scholars could address one another without false pride or false shame. This opportunity for conversation, unspoiled by the need of posturing before other groups, established an intellectual class, or as Coleridge happily named it on the eve of its disappearance—a clerisy.

In nineteenth-century England this class came as near as it has ever done to wielding direct political power, for it subdued to the intellectual life the men who were cabinet ministers, high civil servants, and editors of large newspapers. Read the diaries and letters of the leading men of Victoria's time and you will find what a varied community of talents flourished, bringing together Tennyson and Tyndall, Huxley and Manning, Bagehot and Clough, Spencer and George Eliot, Gladstone and Jowett, Matthew Arnold and Lady Rothschild. The Victorian Age has rightly been called the Golden Age of Intellect because of this remarkable fusion of interests and powers. Nowadays the amalgam is broken up; the bond between a labor leader and his Ph.D. consultant in economics is not between their intellects, but between the information on tap in the one and the vacuum it is to fill in the other.

For men have come to believe that they can link knowledge and action without a regular gradation of intellects to harbor and diffuse ideas, or a common concern about the welfare of Intellect as an institution. They trust to the exceeding fineness and particularity of the information stored in print and made foolproof by formulas. Yet at the very time when the sum of fact on all subjects begins to seem adequate to the demand, a silent panic overtakes both thinkers and doers: 'the problem of communication,' or Babel become an everyday experience.

That same abundance of information has turned into a barrier between one man and the next. They are mutually incommunicado, because each believes that his subject and his language cannot and should not be understood by the other. This is the vice which we weakly deplore as specialization. It is thought of, once again, as external and compelling, though it comes in fact from within, a tacit denial of Intellect. It is a denial because it rests on the superstition that understanding is identical with professional skill. The universal formula is: 'You cannot understand or appreciate my art (science) (trade) unless you yourself practice it.'

This error is briskly propagated by the schools, in the name of scholarship and with genuflections before the menacing heap of knowledge, of which no man can appropriate more than a little. We forget that every age has carried with it great loads of information, most of it false or tautological, yet deemed indispensable at the time. Of true knowledge at any time, a good part is merely convenient, necessary indeed to the worker, but not to an understanding of his subject: one can judge a building without knowing where to buy the bricks; one can understand a violin sonata without knowing how to score for the instrument. The work may in fact be better understood *without* a knowledge of the details of its manufacture, for attention to these tends to distract from meaning and effect.

Even if one sets apart those arts and sciences that require special preparation, there remains a large field to which Intellect has access in its own right. With a cautious confidence and sufficient intellectual training, it is possible to master the literature of a subject and gain a proper understanding of it: specifically, an understanding of the accepted truths, the disputed problems, the rival schools, and the methods now in favor. This will not enable one to add to what is known, but it will give possession of *all that the discipline has to offer the world*. The professional's fallacy, in short, is to make no distinction between knowing the subject and knowing the craft. To be ignorant of what is ancillary, of the scaffolding knowledge of an art or profession, is certainly the mark of the 'outsider,' but by cherishing the doctrine of inside and outside we have split the clerisy without noticeably improving the arts.

Still worse, this illusion about the extent of knowledge and this vainglory about professionalism have destroyed the intellectual audience. Though millions have literacy and hundreds of thousands have 'education,' plus the rudiments of a profession, it becomes harder and harder to find the few tens of thousands who are willing, let alone eager, to attend to intellectual matters.

These ways of denying Intellect give us a foretaste of the utter defeatism which, as we shall see in the next chapter, governs the molders of opinion. Their motive resembles modesty; they profess wide ignorance around their island of knowledge; actually, this hides a desire for distinction. The man who denies that his subject has principles communicable to any receptive intellect, and who says, 'Hands Off! Unless you belong to my profession or will join it, you are nothing to me,' is convinced that the world is divided into the many who know nothing about his specialty and the happy few who know everything. To keep the strain pure, these last require of the newcomer a total allegiance. It thus comes about that the majority of workers in the arts and sciences act like jealous technicians with a strong anti-intellectual bias. It is as if the guild spirit, which is the spirit of trade, had infected the declared enemies of commercialism.

Continuing our tour of the divided House, we come upon a third and final contradiction. It is this: while the scuttling of Intellect has been going on, the dissemination of its products has become a planetary frenzy. It was reserved for our age to see scholarship, science, and art expensively displayed through the loudest means of communication, while an angry chorus of thinkers and artists proclaims the new barbarism.

The facts that call forth these imprecations are familiar: the daily and weekly press enlarging its conception of journalism and taking on the task of encyclopedic popularization; the new industries of musical and pictorial reproduction thrusting down the throats of the multitude not merely the masterpieces of the past, but also their retinue of historical information; the electronic mass media making it their hobby to scatter the small change of scholarship about innumerable subjects. This fever of learning breaks out on the screen as technical jargon and quiz programs, while in the press, the imitation of 'method' inspires graphs, statistics, and scholarly footnotes. One incessantly hears the phrase 'and I quote . . . ,' but few recognize in it the symbol of a cultural revolution.

It is a revolution, and without an end in sight. Consider, for example, what happened on September 23, 1957. According to the *Times,* every bookstore in New York was raided for copies of Stendhal's *The Red and the Black*—raided, not by the police, but by television viewers who had been assigned the book as the first reading in an early morning broadcast called *'Sunrise Semester.'* Here was a marvelous but difficult, inhospitable book being scrambled for in utter ignorance of its contents. The publisher, who in my time has twice dropped it from the Modern Library for lack of buyers, now sends out advertising copies labeled 'Collector's Item.' The ultimate effect is beyond our ken. The point is that dissemination creates demand, and the demand for Intellect—its substance or shadow— appears insatiable.

Under the same moral pressure of the time, every large private collection of books or other valuables of learning is expected sooner or later to become public property. In answer to that craving, our century saw what is perhaps the most astounding spectacle in history—certainly in military history: the armies of the world waging war, each burdened with a corps of art historians for the preservation and classification of *objets d'art,* these same treasures having nearly everywhere been buried at great cost in special shelters. Anyone looking down from Mars would say that our civilization had lost its mind to art and intellect.

But the earth-dwelling artist raises his voice to decry the whole effort as frivolous antiquarianism. He wants support for creation instead of diffusion and protection. He makes clear that regard for the works of the dead does no good to him, who is living, or rather starving, and that if our age wants a good name hereafter, it must give him the means to create. His plea has merit, but the difficulties of his position are not identical with the predicament of Intellect.

Rather, his troubles aggravate the predicament by aligning him, in the name of 'creation,' against 'mere intellectuality.'

In this civil war between art and intellect, numbers and passion are on the side of art. A strong party wants government support for it, as a national concern, and not just as a medium of propaganda. The private foundations develop *tic douloureux* trying to do their manifold duty to creativeness, while the help given by groups and individuals to anybody who shows the slightest capacity for self-expression is touching and tremendous. This is not to say that every artist thrives, but only that no other age has even dreamed of anything like this open-handedness. We are driven to it by our guilty knowledge of history: mindful of ruthless neglect in the past, we worry about the young and the unknown, the handicapped and the hopelessly striving. For them, as much as for the mature and valiant, we organize workshops, bookshelves, exhibits, festivals, fellowships, prizes, courses, camps, colonies, hospital wards, and mobile units, trusting that these will assist the fertile mind in its parturition. Amateurs are coddled into artistry, children stimulated by early acclaim, and in London a chimpanzee has had the first one-ape show.[2] The word 'creative' is so much in honor that it is the clinching term of approval from the schoolroom to the advertiser's studio.* And the quality it denotes is democratically assumed to lie latent in every bosom, only waiting for one of the opportunities we lavishly devise.

· · ·

*Here is a sampling of that approval:

The educator: 'A Report to the Faculties on Research and Creative Thought at Wayne State University for 1957–58.'

The artist: 'The Conductor is Also a Creator,' Milton Katims in *The International Musician*, September 1958, 10.

The physician: '*Beyond Freud: A Creative Approach to Mental Health*, by Camilla M. Anderson, M.D., New York, 1957.'

The bookseller: 'How to Free Yourself From Hours of Drudgery and Give Yourself Time for Creative Work,' Columbia University Press circular, November 1958.

The advertiser: 'Advertising Strategy: The Creative Man—Don't Fence Him In!' Charles W. Hoyt Company in *The New York Times*, June 16, 1958.

Yet all this, far from satisfying our contemporary artists, leaves most of them angered and gloomy amid the orgiastic dispersal of their works. As a result, artists are today the most persistent denouncers of Western civilization; and their lay following zealously presses the indictment. Beside theirs, the political animus against society seems tame. This is something new, in form as well as spirit. For the artistic outcry tends to be vague, abstract, and often absurd. It affects to despise materialism and the world of trade, but the ground of attack is that trade gives artists too little material reward. Being intellectually feeble, these complaints cannot lead to action; they merely poison the air and the lives of those that breathe it.

This autointoxication, which contributes to the modern intellectual's sense of martyrdom, is linked with another social change that has stolen upon us unregarded—the recent education of the artist to the ways of Intellect. In itself, art can exist without learning and, in a sense, without reason. Painters, sculptors, musicians, actors, dancers, even poets and playwrights, resemble engineers and physical scientists in that they can follow modes of thought quite other than those of discursive intellect; some scarcely need literacy, as history proves; and they certainly have no obligation to traffic in established ideas. Some of the greatest have in fact been virtually inarticulate—to cite examples at random: Schubert, Daumier, George Stephenson, Ghiberti.

During the last century, the current has been reversed; artists of every kind have become men of words and ideas, bent on joining the Great Conversation. In youth, they no longer resist a liberal arts training; later, they accept academic posts, they set up as critics and social philosophers, they are caught—sometimes ridden—by political and other systems. This was notable in the Marxist decade and it still is so in the so-called religious revival of today. And now the artists have been joined by an increasing group of natural scientists, late-awakened by the noise of an explosion. In both groups, talent, education, and a fresh appetite for ideas produce an effervescence which has the coloring, though not always the substance, of Intellect.

Nor has the rapprochement been from one side only. The artist turning toward ideas has been met halfway by a public turning aside from words and greedy for speechless art. The new pastimes of the educated amateur are the arts of nonarticulate expression: music and painting. While fiction languishes and the theater is in the doldrums, ballet has risen to popularity, Sunday painting is fashionable, and chamber music thrives. Everywhere picture and sound crowd out text. The Word is in disfavor, not to say in disrepute—which is indeed one way of abolishing the problem of communication.

Nor should we be surprised: This shift in taste has been gathering momentum for three generations. From the Symbolist period on, Western art has been based on the repudiation of what is common—common speech, common life, common knowledge—and its replacement by the singular and indefinable. Excellent reasons can be shown for the choice, and the right of artists to do as they see fit is not here in question. But neither is the effect in doubt, for art has never been so quick and potent in its influence: the revulsion from words, syntax, and coherence accounts for the widespread anarchy in the handling of the mother tongue, as well as the now normal preference for the abnormal in our conceptions of the real. Whereas the 'experimental' in art used to take a generation to be recognized, now we encounter the latest modernisms overnight in the work of the commercial artist and the writer of advertising copy. The public approves and encourages, having learned to swallow and even to enjoy what shocks feeling and defies reason.*

Subtler, but equally strong, has been the result of what we pedantically call 'aesthetic experience.' For many people art, displacing religion, has become the justification of life, whether as the saving grace of an ugly civilization or as the pattern of the only noble career. In sustaining this role, art has put a premium on qualities of

---

*A trade magazine advises professional writers to make use of:
1. *Clever wackiness*; 2. *Exotic, quaint, or off-beat characters*; and 3. *Fresh and unusual props for showing characters*. Follows an example showing the hero's just resentment of his fiancée's mother by the 'symbolic' act of drowning a monkey. *The Writer*, 71:7, 1958, 14.

perception which are indeed of the mind, but which ultimately war against Intellect. The cant words of modern criticism suggest what these qualities are: *ambiguity, sensibility, insight, imagination, sensitive, creative, irony.* All these, in art, declare the undesirability, perhaps the impossibility, of articulate precision and thus defy, counteract, or degrade the chief virtue of Intellect.

The bearing of this observation must itself be understood precisely: there is a difference between the artist and the refugees from life who hide their nakedness in artistic toggery; there is a parallel difference between criticism which is the gateway of understanding and that which is a substitute for artistic work. I do not depart here from my lifelong conviction that art is miraculously precise and communicative in its own domain of fused spirit and sensation. It awakens knowledge of a kind no other means can reach. But that kind is not the only kind, and the means that art uses are always less than explicit. This is the root of the distinction between poetry and prose, between painting and illustration; between narrative or dialogue that 'shows' and the kind that merely 'tells'; in short between Meaning and Information. And the point here is that explicitness in the mode of prose is also desirable: thanks to it, Intellect can steadily pursue one of its great tasks, which is to refine and enlarge the common language for ideas.

Now a devotion to art does not preclude being articulate in this mode, but an *exclusive* devotion, except in a professional, is almost surely hostile to Intellect. For cultivating art out of fear or spite means preferring always what is ambiguous, what touches only the sensibility, what titillates through irony, what plunges the imagination into a sea of symbols, echoes, and myths, from which insights may be brought up to the surface but no arguable views. And this preference is at bottom love of confusion—confusion sought as a release from responsibility. The purest emotions of the aesthetic quest, it is said, are private; one partakes only after illumination, as formerly after mystical conversion. And it is true that the unique messages of poetry, music, painting, and serious fiction refuse to be decanted into common prose. When this is said in contempt of all other uses of the mind, it amounts to a denial of Intellect's declarative powers and social obligations.

That contempt and denial modern artists have not troubled to conceal. 'Every day,' said Proust in the opening sentence of his manifesto *Contre Sainte-Beuve*, 'I set less store by the intellect.' Today, after eighty years or more of this open war, most educated men and women have been persuaded that all the works of man's mind except art are vulgar frauds: law, the state, machinery, the edifice of trade, are worthless. More, men and women feel that they themselves are worthless, they despise their own existence, because it fails in loveliness when compared with the meanest *objet d'art*. The abandonment of Intellect in favor of communion through quartet playing and amateur ceramics has bred a race of masochist-idolaters, broken up into many sects, but at one in their worship of the torturing indefinite.

I dwell at this length on the influence of art upon the intellectual life of today because it is all-pervasive. A member of the educated class nowadays need not have any direct or vivid contact with art to fall under the sway of the aesthetical creed and its emotions. He feels about life, business, society, the Western world, what the art-inspired critics of the last eighty years have felt, and he speaks the phrases appropriate to his borrowed disgust. He may be a minor foundation official living rather comfortably on the earnings of some dead tycoon, but he talks like Baudelaire. Indeed, the attitudes I describe are no longer confined to those engaged in intellectual or semi-intellectual occupations. They have touched the wider public whose exposure to ideas is through the press, where readers find reflected not only the worship of art but also its attendant contempt of the world, both alike taken for granted as the natural response of any intelligent and 'sensitive' modern. A deep unconscious anti-intellectualism thus comes to be the natural adjunct of any degree of literacy and culture; and this at the very time when new social groups, fresh from the educational mills and thoroughly aestheticized, think of themselves as intellectuals and mean to live as artists.

But, it may be asked, is there not a great intellectual force, still more powerful than art and working against it, namely, the force of science? Science is exact, science is strict, science is influential—especially in the press where art must compete with it for attention. Why should Intellect be at the mercy of art?

The question is pertinent, and the answer not encouraging. For despite their differences, science and art have reenforced each other's effect. Through the increasing fantasy of its concepts and symbols, through its diverging technical tongues, science has also receded from the common world. Science too has helped to break up the unity of knowledge. In the name of untrammeled inquiry, scientists have planted citadels throughout the realm of mind, but have taken no thought of the means of intellectual exchange among them. The House of Intellect is lost somewhere in this no man's land. When scientists talk, as they sometimes do, about their supposedly common enterprise, they take one of two contrary views and sometimes both together. One is that science is radically unlike any other intellectual pursuit—in method, language, and type of mind. Science is numerical, objective, certain; nothing else is—as we imply in the common use of 'unscientific.' The second or 'enlightened' view is that the scientist's work is essentially akin to that of the poet. It relies on inspiration and a god-given power to handle symbols 'creatively.'

In spite of this second interpretation—a further tribute to aesthetic propaganda—and in spite of the influence of scientific jargon on common thought, the natural sciences and their practitioners continue to form a world apart. When their representatives meet with those of other branches of learning, the verbal deference does not signify much sympathy. The clans soon re-form and on each side the sense of apprehensive loneliness returns. What will 'they' be doing next? The question is charged with the promise of money and power. Is the public on 'our' side or theirs? I have myself heard scientists speak of a 'conspiracy of the humanities' to blacken science in general opinion, restrict research, and 'reverse the trend of modern progress.' What literary men say of the scientists, chaste ears ought to be spared.

When science won its place in academic and general opinion a century ago, the mutual hostility was perhaps justified, because the claims on each side were extravagant. But there has been ample opportunity since then to codify and make known the ways in which the knowledge of nature is like and unlike the knowledge of spirit. The visitor from Mars would surely suppose that these truths formed part of our elementary curriculum, a *pons asinorum* for all who make the least pretense to the life of the intellect. As things stand, the best that common knowledge can show is a pair of dull clichés about music being somehow related to mathematics, and poetry being 'in its way' as exact as science; but the how and the way are left prudently in the dark.

And this aloofness of the scientists has been seconded by their opponents' ambition. As we shall see more fully later, the remnants of common intelligibility in their work disturb a good many nonscientists and spur them to achieve a scientific separateness. Why can *their* subjects not be rendered esoteric by special terminology and the use of numbers? Scholars, we saw, have improved the art of recognizing fewer and fewer peers, and many think they can do still better by imitating science. Indeed, some artists have also been seduced by science even while blaming it for their ills. In both groups, the imitation begins with externals—a pompous jargon, an affectation of method and rigor, and often also the pose of Truth's martyr crucified.

The motives here are obviously mixed, but among them is a desire for authority, which is not in itself unworthy: the mind should respect what the mind has brought forth and the truth is known by signs: let us multiply the signs of genuine knowledge and increase the respect owed to truth. But in so arguing, the imitators of physical science overlook the fact that every shrinking of the common ground of Intellect lessens the authority of each fragment. I am not speaking here of authority over the unlettered, but of authority among the educated, to whom it matters or should matter that intellectual authority is now dispersed and tenuous. They revere Einstein or Niels Bohr by rote, but hardly with the informed emotion which comes of even partial understanding. Their faith in a thinker's scope is so vacuous that when Einstein's misguided friends publish his nonscientific essays, thereby exposing his intellectual inadequacy, naïve astonishment is soon succeeded by excessive contempt, and another idol is overthrown that never was properly—that is, profitably—idolized.

The prestige of science remains of course pre-eminent, despite the superficial hold that science itself has on the minds of the intellectual class. And it is that prestige, acting as a perpetual goad to imitation, which makes science's share in the decay of Intellect equal to that of art. Each in its way undermines the sense of unity, defeats communication, and throws the individual back on his own resources in a world whose worth, and even whose reality, is challenged by these two imposing enterprises. We may conclude, then, that for a century more or less, Art and Science have been the chief enemies of Intellect among intellectuals. But there is a third and closely related enemy, which is Philanthropy.

I use philanthropy to mean the liberal doctrine of free and equal opportunity as applied to things of the mind. This application has two results. The first, to which I shall return in discussing education, is the corruption of judgment; the second, which forms the subject of the next chapter, is the corruption of the products of intellect themselves. In their corrupted use, 'opportunity' is no longer wholly free and often not at all opportune. Rather, opportunity turns into social pressure, and the desire for intellect becomes part of the urge to share the wealth—a double imperative ceaselessly dinned into our ears: 'Patronize your local library, enjoy a museum seminar in your home, see "what the Zoo can do for you."'[3] You owe it to yourself to have an intellectual life—learn Russian in your spare time, read the 101 classics during the next 1,001 nights, or at least take up the recorder and paint on Sundays. Remember that education should never end: join a class after 5 P.M. Creativity is within you; learning releases it. Education is the best recreation; square dancing is recreation; square dancing is education. Have no fears: in our love is your understanding.'

True to its origins, this philanthropy carries out the behests of pity; its watchword is 'help.' The slightest response to the proffer of opportunity creates a claim to special treatment. Help is abundant, overflowing, and thanks to it willingness in the learner is enough: why distinguish intention and performance? Philanthropically speaking—'in terms of eagerness'—the aspirant is often superior to the passed master. Nor can there be a finer object of philanthropy than struggling incompetence, since evangelical charity says: give to those that want. The opposite, the worldly rule, would give to those that have talents and would take away at least the opportunity from those that have not. But this, proceeding from intellectual judgment, would be cruel; it is indeed a flaw in the reign of love and welfare that Intellect seeks to concentrate its resources rather than spread them as consolations for helplessness.

The connections of this philanthropy with modern art and science are easy to trace. The evils that art discerns in the very nature of politics and business, philanthropy also condemns and tries to make up for. It bars competition, is suspicious of power, and ignores failure. For the usual prizes of Philistine greed it substitutes the guerdons of higher lusts—a certificate of proficiency in French or a scrapbook of two-by-four gummed reproductions of the old masters. Now none of this would be possible without the surpluses that technology has created. The freehanded ways of intellectual philanthropy reflect the abundance of paper, ink, books, schools, photographs, recordings, and freelance lecturers, but also the more general sense of copiousness arising from the pride of science and the litany of numbers, numbers, numbers.

It hardly needs saying that though the whole world is now the playground of philanthropy, its headquarters everywhere are the schools. That their replacement of Intellect by philanthropy is not an exclusively American occurrence can be shown by a British example: 'Mr. G. H. Bantock expresses the concern that all thinking educationists are troubled with when they consider the present chaotic state of education in our society. Rightly, he considers it will fail to produce "the educated man"—though he carefully does not define this phenomenon. It concerns me more that the present system will lead to failure, not to produce the educated man, but to produce human beings with a capacity for life.'[4]

These last words tell us much. The talk of 'education' where none is wanted or needed, or where something else is meant, is characteristic of our time. But even more illuminating is the identity suggested between education and psychology or psychiatry, two demisciences ridden by philanthropic moralism. The doctrine of pity and help, originating in the church, the settlement house, and the clinic, has found in the modern psychologies a convenient means of carrying abroad the war against Intellect. Though the genius of Freud was unswervingly intellectual, it has given birth to a large progeny of adapters who, from generous as well as selfish motives, put philanthropy first. They mean to cure, or at least to 'help' at any cost. They respect, certainly, no intellectual limits or principles, and one by one the chief elements of our culture have fallen within the area of their devastation. Thus the school is not to teach but to cure; body and mind are not to use for self-forgetful ends but to dwell on with Narcissus' adoring anxiety; the arts, not to give joy and light but to be scanned for a 'diagnosis' of some trouble, a solution of some 'problem,' or else exploited for the common good in occupational therapy; and all other social or political institutions are not to serve man's material needs but to be brought to the bar of cultural justification.

The final twist in this transformation is that the clinician-publicists who carry on the war breathe love in hostile phrases while finding in Intellect untold aggressions to condemn. Their love hates Intellect because they feel and disapprove its impersonal calm, and also because its triumphs look like conquests not so much by, as over, common humanity. *Avant-garde* psychology, *avant-garde* art, and the philanthropy that is coeval with them, alike cherish the warm confusions of animal existence.

These foes of Intellect nevertheless make stern demands. Art, like professionalism, claims of its devotees exclusive allegiance. Science reserves the right to apply its method where it chooses and hopes for world empire. Philanthropy leaves no one alone, and its educational and psychological allies, taking universal welcome for granted, turn vindictive when challenged. For Intellect to say that its duty is clear and limited, that it cares little for happiness, that it puts other virtues ahead of good will and does not seek world peace, convicts it out of its own mouth. So much sobriety is not in fashion, it looks like provincialism, a refusal of enlightenment—complacency.

The anti-intellectual emotions at work here being even more complex than usual, one can easily mistake them. Yet it does seem as if the prevalent desire to embrace the whole world in some benevolent imperium of love, science, or art expresses chiefly a rooted aversion toward the immediate and actual. Living habitually at the full stretch of their perfectionist fancy, modern men of ideas loathe the world they know. If proof were needed, one could cite the utopian passion which governs nations in the East and the corresponding Orientalism which works as a ferment in the West. War and travel in Asia have made Western intellectuals once more preach the wisdom of the East; they do this because they can thereby belittle the too familiar West. Writing of Toynbee's *Study of History*, Mr. Lewis Mumford says: 'I would point out that no book that deals with human affairs has been more free from the blatant parochialisms of our age and our civilization: the obsessions of nationalism, the exaltation of Hellenic and later European civilization at the expense of nineteen other significant societies . . . [and] the notion that our age is the climax of human existence and that its ephemeral values are eternal ones.'[5]

One may wonder at the causes of this self-laceration and ask in what sense, other than the historical, the vanished among those nineteen other societies are significant, and how our indispensable concern with our own has been *at the expense* of the others. What obligation has been left unpaid, once we have discharged the intellectual debt by doing what no other civilization has ever done—

systematically studied the rest? Far from being parochial in that regard, the West may claim the merit of immoderate hospitality for its House of Intellect, which is so far the only building of its kind.

The Western Intellect has been and continues to be favorable to the study of Oriental thought and culture. But it is one thing to study and another to adopt, and even the attempts at adaptation may be regarded critically without its implying provincialism. The motive which brings an image of the goddess Kwannon into the window of a Fifth Avenue department store, and which sends American women to club lectures on Zen-Buddhism is but the fashionable curiosity that is always shifting from one source of new slogans and sensations to another. To prefer the exotic to the home grown is a usual form of 'sophistication'; and when, as in the present fad for Zen-Buddhism, the fashion enjoins contempt for Intellect, the pleasure is double.

But Intellect is not abashed. It goes to work on anti-Western arguments such as I have reproduced and easily shows how false is the warm, generous, philanthropic attitude which they affect. Taking up the charge of 'blatant parochialisms' and 'obsessive nationalism' leveled at 'our age and civilization,' Intellect asks: how is our detestable pride to be measured—by Arab tolerance, African neighborliness, Chinese humanitarianism, Japanese indifference to gain, Egyptian humility? Where is the model state and people? And where have empires more or less voluntarily given up their alien possessions, and governments their oppressive powers—in the East or in the West?

The love for all peoples far away has in it also a touch of self-pity, occasioned by the presumed 'decline of the West.' The phrase may mean many things, but in one of its meanings, Intellect points out, it is exactly matched by the decline of the East. Every piece of machinery found east of Suez, every word of English spoken, every pair of trousers, every bad movie, must be accounted a 'triumph' of the West over the declining East. To say this is to show the absurdity of the phrases which pass for 'intellectual' comments on Western civilization and for signs of large comprehension on the part of the users. The only importance of these pronouncements is that they are inspired by 'other-worldliness' in a new sense, one which associates all the evils of life with our historic past and our characteristic modes of thought, in an effort to repudiate them both.

For it is true that Intellect as I am defining it belongs largely to the Western tradition—the tradition of explicitness and energy, of inquiry and debate, of public, secular tests and social accountability. What Intellect satisfies in us is the need for orderly and perspicuous expression, which may lead to common belief and concerted action.* Eastern philosophies and religions undoubtedly contain ideas that are valuable to persons and peoples outside the East, but one cannot help noticing that the first signs of a Westerner's involvement with Oriental thought, whatever inward good may go with it, is a toxic condition of the vocabulary—every word meaning not only what it denotes but its opposite as well†—complicated by serious lesions in coherence and a rapid lowering of the logical pulse. With the loss of articulate precision, Intellect as the West has developed it—the social and publicly responsible Intellect—sickens and dies. Whether this is desirable is not the point. The point is that, until we choose to go under, we must look upon all philanthropic gestures, and especially upon amateur Orientalism, as a warning. The signs of these effusions are unmistakable—easy indignation, the throb of pity, portentous promises, and still more generally: vague words, loose thoughts. The state of the mother tongue is in fact the index of our control over destiny.

· · ·

*Without wishing to prejudge the difficult question of how to compare radically different cultures, I may cite as a sample of that difference the kind of utterance which many Western inquirers about Zen find a refreshment and a lure: 'What,' asks the seeker, 'is the entrance to Zen?' The master replies, 'Do you hear the sound of the stream?' 'Yes.' '*There* is the way to enter.'
†Anyone who has been close to Oriental scholars knows the difficulties they encounter in interpreting texts, especially the Chinese and Japanese classics. The characters may mean widely different things, and competent men disagree on points the like of which seldom occur in Western exegesis. During the last war the Japanese military found similar obstacles to clear communication among themselves. The adoption of the alphabet, fundamental to Intellect, as we saw, is now being debated by the Japanese government (June, 1958).

These three great forces of mind and will—Art, Science, and Philanthropy—have, it is clear, become enemies of Intellect not of set purpose, not by conspiracy, but as a result of their haphazard assimilation within the House of Intellect itself. The intellectual class, which ought always to remain independent, even of Intellect, has been captivated by art, overawed by science, and seduced by philanthropy. The damage done by each has been that of heedless expansion combined with a reliance on the passage of time to restore order and decency. But time mends only by blotting out. In the modern riot of art and science and loving-kindness, Intellect has seen decline the virtues that make it what it is: unity, concentration, communicativeness, and knowledge of itself. Few even among intellectuals think of the intellectual constituency: most think of particular artists, scientists, educationists, psychiatrists. Few acknowledge a proper sphere and matter of Intellect: most dream distractedly of sublime artifacts and antisocial fantasies, of scientific wonders and nuclear threats, of benevolent programs and civil conspiracies. Few appeal, or could appeal, to any common principles. The identity and integrity of Intellect seems a memory of what could never be.

Doing duty in its place is the conjunction just referred to—art, science, good will, fired by the prodigal Id, and whose characteristic bias an example may serve to make vivid. In 1955 there appeared among the publications of the Museum of Modern Art a catalogue of 192 pages entitled *The Family of Man*. It reproduced an exhibition of five hundred photographs gathered from sixty-eight nations to represent the multifarious activities of the species. Quotations from James Joyce, Tom Paine, and others put into words the fraternal outlook implied in the title. The volume enjoyed an unusual popularity.* It was seen and talked of in many places outside artistic circles and always, as it seemed to me, with that warmth of praise which greets the objectification of strong contemporary feelings.

*It has now been reissued as a small paperback at fifty cents.

Presumably, then, *The Family of Man* gave visual pleasure coupled with the confirmation of a philosophy of life. The ground of that philosophy is best indicated by the cant phrase 'the human condition,'* and its setting forth in *The Family of Man* is seen in the many variations played on but a few themes—those of sexual love, misery, poverty, and the innocence of childhood. Also emphatically represented are: birth, death, motherhood, toil, music, and dancing.

One may of course take these scenes as direct evidence of what is. Yet it is hard to resist the impression of sentimental bias that they create by repetition, which one suspects is not exclusively the work of the local editors. Photography is a minor art, but it readily transmits—this is no frivolous play on words—the views of the photographer. And in this portfolio the views disclose a worldwide concentration on the helplessness of man, and on its excuse and anodyne—his animal needs and sensual pleasures.

The book opens with a rather tendentious female nude, prone amid the ferns of a forest glade. This is followed by episodes of kissing and caresses in public places. Next, in the middle of a black page, is a small square transom through which one sees a shoulder, face, and hand belonging to a couple making love. The vignette is printed horizontally so that there shall be no mistaking the subject. The theme of copulation is frequently repeated, notably as a restorative after the half-dozen pages devoted to schoolwork. The only other image of man that receives comparable insistence is that of suffering, as shown by faces of misery, worn limbs, and postures of dejection.

The rare views more or less related to Intellect are almost all of effort, chiefly by the young. Accomplishment and embodied power as they might be shown by the faces of great men and women are absent—except for a small snapshot of Albert Einstein, looking

---

*Its originator, Montaigne, would undoubtedly repudiate the intention that the phrase almost always carries today—that of 'the detestable human condition.' Montaigne knew the wretchedness of man's lot as well as anyone, but strength of intellect kept him from infatuation with misery.

innocent and bewildered, and a truly magnificent full-page portrait of Judge Learned Hand. Here Intellect shines out for one five-hundredth of the kaleidoscope, though from its placing and its anonymity one surmises that the portrait is intended to represent not so much Mind as The Law.

Yet the law in action, a model of articulate precision, is also skimped, and government as well. Except for a view of the United Nations Assembly—the least of governments—one would scarcely know that man had fashioned the state and that it had value. The pictures that allude to it are of riots and mass deportations. An isolated sentence from Jefferson suggests that only the unorganized people are trustworthy, and a passage from the diary of Anne Frank asserts that they are all good. Elsewhere, the extracts from the Bhagavad-Gita and from Sioux, Kwakiutl, Maori, and other folk literatures stress the simplicities. Primitivism is preferred. There are superb views of aboriginal nature, including a pair of nebulas as frontispiece; there are none of architecture as such. The book ends with yet another group of small children at play.

Whatever is formed and constituted (the work seems to say), whatever is adult, whatever exerts power, whatever is characteristically Western, whatever is unique or has a name, or embodies the complexity of thought, is of less interest and worth than what is native, common, and sensual; what is weak and confused; what is unhappy, anonymous, and elemental.

The rhythmic return of the main themes makes it evident that questioning the proportions of the work would be met by the statistical argument—there is in the world more fornication than philosophy; and by the documentary argument—all facts are created equal. Science, or a hankering for it, shows why it seems important to record the facial expression and gripping fingers of a woman during sexual intercourse. And art, that is, the works of the last half-century, have put us in the mood for this and all other primitivisms by giving us a peepshow as deceptive as the dark little square on page thirteen.

The pictorial art of the volume, which Carl Sandburg in his Prologue calls 'a camera testament,' has the ambiguity of photography itself. Message and composition do not always jibe, and at times one suspects that the exhibitors, bewildered by 'over two million photographs,' forgot one of their aims. For on the cover we are told to expect 'the greatest photographic exhibition of all time,' which promises a mainly aesthetic criterion. But inside, the purpose turns sociological, not to say philanthropic, as appears from the chief editor's absent-minded jargon: 'the gamut of life from birth to death with emphasis on the daily relationships of man to himself, to his family, to the community, and to the world we live in . . . Photographs of lovers . . . of the family unit . . . of the home in all its warmth and magnificence . . . of the individual and the family unit in its reactions to the beginnings of life and continuing on through death and burial. . . . Photographs concerned with man in relation to his environment . . . the good and the great things, the stupid and the destructive things. . . . '[6]

It is easy to believe that *The Family of Man* has been 'created in a passionate spirit of devoted love and faith in man,'[7] but one may be permitted to ask whether that love was not blind—blind to whole ranges of man's life, blind to the effect of certain iterations, blind to the requirements of sense and manly pride, blind to the discretion which judgment owes to even the sincerest faith.

If one asks further why the directors of a leading museum, rightly prized for its intellectual courage, should so meekly conform to the unspoken demands of public opinion, one must turn for the answer to that public opinion itself.

II

◈

The Public Mind and
Its Caterers

Writing in the same liberal tradition which assigns ultimate wisdom to the people, and which was quoted approvingly in *The Family of Man*, Thomas Jefferson set forth in his *Notes on Virginia* a plan of elementary schooling by which, he said, 'twenty of the best geniuses will be raked from the rubbish annually.'* It is inconceivable today that anyone should publicly describe any group of people as intellectual rubbish. I am not myself suggesting that we should, for I am a child of the age and I shrink from giving pain. I only illustrate by this taboo our changed outlook, which gives a clue to public feelings about Intellect at the present time: the democratic treatment of Intellect is not determined by any conscious valuation of it on anybody's part, but by attitudes designed to protect everybody's tender ego.

Since Jefferson wrote, thanks to inventions he would have

---

*The idea of early and rigorous intellectual selection recurs in Jefferson's other writings, notably the 'Bill for the More General Diffusion of Knowledge' (1779), Sections 16, 18, and 19.

approved, the register of public opinion has been greatly enlarged; we have thicker newspapers and an entirely new apparatus providing through eye and ear what we call mass communication. Yet the tenor of public opinion on intellectual matters is remarkably uniform. Throughout the multitude of clashing interests the tone and the assumptions are the same. This is true even in what we like to think of as different layers of taste, from the popular and tabloid to the highbrow and educational. Those who fill the organs of opinion with their words are of course alike in having received the standard dose of literacy. Almost all have had a college education, and many some special training in journalism or 'English.' The presumption, to a Jefferson who might revisit, would be that these molders of opinion would show a bias in favor of Intellect. But this is not so, both because education does not impart any such bias, and because confused emotions smother any latent desire to champion the mind.

In consequence, publicists, reporters, editors, and other makers of opinion are almost invariably defeatists. Though they are educated men and women, and some have a high conception of their calling, they feel no need to define for themselves the rights of Intellect or to ponder its role in the national life. Such a meditation would probably strike them as artificial. Unschooled on this point, they follow the common yet subtle interpretation of equality which allows 'encouraging the arts,' but would make anything like homage to Intellect seem arrogant, pompous, or absurd. Even when stirred to cry out against 'anti-intellectualism' in the narrow sense, and while defending freedom of speech or press, speakers and writers take it for granted that their opponents have ulterior motives. These enemies, they think, attack ideas to protect interests. This may be true, but it also ignores both parties' complicated emotions regarding Intellect.

What is the tangle they fail to unravel? The loose end of it is uncertainty. Since it is seldom clear whether intellectual activity denotes a superior mode of being or a vital deficiency, opinion swings between considering Intellect a privilege and seeing it as a handicap.* As a privilege it must be assailed; as a handicap it seems so easily remedied that it is scorned. In neither phase is the feeling whole and assured, for the attack and the derision alike testify to a quality that gives no hold to the philanthropic impulse. This is why the 'egghead' and the 'grind' are not pitied like the physical cripple, even though all three are deemed miscarriages of nature. Intellect is thus simultaneously looked up to, resented, envied, and regarded with cold contempt.

This chasm between physical and mental, which freezes good will, is part of a larger reality always present to the popular imagination. Physical events are easily seen and judged, so that wherever it is possible to rely on the evidence of the senses, as for example in sports, public opinion demands performance. The philanthropy bestowed upon the physically weak does not go so far as to give them a place in the Olympics. Likewise in acting, mountain-climbing, or bridge-building, people are willing to discriminate and reject, regardless of sentiment. Rigor in fact governs the lives of all whose work is subject to judgment by counting: a politician who fails to win the requisite number of votes, a salesman who falls below the expected minimum of sales, a bookkeeper who cannot ever get the books to balance, is treated like a boxer who is outpointed. However much these unfortunates may feel it as cruel, no one dreams of giving up for their sakes the aim of success.

Public opinion, then, by the very fact that it is public, develops the habit of judging by tangibles. And the habit, growing in strength with every new tangible standard, necessarily leads to a greater suspicion of Intellect for its seeming evasion of measurement. On its side, Intellect is bound to think public opinion crass for always seeking material tests. Much of the criticism of our 'materialistic society'

---

*This doubt is not new, as was intimated in the last chapter. The anecdote of Dr. Johnson's pride as a rider is in point: 'He was, however, proud to be amongst the sportsmen; and I think no praise ever went so close to his heart as when Mr. Hamilton called out one day upon Brighthelmstone Downs, "Why, Johnson rides as well, for aught I see, as the most illiterate fellow in England."' Mrs. Piozzi, *Anecdotes*, London, 1786, 206–7.

and of its decisions based on money, popularity, or some other use of raw numbers, actually strikes at the pathetic uncertainty of minds that cannot judge the intangible yet want to be right.*

What supports this view is that one detects a kind of revenge, a turning of the tables on Intellect, in the common desire to disregard what evidence of mental powers there may be and prefer the duffers. In the school system, as in business, government, and social inter-course, this ready generosity seldom fails. Amiable stupidity is pro-tected, being no threat; a pleasantly retarded mind contributes to everybody's ease. Character, everyone cheerfully repeats, is of infi-nitely greater worth than brains: 'Be good, sweet maid, and let who will be clever.' Charity of this order often begins at home, every man believing that he has enough Intellect for all decent purposes. To be sure, he professes to be a 'plain man,' and lays no claim to brilliancy or depth of mind; yet the sincerity of this disclaimer is not of the same strength as that with which he concedes that he could not swim the English Channel.

In short, the characteristics of Intellect—its scarcity and superior-ity, its eccentricity and intangibility—prevent the democratic public from entertaining about it a just view or a straightforward emotion.

That is why those whose business it is to put before the public the products of Intellect are in the ambiguous state I have termed defeatist. The defeatist does not really want his country invaded, but he would rather not keep on fighting: he is tired, and he thinks there is much to be said for the enemy's point of view. The small daily betrayals of Intellect in the large record of public opinion reflect in a myriad ways this weariness of doubt, which it is a mistake to ascribe to bald commercialism. The promoters of merchandise are in fact much more single-minded, self-confident, and happy about their products than the 'thoughtful,' apprehensive, ulcerated purveyors of news and ideas.

*In the 'spiritual East,' it is of course just as common to judge by signs: the holy man is known by his garb or his emaciated body, which tells of fasting, or by his physical location, in a temple or on a bed of nails, or by some sym-bol of caste or religion.

But should we not distinguish these purveyors from the amorphous being called Public Opinion? There is no need, for they could not be what they are without forming part of public opinion and being unusually responsive to its cross-currents. But they are also loosely allied to the tradition of Intellect, to which their education introduced them in passing, and hence their lifelong discomfort. They must, in the midst of Babel and under the eye of conscience, choose which book or news story to publish, which article to write or editorial view to adopt.

These choices remind us that public opinion is made, or at least led, by two classes of persons—producers and middlemen. Their mutual influence is as decisive for Intellect as their joint action on the reader or listener, but the middleman is in the short run more influential than the producer, who can forget the world and take his chance. The middleman is a caterer who learns whimsicality from his customers and ends by living a fantasy within a fantasy, the unknowable public mind entwined with the picture of it in his head.

Having taken little thought about Intellect as such, the middleman repeats the fallacy of the professional, who sees no mediation possible between his knowledge and the layman's ignorance. The editor more crudely thinks: '*I* can stand this, but *they* can't.' When such an entrepreneur is moved solely by greed, there is nothing more to say: everyone admits that to hold the attention of large numbers one must strike the one note of perfect vulgarity. The life of Intellect is not at stake. But what is one to think of the middleman who professes devotion to the highest standards, whose product, often, is subsidized, whose following is docile, and who yet boggles at things that do not arouse in his mind an immediate echo? Here is a periodical that boasts of being advanced; the editors receive an article about a writer, living or dead, who is scarcely known. The article is informative, full of lively or moving quotations from the unknown's works, and all other details are satisfactory, but—but who wants to hear about somebody who is not Joyce, James, Gide, Rilke, Yeats, Proust, Keats, Kafka, Dostoevsky, or Melville? The list is closed. Well, maybe Hölderlin belongs. In any case, the possibility of extending the public range of pleasure and awareness is also closed, not from a pledge of conformity, but from defeatism before the unknown.*

One degree lower, the same principle governs all the anxious cutting and changing that goes on. Since all this labor is undertaken in the public's behalf, there are many commandments. One, for example, requires equal elaboration throughout: an author who has a darting mind will, without losing the main thread, suggest some original points by the way. But the reader's attorney in the editorial office is watchful and says: 'Explain or omit.'† One has even heard him object that in a certain writer's work 'there is a thought in every sentence.' The ideal seems to be 'five thousand words with but a single thought.'

Other required changes are still cruder in form and motive. I have told elsewhere of the suggestion I once received from an editor to substitute Newton for Descartes in my text, regardless of meaning, on the ground that Newton was better known. More recently, the title of an article of mine about the humanities, originally commissioned on the strength of that title, had to be changed because it is axiomatic that the word 'humanities' presents a forbidding idea. Science, now, is not forbidding; it is everybody's meat; to bring it in would rouse the common man's curiosity and spirits too. The trouble was that the new title no longer fitted the subject, as a number of intellectual readers noticed. What embitters the defeat in this episode is that the magazine in question was making a venture in Intellect, had guaranteed (and respected) the inviolability of the

---

*The same weakness amid pretensions is illustrated by the request the readers of a leading literary quarterly received some years ago from its editor: 'Any comment you may care to make or any suggestions that may help us make the —— a constantly better magazine will be heartily welcomed by all of us here.' After this, why pay an editorial staff, or criticize the advertisers who make an obsequious show of 'service'?

†The attitude is catching, and soon a reviewer writes: 'He has thrown out an idea that is arresting, in fact startling, and that may be highly significant; but he has not elaborated it far enough to permit one to judge. . . . ' *Herald Tribune Book Review*, June 3, 1956.

author's text, and was widely advertising its own courage. But at the last minute the editorial knees buckled—and transmitted some of their weakness to the author.

The incident brings out the inevitably collective method of journalism, which modern practice interprets according to the purest democracy. In mass publishing, a book or article contains all the ideas, judgments, and wordings that one or two dozen people, and sometimes the entire staff, can contribute. This includes—as I can testify—the opinion that the stenographer or office boy entertains of a jacket design or picture caption. And that opinion, I need hardly add, tends to overrule any other, for the aim of self-protection by 'testing' democratic opinion means submitting on matters of taste to the unspoiled judgment of the delegate from the majority.

One need not quarrel a priori with the system. Molière and other great writers are said to have consulted their cooks on points of usage and art. But presumably those writers retained editorial control as well as responsibility. Where Intellect is harmed by modern collective journalism is in the strengthening of two fallacies—one, that the way to settle the great uncertainty, 'Will they like it?' is to rely on artless, unpremeditated judgments; the other, that to hedge against failure one should combine the good points of divergent schemes. This second fallacy, the fallacy of false perfection, becomes the worst enemy of intellectual work. The effort may contribute to surface finish, but it does so at the cost of inner solidity. Nothing replaces the force imparted by oneness of conception. And its unmistakable charm—that of individuality—comes, as the word itself tells us, from undividedness.

At a time when they complain of being swamped by the anonymous mass, intellectuals cannot be indifferent to these considerations. Depth, surface, unity, technique are not mere aspects of an unchanging core of thought. They are the incarnation of the thought itself. Yet intellectuals submit without protest to the devices by which democratic collaboration destroys—from unnecessary lunching and pathological conferring to following house rules of English and yielding to the alterations that remake the finished work as in a clothing shop, to suit the arbitrary customer. It is faith in unlimited improvement that inspired the adulation authors and publishers showered on the late Maxwell Perkins, the indefatigable editor of Hemingway and Thomas Wolfe, and that persuades publishers that no editor would soon mean no literature. The best of firms declare their main function to be the bringing to book of wayward authors, by a joint effort in which knowledge and judgment are on the side of the firm. So true is this that publishers spend a good part of their time in devising subjects and cajoling writers into doing the work—that is, half the work. The consequence at large is that the fruit of intellection, be it literature or scholarship, comes to be conceived by everyone as a product answering exactly to specifications, not only the inevitable ones of length or the adopted ones of genre, but the specifications of tone, manner, speech, and mode of development.

With so much pains taken to protect the clientele, it is not surprising that it should be fussy and weak of stomach. This in turn prompts the middleman to greater solicitude, and so on in a vicious circle. The effort to please becomes negative—the avoidance of rough texture and all other causes of pain. The molders of the public mind thus come to rely on two fundamental criteria: ease and freedom from error. These two define for them technical perfection, constitute, in fact, the supreme ideal of Technique.

Everything in our life encourages this conception of what is admirable and fit: mechanical inventions serve the inclinations of ease, and advertising spurs the desire for it. Science makes a crime of factual error. Machine industry produces the smooth in place of the rough-hewn. Mass output calls for the unvarying repetition of steps which we call technique. Middlemen, producers, and customers are but reproducing in mind-stuff what the material world gives them as models.

The question is whether men are bound to act like robots when they can set themselves independent goals that are preferable. In dealing with error, Intellect is able to discriminate between trivial and important. Modern readers, as we know, take all facts as equal and rush to fill the correspondence columns with indignation whenever they catch any small mistake in print. For these slips, writers and editors apologize with a humility not seen on earth since the early Church. The expensive apparatus for detecting error before publication grows nearly infallible about trivia, and nearly blind about what matters. A wrong initial in some obscure name is set right, while a colossal nonsequitur is overlooked. In the end this unsuspected lack of balance regulates (if that is the word) the public mind, which then wonders at the state of our education and the quality of our politics.

Like error-hunting, the love of ease in intellectual matters goes with the Lilliputian outlook, whose typical handiwork is the digest. Whether of an article, a book, an opera, or a philosophy, the digest anticipates collective judgment by eliminating what is unexpected and difficult. Take out everything that anybody might object to or stumble at, and you have reached your goal: the old bare bones, the one simple point, the upshot—all that is worth passing on. The word we apply with a mystic's confidence to this residue is 'basic.'* When we reflect how often padding and repetition pass for thought, the wish for what is basic, for the digest, may seem legitimate. But this is only because in their intellectual weakness the schools and other centers of learning do not enforce brevity. The magazine's rule of elaboration—one article, one idea—is also bent on ease, though in the opposite way of length. It thus causes the impatience which the digest relieves at the expense of thought.

But there is another sort of impatience with length, which comes

---

*It is said that at an editorial conference where a serious treatise entitled *Perversion* was being considered, an experienced publisher suggested that the impression of scandal or, alternatively, of fiction, could be turned into irresistible appeal by changing the title to *Basic Perversion*.

from discomfort when the professional formula is flouted. It was in response to this uneasiness that Mr. Somerset Maugham, at the request of a publisher, permitted himself to cut *The Red and the Black* and nine other 'great novels.' The omitted parts were unnecessary. To whom? Desires and dislikes are imputed to a public imagined as restless or critical of technical faults, though in reality it is only the middleman with a jaded appetite who nervously narrows his public's tolerance. More often than is supposed the public would accept originality full strength. But daring is discouraged early in life by the first purveyors of print: 'See what we have for you, dear—not a word in this book that you cannot understand.' Later, it is the journalist's or broadcaster's throaty assurance that the coming touch of Intellect will not hurt: 'A book about philosophy that people actually want to read.' And everywhere formula, technique, cliché, reconcile the desire for novelty with the comforting experience of sameness. By distracting attention to external forms, to ritual words and gestures—to packaging, as it were—much that would shock or bore slips by. This holds true for all kinds of performance; it is not limited to the journals of large circulation and corresponding rigid techniques, but governs the cant words and editorial poses of all organs of opinion, from the *Wall Street Journal* to the supercharged ephemerids that choose names like *Flout, Styx,* or *Nil.*

On reflection it might seem as if the various devices I reprove under the general name of technique were no different from the conventions I have commended as the handmaidens of Intellect. They differ in this, that the technical tricks I point to are temporary expedients having small intellectual relevance to what they disguise or adorn. Notice, for example, in broadcasting, the needlessness of exact timing, the horror of silence. When a program stops forty seconds short of the hour, what self-reproach in every breast! But why should a panel discussion represented as 'free' and 'informal' end 'on the nose,' with a pat utterance by the chairman? What have the rigorous adjustments of industrial mass production to do with conversation? Nothing is so revolting to Intellect as automatism.* Yet it is such false shows of discipline that the middleman in his uncertainty calls for, and teaches the public to regard as the mark of professional competence.

Even when put in uniform, Intellect continues to make the middleman nervous. That is why he so often presents it to the public or retraces its history in a faintly derisive tone which dissociates him from the thing he proffers. Thus the periodical press habitually invites the reader to side with normal men against eccentric Intellect: 'These queer marks don't seem to bother the professor: they are the symbols he has devised for his peculiar researches.'

The variations on this attitude are many. A writer, for example, can imply that Intellect is an alien world, as in the *Times* obituary which said of a businessman: '[He] was an intellectual, who quoted Aristotle in an argument with the late Count Alfred Korzybski, the semanticist, and was a close friend of Mortimer J. Adler, the metaphysician.'[1] Here the solemn words make clear that the writer is no familiar of the household he describes, where Aristotle was quoted, apparently, once in a lifetime, like going to Mecca; and where Drs. Korzybski and Adler bore titles that suggest at once a trade and a monopoly.

Dissociation can also be achieved with hostility and an air of brooking no nonsense. This is especially effective in dealing with so-called controversial thinkers. Thus *Time* informs its readers that 'Friedrich Nietzsche was a pale, crabby hermit who sat in a cheap Swiss boarding house peering beyond good and evil and demanding, at the top of his apocalyptic voice, the rearing of a daemonically driven breed of superman. Just when the world began to get wind of his prophetic fulminations, he went mad. For the last tragic eleven years of his life, he was a myth—and so he has remained.'[2]

More dull error could not be compressed into so few words—

---

*A simple example is the cliché or bromide. The man who cannot speak of a dim light without calling it a 'dim, religious light' offends both by the pointlessness of the second adjective and by the conviction he creates in the listener that the remark has become a pure reflex.

words which were undoubtedly put together by an intelligent, literate, college-bred writer and 'verified' by a no less qualified 'researcher,' probably a graduate of one of the country's best colleges for women. The joint product illustrates what reference-book information will yield when unlit by Intellect. We may imagine the simple analysis actually needed. If Nietzsche was a pitiable fool, he deserves no more than a mention to that effect. If he is still a living menace, describe that menace with precision and condemn it if necessary. In a word, tell us what you know. It is not irrelevant that the magazine from which the paragraph is quoted rents full pages in the newspapers to praise the delights of knowing, on one occasion reproducing in large type a column of the Oxford dictionary on the verb 'to know.'[3] Being invited to share those delights, what we want to know first is the meaning of 'to sit in a cheap Swiss boarding house peering beyond good and evil.' All one is sure of is that the ridicule would persist regardless of the facts: if Nietzsche had lived in an expensive hotel, the knowledge would come out as 'peering at good and evil between the potted palms of a garish palace.'

The sincerity of the writer and his editors is not the point at issue. The issue is whether the attitude adopted and conveyed to the reader is appropriate to any intellectual subject whatever. A weekly news magazine is not required to supply intellectual opinion, but when it does, it comes under intellectual judgment: is the thought genuine or counterfeit? One suspects that not even the writer's dislike of Nietzsche is genuine; it is put on to 'create interest,' to stir up the dumb beast of a public to the delights of knowing. But the prodding is mechanical and falters before the end of the paragraph, as we see in the reference to Nietzsche's 'tragic' last years. If the man was such a pantaloon, what was tragic about his madness? Only a great mind overthrown yields tragedy. 'Oh, but you surely know—to the public every mishap is tragic.'

This sample of intellectual journalism proves moreover that the public will not mind being thoroughly muddled—or does not know when it is. For the story is a report of the new German edition of

Nietzsche's works by Karl Schlechta. Starting with abuse, to make Nietzsche a spectacle, the reporter is soon forced to defend the philosopher against common prejudice, for that is the purpose of Schlechta's edition. The reader, still with the induced sneer on his lips, is now gravely asked to rejoice in the discovery that Nietzsche's Will to Power, a bugbear only yesterday, 'emerges not (or not alone) as man's will to mastery over other men, but as his will to a sort of excellence or virtue in his own inner being.' And so Nietzsche 'may find his place in Germany not as a national but as a universal ancestor of a troubled age.' Thought here has given out completely, but one gathers that the 'crabby hermit' shouting 'at the top of his apocalyptic voice' has been absolved.

Perhaps it is too much to ask for both news and sense. But did we get even news? It so happens that what *Time* says of the Will to Power in 1958 has been a commonplace of scholarly criticism for fifty years. Yet if we except the anti-intellectualism of the intellectual, there was no barrier between the writer and the facts. Anyone, including journalists and researchers, can read Nietzsche's words in translation or can consult the lucid and authoritative *What Nietzsche Means* by the American scholar, George Allen Morgan. The journalistic excuse for not doing either is probably that time does not permit. If so, one must conclude that the weekly shortcut to the delights of knowing is misinformation trimmed with insults.

The article that makes us so conclude should not lead us to think that intellectual misdeeds occur only in the type of magazine where it appeared. The case is made out here by exposing the best of one kind, but it could also be made out with the best of another kind, say, the liberal *New Yorker* to match the conservative *Time*. The *New Yorker*'s technique of casualness and the spirit of its celebrated profiles partake of the same attitude—derisive, suspicious, faintly hostile—which characterizes the democratic ego when faced with Intellect. This attitude will be found in poets as often as in journalists; it is now part of the public mind. Intellect, unless redeemed by the mystery of science or art, or again by the courage of adventure, as in the successful voyage of the Kon-Tiki, is equated with pretension and must, even while acknowledged, be 'whittled down to size.' This is done by clever doubt—'raised eyebrows'—by understatement, or by interjecting a biographical fact calculated to lessen or inhibit admiration: the Nobel Prize winner wears a dirty sweater before lunch. This does duty for criticism and makes the subject seem 'human.'

Never, in truth, has the educated population needed to be so often reassured about its distinguished fellow members' being human. The world greets with approval any discovery of a shortcoming, applauds the confession of mistakes, and indemnifies the spectator for any fleeting sense he may have of diminution by someone else's accomplishment. A truly modern dictionary would add an entry under 'human': 'the opposite of admirable'; and religious critics who repeat that a godless world falls into the worship of man should open their eyes to the demonstration of the contrary.

This grave subject does not take us away from our concern with public opinion. To admire is an expression of freedom that is denied by envious equality, and admiration depends on fame. But the apparatus of public opinion, responding exclusively to what it considers news, can no longer sustain fame. What it gives instead is publicity. Newcomers and others receive notice, according to formula, as news merely, and sometimes in such an overdose that it destroys the beneficiary. He is driven from his emotional base or from his proper work and ends as a burnt-out talent or a suicide.* If he survives as a talent, he still has to forego the attribute of wonder, or fame. The result is that the House of Intellect today numbers few

---

*Giving examples would be painful, but the outcome I describe is so frequent that it has become a commonplace of public discussion: 'Will Success Spoil Van Cliburn?' asks a writer in the *Times,* who details some of the artificial perils of notoriety. *New York Times Magazine*, June 22, 1958.

great figures and virtually no grand old men. Past achievements do not secure anyone a place, and this not because of the multitude of new achievements, but because to consider a reputation established would be to confer status, privilege. A master in his old age must therefore continue to 'be news' or go without public attention. Picasso by political murals, Frank Lloyd Wright by lectures on public affairs, can hold their places in the public mind. But Mencken, who was retired and stricken, received on his last birthday exactly thirty messages of congratulation.[4] Comes the obituary—the ultimate news—and the account is closed. Next!

To be sure, this city-room disposal system is not premeditated. It is natural to minds trained in the old ideal of the political press and the modern conception of news. The press, as the gainer and guardian of our liberties, stands rigid in the posture of fighting; it is automatically against. To say this is but to make an historical observation. Liberalism grew with the press, and both are traditionally skeptical of whatever suggests power, whatever is established and claims authority. Indispensable as this critical method is, grateful to it as we must be, it is also true that it turns obscurantist when the mood of the minuteman is coupled with the cynicism of the newsmonger. Puritanical and prurient as regards the private life, and professionally blasé as regards the public mind, the daily writer is sure that readers respond not to truth, but to a few of its incidentals: exposure, sentiment, jocularity, and whatever can be described by superlatives.

Behind this creed lies a vague premise having to do with modernity—with being at once bewildered and impatiently alive. As such, the reader is thought unable to take mere newness as news; for, on the one hand, nothing is harder to grasp than the genuinely new; and on the other, events of moderate novelty and magnitude are too numerous to report. But some give more scope than others for a 'news angle.' On the manufacture of these angles is lavished, in the editorial rooms of the world, a ruinous amount of intelligence, imagination, and literary skill. Given some facts and the categories of interest listed above, 'blow up' the fact which fits under one of the categories and omit the rest. Thus in the course of an all-day conference on an educational problem, one of the participants, the director of a national fellowship program, mentioned in passing that the son of a wealthy family had applied for an award. The story in the *Times* the next day devoted its headline and most of the full column to this disclosure.[5] From this example, which still leaves the particular newspaper preeminent in its 'coverage' and a respecter of Intellect besides, one can gauge the reliability of the rest.

It is only fair to add that the *Times* has a posted rule limiting the distortion requisite for news. This is the rule: 'In all stories that deal at considerable length with one speech, let us try to include one paragraph that will give the theme of the address.'[6] When the try is successful, that paragraph is the thin line of communication by which the public mind can keep in touch with the reality of intellectual events.

Editors will reply that they are swamped with 'world news' and do the best they can. But, let me say it again, a daily paper is not obliged to deal with intellectual matters, any more than a political weekly. The attention to art, science, and knowledge generally, which has transformed the press into a haphazard encyclopedia, is recent.* But new pretensions entail new duties, which cannot be discharged simply by intimating that Intellect is lucky to be noticed at all. More

---

*An early form of this expansion was repudiated by the London *Times* a century ago: 'The majority of mankind have but little strength or interest for reading. For the half hour at the end of a fatiguing day they must have something that does not burden their attention or keep it too long on one strain. . . . Some of the papers published in the manufacturing districts . . . aim more directly at supplying the place of all other literature than we can pretend to do. With the vast quantity of intelligence which we are obliged to insert . . . we have little room for those copious extracts from new publications and other like matters that make some papers rather daily magazines than journals of news. . . . Whatever our faults, we shall not be thought guilty of relaxing and unsettling the youthful reader by too light an entertainment. . . . There is no doubt that such a combination of news and amusement . . . is very suitable for a large class of readers, and dispenses with the necessity not only of well-stocked shelves, but even of the circulating library.' (February 1, 1851.)

and more journals of large circulation and small cerebration seem bent on flirting with Intellect, but this puts Intellect under no obligation except the burdensome one of survival. And the strain is great, because the defeated hope of creating and holding interest by honest means leaves only the 'angle' and the 'gimmick' as a resource, and this in turn adds to the relation of middleman and producer a painful ambiguity which puts Intellect once more on the defensive.

Thus when a periodical founded for entertainment, and which educated people read (if at all) at the barber's or the dentist's, wants to signalize its coming of age, it seeks out an intellectual contributor and asks him to treat 'in perfect freedom' some subject of present concern in the world of ideas—usually some aspect of 'the' situation, social, moral, artistic, or international. The editors are as honest in their proffer of freedom as in that of abundant cash, but they are noticeably nervous about the freedom. They must lunch about it, and more than once, for they can 'see both sides': they have read the contributor in some quarterly which they admire but think ponderous, and they know the lightweight material that has worn well with their own readers. What can they do but try to urge the contributor to reduce his specific gravity, to supply or, if this is beyond him, to tolerate, a sprinkling of light touches in his otherwise relentless prose—nothing against his wishes, of course, but something for the willing readers who have not had his intellectual disadvantages.

If he refuses, he has denied his thought the opportunity to reach the millions—so he is told. If he complies, he has dealt Intellect another blow, light it may be, but whose repercussions he cannot gauge. Take the superlative, which has become the placebo of mass journalism, written and oral. The superlative seems transparent and harmless. How does it corrupt? By the insidious suggestion, which is soon common belief, that among all the things that fill the world the only notable specimens are six: the first, the last, the largest, the smallest, the oldest, and the youngest. Journalistic art consists in making every story a vehicle for one of these mental aphrodisiacs. No law as yet enjoins the warning: 'Irrelevance and false excitement added.' And so the captions continue to tell us of 'the largest single fragment of statuary . . . Though not the first, it is the heaviest . . . brought up by the expedition, which includes the youngest archeologist ever to, etc.'

But surely everybody takes this with a grain of salt? Not at all: there is not salt enough on earth. To the unprotected mind, even though 'advanced,' only the superlative deserves attention. One observer has with good reason called this 'The Paragon Complex': 'The supreme novelist of all time is Thomas Wolfe. The greatest American poet is Wallace Stevens. The most significant influence upon the development of British drama is Beaumont and Fletcher. Katherine Mansfield is unquestionably the finest short story writer in our language. No writer possesses more sensitivity and power than Federico García Lorca. Laurence Sterne brought the novel to heights unequalled before or since. The outstanding poet of the past three centuries is William Butler Yeats. Contrariwise Dylan Thomas is the outstanding poet of the past three centuries.

'How do I know all this? Very simply: I have been reading a number of recent M.A. theses and Ph.D. dissertations. Picking up more of them, I discover that Emily Dickinson is the acutest woman poet of history; that Gerard Manley Hopkins has no peer within the past several centuries; that Virginia Woolf is the most valuable novelist of our time; that James Joyce is the most valuable novelist of all time; and that the supreme thinker of the modern world is John Henry Newman. Continuing with the theses and dissertations, I learn that W. C. Williams possesses more insight into the modern condition than any other contemporary; that George Santayana hit closer to the nub than any other philosopher; that John Steinbeck reveals more knowledge of modern life than etc., etc.

'One other thing is sure: if anyone doubts or disputes these judgments, then he stands self-condemned as ignorant, uninformed, and naked to laughter. . . . He is—to be cruel but true—insensitive. The Paragon Complex deals only in superlatives.'[7]

The superlatives of the mass media, borrowed in part from the advertiser, need not be the direct cause of the like absurdity in scholars. It is enough that the public expects and relishes the shabby uniqueness. That the effect on academic thought should follow so impalpable a cause shows once again the dependence of Intellect on its surroundings. The world has long observed that small acts of immorality, if repeated, will destroy character. It is equally manifest, though never said, that uttering nonsense and half-truth without cease ends by destroying Intellect.

One reason, perhaps, why the educated men and women who professionally address the public can daily flout their own powers of reasoning is that they think of themselves as manipulators; that is, as users of a make-believe which will take effect on others but never on themselves. This illusion they have always shared with other practitioners, notably actors, teachers, and psychiatrists. But nowadays the example of applied science seems to say to everyone: 'Find the right formula and you will produce any result you desire.' This is the magic of advertisers and the hope of politicians; all the more natural that it should become the creed of writers and middlemen, who are nothing if not dealers in formulas.* Unsure of the fickle public, defeatist by habit, they come to believe in their catchwords with the superstition of an old sailor.

*These today include a large number of unrelated devices whose use would be hard to rationalize on grounds of either pleasure or utility. I have in mind not only the affectation of footnotes in weeklies and dailies, but the mechanical attention paid in the news to peoples' dress, facial expression, and hair (usually 'balding'), and the like.

Lately, these novelisms and other bookishness have led certain reporters to describe every attendant detail and to name half a dozen secondary characters, with their titles, before giving the clue or stating the point of the story. See for example the account of Maria Callas's refusal to sing at La Scala, *New York Times*, January 3, 1958—thirty lines before the reason or pretext was mentioned; again, the announcement of a prize for conductors (*Ibid.*, May 23, 1958)—twenty lines, containing the names of the judges, of the presiding Lord Mayor of Liverpool, and a comment on the performers, before the three winners were named. Trivial, if you will, there is in such 'news' a deep resistance to understanding. In some magazines it is now a rule that an expository article must not develop its subject in orderly fashion but must go 'banging about' (a technical term), so as to keep up suspense.

Or—one might also say—of an old artist. For wherever an effect cannot be related to a clear cause superstition thrives. And art, according to modern analysis, produces its magical effect by unconscious means, by underlying symbols and myths, of which neither the artist nor the beholder is fully aware. These hidden persuaders the creator himself merely gropes for. Intellect serves him not at all. When some sign gives the maker evidence of success, he clings to the sign. He is a manipulator, like the propagandist, advertiser, or middleman. The difference between the artist and them is that he trusts passion and seeks truth, whereas they repress both, disbelieving their existence in the public.

A good example of this absent-minded reliance on meaningless signs can be seen on the jacket of almost any book. By formula, blurb writers make all books of a kind resemble one another. All novels are 'sensitive' and 'moving'; all essays are 'brilliant' and 'provocative'; all narratives of adventure are 'thrilling' and 'incredible.' And all books whatever are 'stimulating.' The *difference* between one book and another, which is the only reason why a reader should want more than one book, is rarely brought out. Sometimes it seems deliberately hidden: a modern biography of Bertillon, which carefully explains that he did not invent, and was in fact opposed to, fingerprinting, is advertised on the jacket by means of a huge fingerprints.[8] This is the germ of the 'thought-cliché,' of which I shall speak in a moment.

The argument that book buyers pay no attention to blurbs once again misses the point. The ritual which goes on, paid for by the consumer, represents the abdication of judgment where judgment is called for and ostensibly offered. The misfitness is not even a profitable hoax, since it is admitted by publishers that blurbs and advertisements do not sell books. The words are written because it is a routine, a reflex—as is becoming ever more frequent in other parts of our intellectual life, for example, in so-called educational television. I do not refer to the use of the apparatus in schools, but to the programs for the educated. The begetters and floor managers of these panels and interviews, not knowing what form the substance should take, want them to resemble the 'regular' programs. To achieve this illusion, those invited to perform are given endless instructions—they must sit and look thus or so; they must be sure to interrupt; they must act casual and human, smoke if possible, and frequently mention household names—in short 'enliven' the program and ooze ease, even at the cost of forgetting what they came to impart. The possibility that the subject was alive in itself, and that its normal mode of presentation is part of the educational effect, cannot make headway against the ritual. The learned participants are themselves overawed by the claims of 'technique,' and think that their educational role is to wheedle the public out of its undeviating tastes.

In sober moments, everyone counts on the 'intelligent reader or listener' to overlook all these offenses against him. But resistance to folly takes strength beyond the common measure, so that corruption ends by infecting everyone in greater or less degree. Manners, conversation, intimate thoughts and feelings, (as we shall see in the next chapter) are muddied by what starts out as a trick of technique, a manipulative device, a ding-dong on Pavlov's bell. They all 'work,' indeed, but not toward the end proposed. Meeting at every turn the same bland, patronizing treatment, the man who feels within himself the wakefulness of Intellect comes to think of it as peculiar to himself, a somewhat shaming oddity. He too joins the ranks of the vanquished.

If by chance he has more than a taste for Intellect, an appetite, perhaps a passion, the habits of public opinion may strike him as so stern a rebuke that he succumbs to the common disease of denying in oneself what one finds denied outside. And that is how the intellectual comes to hide and suppress his powers. He pretends that he is harmless because powerless, yet he rebels against this self-imposed emasculation, the current name of which is conformity. In no sense positive, conformity expresses lack of power—not duress after struggle and loss, but lack of what one has consented to destroy. Seeing everywhere the color of compromise and accepting defeat as the gateway to influence over other minds, all but the strongest intellects neutralize their energies in vague protest, repudiate through false bonhomie their expensive education, and smother in collective indignation all efforts to end particular abuses.

Tocqueville described the cause of the distemper at the beginning of the scientific *coup d'état,* a hundred years ago: 'We love to think that effort and struggle will henceforth be futile and that our blood, muscles, and nerves will always be stronger than our will and our virtue. This is properly speaking the great disease of the age.'* Believing in 'forces' and the statistics which publicize them, thinking men ascribe to fashions the fixity of natural law and create the paradox that in a free society full of rights, intellectuals are sure that nothing can be done. By dint of talking about complexity and the age of woe, the men of ideas convince themselves that unless they move the world—or at least 'make the headlines'—they are paralyzed. Anger and cynicism and the chatter about crisis in every department of life are but varying ways of rationalizing the absence of public hope.

The ultimate conformity, abdication, what you will, finds expression in what I may for convenience call the thought-cliché. I used the term in speaking of the misleading image of a fingerprint that advertises a current book, but its like is to be found in all the forms of written or spoken opinion. The thought-cliché is an idea or a phrase contrary to fact, which is clung to because it sounds familiar and feeds a half-attentive wish for thought. This double appeal makes it indestructible. Against stereotyped *feeling,* the intellectual reader has long been on guard. As the motive power in political propaganda and cheap fiction, it has been frequently analyzed and ridiculed, nowhere more neatly than in Shaw's *Doctor's Dilemma,* where the newspaperman, who has heard the dying artist urge his wife to wear no mourning and not fear to remarry, says: 'I thought it showed a very nice feeling, his being so particular about his wife going into proper mourning for him and making her promise never to marry again.' But nothing so simple and entertaining can dispose

*To Gobineau, December 20, 1853.

of the thought-cliché, because it looks plausible and correction sounds pedantic. No matter how often convicted, the thought-cliché springs back, fresh, strong, and unconscious of offense.

We saw the shadow of this intellectual changeling in the paragraph on Nietzsche; a common example is found in the half-ironic assumption that a scholar or intellectual is a great mind,* and another in its corollary that intellect is a bar to success in business and politics. This cliché still clings to the fame of Woodrow Wilson, in spite of his achievements, which indeed are obscured by it. The opposite fame of Theodore Roosevelt for physical prowess proves the same point, for his intellectual interests and abilities are kept out of sight, out of respect for the soldier, hunter, and trust buster. The cliché has dogged the steps of Mr. Adlai Stevenson, and it survives the daily instances in which the lives of comparable men show it to be false: the 'exception' is cited in a tone of surprise and the cliché lives on. Thus a new president of the Teachers' Insurance and Annuity Association is presented to the public as 'Professor at heart, but a businessman in action.' The article gives his academic background in full, but before the end the reader is reassured: 'A book on the Einstein theories simplified put him to sleep a few nights ago.'[9]

The thought-cliché fulfills a tortuous purpose. At the outset it is deliberately contrived to spare the reader the effort of learning something new: my intelligent, cultivated editor wanted to print 'Newton' instead of 'Descartes.' But another and a subtler intention is to afford the pleasure of recognition and earn the gratitude that goes with it. 'Ah, yes, of course,' says the reader; 'I know all this: what an intelligent and pleasing writer!' Contrariwise, to utter the unexpected is to be bumptious, arrogant, undemocratic. 'What did you say? Never heard of it!' And woe to that other, who tries to steer a middle course by offering the new with an apology and incurs the charge of patronizing! It is, after all, so easy to give the impression of

---

*'On these pages are pictured members of Chicago's faculty, one of the most awesome collections of brains ever set before the camera.' *Life*, July 16, 1945.

weighty but painless novelty by dressing up the cliché skeleton. Darwin, for example, is about due for celebration, a hundred years after the appearance of the *Origin of Species*. The bare bones of the thought-cliché, the *digest* of Darwin's labors, is: he discovered evolution and his theory was the survival of the fittest. This is the dressing up: 'Darwin developed the theory that nature selected for survival only the fittest during a voyage around the world in the *Beagle* between 1831 and 1836. During that time he noted that while nearly all the plants and animals seen in the old and new world were different, the larger groups . . . were the same. This gave him the idea of evolution. . . . '[10]

For this series of misstatements, the reader has nothing but an approving nod—though he would take up arms for an error of nine feet in the height of the Chrysler Building. The nod means: 'I knew it all along.' He knew, namely, what is not so and what has been corrected in his presence again and again. But his mind is elastic, like that of Shaw's reporter. He clings to Darwin as the great originator and hence cannot believe that biological evolution antedates Darwin by about a century. To remember the names of Erasmus Darwin, Lamarck, and Lyell is too much to ask. And so would be the effort needed to perceive that the survival of the fittest, so far from being a theory, is either a fact or a tautology. Darwin's 'theory,' which he called natural selection, can only refer to the *result* of that survival.

I dare not add a word of Darwin's belief that natural selection was only one of three distinct means by which the rise of species might be explained. For the middleman at this point says that the truth is 'too complicated' for 'the average reader.' Thanks to this assumption—the opposite being seldom tried—the thought-cliché is assured of long life. With its backing, the forces of public opinion can maintain their successful resistance to learning, and the reflexes stimulated by 'enlightened' organs of opinion can circumvent thought.

That struggle explains why even on subjects of general interest there is a handful of informed specialists and a mass of misinformed or ill-informed 'educated' men. The barrier of difficulty is not in the subject; it is in the opinion that has fastened upon the subject. It is idle to speak of popularization as if we knew where it could be found. We lack a respectable tradition about it and find only two choices open—improvising an embarrassed idiom each time scholarship breaks into the news, and warming over a few thought-clichés.

The prevalence of the thought-cliché does more than misinform; it weakens attention, curiosity, and the critical sense. Where all is familiar, nothing arrests gliding and starts thought. And smooth progress permits any group of words, provided they are recognizable, to 'explain' almost any situation. In moments of political stress it is this condition of the public mind that makes scapegoats believable. The following example is not dangerous, merely silly, but it illustrates how mindlessness coexists with 'ideas,' indeed wants them nearby. An employment agency for college graduates explains in a newsletter why jobs are fewer: '1957 was a year of contradictions. A man-made satellite explored the heights of outer space, while sales on the stock market reached a 15-year low. The Wimbledon Singles Tennis Championship was won for the first time by a Negro, while integration problems were conspicuous in Little Rock. . . . [The agency] reflected the impact of events. The second six months showed the unsettling effect of Sputnik. . . . '

The more the task of leading or informing public opinion turns into manipulation, the more thought-clichés are required and produced, and the more certain subjects are dealt with in one invariable tone—perhaps to cover a lingering embarrassment. Thus the theme of intellect in politics calls for the playful and jocose.* Any reference to art, especially music, calls for a play on words, if only to show that

---

*'Professor Sows Political Seeds—A Williams College Professor of Political Science is conducting an experiment in practical campaigning this year. . . . He has been sowing political seeds since January in the fields and hillsides of the First Massachusetts Congressional District.' *New York Times*, May 4, 1958. Again: 'A Republican egghead is trying to leap from a college to the Iowa Governor's chair.' *New York Times*, March 16, 1958. Ever since 1898 (see above, note, p.1), the spectacle of several intellects together has been a subject of fun: 'A quaint little war of intellectuals is going on here to determine who among the Soviet eggheads is the least ethical.' *New York Times*, December 1, 1957.

the seriousness which belongs to bridge tournaments and the trade in baseball players is here out of place.* In a word, anything tinged with intellect must be 'enlivened.'

One could write an instructive fantasia on the subject of 'enlivening.' In defeatist theory public opinion is always on the verge of coma. Consequently, serious writers themselves must treat serious subjects in a special tone, a mixture of slang and verbal aggression that will galvanize the moribund.† Here is a learned critic writing in one of the two most intellectual Sunday newspapers: '*Measure for Measure,* that grimy tale of candid deviltry and secret lusts, is one of Shakespeare's so-called "dark" comedies, and when the Canadian Festival took a whack at it a couple of years ago the stress was squarely on its steamy and cynical back-alley atmosphere.'[11] Again, an austere publishing house announces that it is 'not bringing out just another *Gulliver*' but using 'the medium of the modern drawing to interpret the book and to bring it more alive.' The common assumption appears to be that the products of intellect are all dead, but that it is possible to inject them with life before they reach the receiving mind. This is one of the main causes of the present educational stasis. The teacher or textbook is expected to 'enliven' the subject while the pupil looks on in passive discontent. This passivity is not native to the mind; it is induced by the atmosphere of public opinion, and particularly by the manipulations to which middlemen resort, in the belief that they need to overcome indifference only in others.

· · ·

*'Musicians Sound Off at Soviet Writers,' 'Expert Music Teacher Finds He's Out of Tune' [i.e., lacking a teaching certificate], 'Tammany Leader's Conducting Is Not Meant as a Political Overture.' Not even ordinary physical operations connected with music can be spoken of in plain words: 'Lewisohn Stadium Put in Tune for Concert Opener on Monday.' *New York Times*, June 21, 1958. The thought-cliché carries over to the titles of musical biographies, essays, and memoirs, e.g., *With Strings Attached, Notes and Crotchets, Music Ho!*
†Its vocal parallel is the breathless and bumpy delivery of the news broadcaster.

In public affairs the means of enlivening are a fight and a scandal.*
Not surprising in itself, this intellectual limitation is of grave import
to democracies. Judging from the way fights and scandals are
received, we can guess how near dead center the public mind was just
before the news 'broke' and excitement filled the void. We have on
this point the testimony of an admirable journalist, Mr. James
Reston:

> WASHINGTON, June 12 [1958]—The Capital is in its glory
> tonight. After being bored to death with the economic cri-
> sis of the Western World it finally has the kind of simple po-
> litical personal conflict it likes: a partisan argument about
> who paid Sherman Adams' hotel bill in Boston. This is not
> likely to decide the future of the Republic or change the
> balance of power in the world but anyway it is interesting
> and it takes Washington's mind off the big complex ques-
> tions.[12]

One cannot help sympathizing—with the delighted relief and
with the strain of the 'big complex questions.' But one also remem-
bers that 'the Capital in its glory' refers not to the ancient plebs, not
even to the unassuming mass of the modern population, but to men
and women whom sanguine sociologists call 'opinion leaders.' This
fact should find a place in our thoughts when we consider extending
to all a free college education.†

A still nearer concern is the bearing of the unenlivened pulse
upon the quality of political debate. The press duly reports a clamor

---

*'Dispute Enlivens Sports Hearing: Celler and Keating Clash on "Objectiv-
ity" Issue as House Unit Starts Inquiry,' *New York Times*, June 18, 1957.
    'Occasional clashes between Senators Herman E. Talmadge, Democrat
of Georgia, and Jacob K. Javits, Republican of New York, enlivened a Senate
Sub-committee hearing today on anti-filibuster proposals.' *Ibid.*, June 25,
1957.
†We shall see later how necessary it seems to teachers and educators that
their daily tasks be 'exciting.'

of voices that 'score' and 'rap' and 'bar' and 'ban' something or somebody at great expense of words. A democracy rightly takes pride in this manifestation of free speech without reprisals. But raucousness is not an end in itself. Criticism is supposed to demonstrate an opponent's error or the merits of a better idea—intellectual work par excellence. How adept are the 'opinion leaders' at this kind of work—or rather, what forms and traditions can they follow in public give-and-take? The answer is, none. Intellectual forms have been replaced by psychological ploys. When lawyers in important professional posts have attacked or defended recent Supreme Court decisions, the discussion has chiefly brought forth mutual accusations of hysteria, panic, and irresponsibility.[13] Granted that newspapers made the most of these enlivening suggestions, they were there to be made much of.

That political argument properly so called is extinct can be seen by sampling first the current newspapers and then the Lincoln-Douglas debates of a hundred years ago. Simple in language—for they were directed at the plain people of Illinois towns and farms—those speeches contain reasonings on moral and constitutional points which today would tax the attention of graduate students. This is not to say that 'thoughtful men' today are less intelligent, but that their powers have habitually been put to other uses than reasoning. They are 'sensitive' minds, quick to suspect hidden bias, to note an odd turn, to assess unconscious motives in spoken and written words. All this they do with much expenditure of feeling and a penchant for communicating to their friends not their thoughts but their anxieties.

The apprehensive mood explains in part the exaggerated vindictiveness frequent in intellectual circles and the herdlike urge to coerce. One such disgraceful instance of mob action in high places was the pressure put on a publishing house some years ago after it had brought out a book on cosmogony by an unorthodox but plausible writer. A number of scientists threatened to withdraw their textbooks if the firm did not withdraw the offending work. The publisher yielded. The editor, who had not chosen but only edited the book, was dismissed. In short, the scientific treatment of the case was successful. The worst of the incident is that to this day one cannot persuade a good many scientists that the rightness or wrongness of this writer's views is totally irrelevant to a judgment of the scientists' behavior, and that that behavior is the negation not only of civil rights but of science itself.

The dangers of such anti-intellectualism in a republic are evident. Its members tend to lose the sense of the actuality of issues and certainly of the weight of arguments. Any conflict is a game, and probably a dirty game, in which the spectators weigh only the forces for or against the side they fancy; they impute motives and think abstract hatreds, as in a state of war. A sign of this is that in giving up the lawyer-like liberal tradition of debate we have changed the meaning of the word 'controversial.' It now means something (or someone) about which we cannot afford to engage in controversy—virtually the opposite of the former meaning. Even for lawyers, controversy is made to sound like a disreputable thing, as this description suggests: '[His background] has not prevented him from building a lucrative legal practice, mainly with respectable trade unions but with some controversial ones as clients.'[14] Again, a radio forum run by a university in the national capital publicizes its programs on public affairs with the motto: 'Clarification Not Controversy Has Its Reward.'[15] In the legislature, too, the futility of such speeches as are still to be heard is acknowledged by the rules which have made the *Congressional Record* no record at all, but a wad of harangues largely unspoken and equally without effect on those near and far. The journal resembles the posed newspaper photograph showing the public official and his aides poring over the state paper just drafted—a ridiculous huddle and a falsehood masquerading as news.

The temptings of defeatism and the devices of manipulation lead everywhere to a like result: argument taxes the mind, whereas suspicion or psychologizing excites it; make-believe ideas, made-up pictures, and a cloud of irrelevancies—scholarly, novelistic, philanthropic, and other—refresh or divert anemic thought. Or to put it 'constructively,' thanks to improved means of communication, social life and the work of Intellect within it have been decently replaced by the phantasms of public opinion.

III

❧

Conversation, Manners, and the Home

In private life, the counterpart of public debate is conversation. The word sounds old-fashioned and its meaning is blurred, because in the years since conversation was given a name and made an ideal, its nature has changed as much as that of public debate—and for the same reasons. Yet whether we use the word to mean all forms of verbal exchange or, more narrowly, the sociable sifting of opinion for pleasure, conversation is the testing ground of manners. This is so because manners are minor morals which facilitate the relations of men, chiefly through words. When those verbal relations are deliberately staged, for no other purpose than pleasure, men find themselves engaged in an intellectual exercise that is one of the delights of life. Manners, therefore, are not solely a clue to the deeper moral assumptions of an age, they are also a strong or weak guardian of Intellect at its most exposed.

Conversation being difficult, the reality of it has always been inferior to the ideal. We can nevertheless deduce almost as much from the ideal—or the lack of it—as from the audible reality. The reader will have noticed that I did not speak of sociable conversation as the *exchange*, but as the *sifting* of opinion. The 'exchange' view is a nearly correct description of modern practice: A delivers an opinion while B thinks of the one he will inject as soon as he decently can. It is an exchange in the same sense that we 'exchange' greetings: we offer a formula and are offered another, but generally go off with our own.

In this rudimentary game Intellect plays a small role. It contents itself with finding words adequate to the belief or impression of the moment, while navigating a passable course among other ideas suspected of being afloat in the vicinity. The genuine exercise or true conversation sifts opinion, that is, tries to develop tenable positions by alternate statements, objections, modifications, examples, arguments, distinctions, expressed with the aid of the rhetorical arts—irony, exaggeration, and the rest—properly muted to the size and privateness of the scene.

In modern life this discovery of opinion by conversing is supposed to have more than pleasurable uses. We are addicted to 'panels' and 'forums' and 'round tables' on given topics. When broadcast, such performances are supposed to interest, and even instruct, millions of listeners and viewers, also in living rooms. That these conversations in public most often fail is a proof of the lack of conversational skill among the educated. After one such failure on a national network, an introspective member of the group, a psychiatrist, tried to state the causes, for the use of program directors. He blamed the latter as well as the speakers: 'Every one . . . did a bad job. Our inept efforts at discussion reminded me of a lot of falling-down drunks trying to shake hands.' He then listed the requisites of success: 'not a group of yes-men, but of men who are on a par in their knowledge of the field . . . so that they can communicate without such purely verbal confusions as clouded our interchange. I will say flatly that unless any panel . . . is given lots of prebroadcast time for free discussion, and repeatedly, the group cannot be expected to talk effectively in front of the camera. . . . An unrehearsed poly-disciplinary group lack a common language. . . . We had assembled for an hour and a half before the broadcast, but failed to take advantage even of that meager time. This was because after about ten minutes of groping talk, further discussion was halted lest we become stale. . . . Similarly, during the conduct of the discussion, just as we would begin to join issue around some problem, our moderator would abruptly change the topic. . . . Everybody on the panel felt increasingly frustrated and the audience was confused and unenlightened.'

Most participants in public conversations would agree with the critic and would welcome one or two hours of warming up. But in a practiced conversationalist a prolonged rehearsal would kill interest and spontaneity before the broadcast. The director's fear of staleness was therefore justified; his error was to suppose that his experts— lecturers and writers though they were—were conversationalists. Our use of panels and other discussion groups offers a curious instance of a social form that does not produce its adepts. The cause must lie in the existence of a stronger contrary force.* In a discussion of 'Political Communication and Social Structure in the United States,' Mr. David Riesman makes clear that the eliciting of opinion, notably by interviewers, is universally considered the very opposite of conversation. That name is reserved for 'chit-chat about health, personal relations, the job.'[1]

A German writer, noting recently that in the title of the latest edition of Brockhaus, the term 'Konversations-lexicon' has been dropped, attributes the general decay of conversation to the lack of an idle class, or more simply, of leisure.[2] But leisure is increasing, and enough time, surely, is spent by persons with a college degree in 'exchanging' ideas, on social as well as on public occasions. It cannot be our material circumstances alone that hamper us, but rather our manners, that is to say, at bottom, our emotions.

For the starting point of conversation is contradiction, and this democratic manners do not tolerate. Contradiction implies that one

---

*The program called "Conversation" and led by Mr. Clifton Fadiman was, it is true, generally successful as conversation. It received several awards and a good deal of written approval. But it did not commend itself very long to NBC, nor to any advertising sponsors, for whom monologue has an obvious advantage.

or another of the conversing group must be wrong, and under modern manners, as I said earlier without trying to explain it, peculiar feelings cling to error. Perhaps science has made small accuracy sacred to all, though everybody thinks that to be caught in a mistake is necessary to prove that one is human. Or again it may be that business and industry lead us to overestimate the interest of facts, about which contradiction is foolish. I think it more likely that the fear of being wrong which prohibits contradiction has in view, not error as an intellectual mishap, but the punishment that follows a breach of group unity. If your hostess says that the latest play by Mr. Kentucky Jones is very fine, and you contradict her, no matter how sweetly, one of you will have the majority in opposition. And this, regardless of who is the odd man out, nobody will enjoy. The reasoning goes: you are one against several=you are wrong=you are a fool. In some companies, the series of inferences would run: perverse=showing off=a snob; and the rejection would be no less complete.

In either form, the syllogism is bound to be hard to refute when the first premise of a society is that the voice of the people, ascertained by majority vote, is the voice of God. All the great men since Socrates may have asserted the contrary, but their assertion was evidently self-serving. Virtue in modern politics is against the solitary dissident. It is assumed that he too wants the backing of a majority, and having gained it will enjoy power. This is never allowable in a populist culture. Even in the Soviet Union the 'cult of personality' has been denounced, which is comic but indicative.

By confining conversation to facts or to the exchange of bland opinions, trouble is avoided. This is elementary self-protection in a system where the absence of fixed place and privilege puts one at the mercy of the group. When we quote what Tocqueville said: 'I know of no country in which there is so little independence of mind and real freedom of discussion as in America,'[3] we must not ascribe wholly to timidity what is in part sensible self-restraint. Even in the great days of militant liberalism it was decreed that politics and religion should be excluded from general conversation. This is a tribute to the power of words, in that people take them as the signs of instant action, of treason, rape, sacrilege. One does not know whether to wonder more at the imagination of the listener who is so readily hurt and alarmed, or at the skill of the speaker who over a cup of tea can with a few phrases produce flushed faces and the grim ardor of a militia defending hearth and home. However it comes about, the motive of curiosity about ideas, the play of mind, is not accounted a social possibility. But subversion is.

That is why full democracy has simply extended the no-politics-or-religion rule to any strong opinion. Yeats, moving in circles full of intellectuals and full of ideas, could yet long for the conversation of a *society*, for gaiety of mind and the fantasy that prepares matured convictions, for the kind of agreement that comes with, and not instead of, the free play of Intellect.[4] What he found and what we have is the political judgment of dissidence carried into the living room and using the threat of mild or harsh ostracism to prevent even the shadow of conflict.

In putting first the political, I do not mean to overlook other impeding emotions. Good conversation, like any game, calls for equals in strength. But in a social system where movement is easy and frequent, one meets mostly strangers, whose equality other than legal and abstract has to be presumed. To safeguard that presumption, democratic manners prevent a jousting in which somebody might appear stronger, brighter, quicker, or richer of mind. This is not to say that democratic society is without snobbery. But like our public opinion, our accepted snobbery seldom ventures outside the tangible. It relies on differences that are not subject to dispute, such as disinfected wealth or descent from a famous historical event. Otherwise, the assumption of social equality indispensable to our life is preserved by blinking or suppressing all signs of the contrary.

This description may suggest that underneath its amiability the democratic group hides ugly sentiments. This is rarely true. Whatever his unconscious fear of Intellect, the democrat's conscious desire is philanthropic; he wants love to prevail; he wants to add friends to friends and find them friends to one another, as in Euclid; he wants, above all, that everything and everybody should be agreeable, by which he means interchangeable, indistinguishable—like a prefabricated part—until the taste for human encounters is purified and uplifted from the social to the gregarious. The highest merit and pleasure is to love people, to want to be with people, to be 'good with people.'

Only a churlish man could profess insensibility to so much warmth and such regal indifference to the marks, precisely, of difference. For the true-born democrat, origin, education, and intellect matter no more than clothes, speech, and deportment. He no longer sees them, or he feels remorse when the thought of them breaks through his proper manners to his conscious mind.

The philanthropic motive thus generates its atmosphere and chooses its goals. The hope being to found unity on a simple similarity among men, the search is for essences. Not externals, depths. The taste for psychologizing takes it for granted that depths are more real than surfaces, and since depths will be shown only to the face of love, each person seeks out the other's heart. No longer does anyone think or say of a new acquaintance: 'I disliked him, but we had a fine conversation.' Rather, we guard against this discrepancy by prefacing the slightest reference to disagreement with: 'Please understand, I'm very fond of Ted, but I think he's wrong about transplanting irises.' Face to face, we say: 'I entirely agree with you, but—' This means, surely, that knowing the weakness of our intellects, we confess that we might disagree unreasonably, out of dislike. So strong is the belief that to differ is to endanger the budding love of new friends, that the word 'candid' has become synonymous with critical: 'I was candid with him. I told him—' As everybody knows, the desire for personal rapport knows no bounds or season; it is just as passionate in the committee meeting as in the living room. Indeed, who can now tell the two places apart by manners or subjects of discourse? On the occasions called sociable, the sought-for communion untroubled by ideas—that is, the discovery of the stranger's essence—brings forth the ultimate praise: 'She's a real person,' 'I found him very real.'

To reach that reality quickly, the preliminaries must be reduced to a minimum—hence the supreme duty of informality, the casual style. Its contrary, politeness, would be sniffed at as 'formal manners,' rebuked as 'aloofness' and 'reserve,' or condemned as 'superiority.' This is one more reason to bar Intellect, which incurs all these disapprovals: it has and is form, and it is superior to nonintellect as any skill is to the corresponding incapacity. Aware of the burden, some possessors of Intellect try to mask or apologize for it. They exhibit a rough, boisterous simplicity, or they belittle mind, disclaim it, and patronize by turns. In this self-consciousness begins that shuffling which is the characteristic manner produced by our manners.

Shuffling is what one cannot help doing when one is pulled by contrary feelings or chaotic perceptions, and unwilling or unable to make any prevail. To occupy this position might be mistaken for the self-awareness I call an attribute of Intellect. But there is a distinction between the shuffling of the self-conscious and the act of choice of the self-aware. The conventions that informality condemns were invented to facilitate this choice until it becomes second nature. To the lack of such habits under the reign of casualness can be attributed the painful extremes of tact and rudeness that characterize the modern scene.

To be sure, the rudeness exists only from the point of view of Intellect. Its opponents find natural the use of conversation for quick intimacy through probing and diagnosis. They scarcely attend to what you say in their eagerness to discern what you are. Their antennas and instincts are at work and not—as is soon plain—their ears and their reason. This accounts for the incoherence of the panel discussion and for the difficulty of maintaining general conversation among six or eight people. They break up into tête-à-têtes for mutual auscultation. Odd little indelicacies follow: people do not hesitate to ascertain your circumstances in full detail. They expect the same interviewing in return, to which they say: 'That's a good question.' You are evidently a bright, engaging specimen; they are noting down points. They remark: 'You said something just now that interested me'; i.e., the rest was useless for my purpose. No one thinks it improper to *personalize* in this way, but would deem it stiff and artificial to address himself to a theme that, like an object in the midst of the conversing group, stood at a distance from each participant.

It being accepted practice to start conversation by asking people what they do, one hears what is uppermost in their minds, and one is not always pleased. The lawyer's or the doctor's case, the businessman's or housewife's worry, can be as trying in talk as in reality. But it is wrong to conclude that shop talk is boring and should be ruled out. People seldom object when the shop is their own—the men on one side 'exchanging' stock-market rumors and opinions; the women on the other comparing children, schools, and clothes. These concerns being the stuff of life may be talked about in society, provided the speaker keeps his distance from them and *makes* something of his facts or views. He must, that is, mix the raw material of experience with some thought that gives a handle to further thought, to disagreement, to speculation—Yeats's 'phantasy.' Any subject—a lost button—then becomes matter for conversation and a source of delight.

Achieving this calls for effort and a practice we now lack. Even if the personal view of sociability did not bar impersonal Intellect, the exercise would prove too taxing for minds atrophied on the side of reasoning, helpless to judge what is fitting. Sometimes in a gathering an idea does emerge in spite of everybody, stopping all other talk. One then sees how unprepared for this virgin birth intelligent people can be. They have thought the thought but never reflected on it. They are forced to improvise; but their span of attention hardly takes in one or two modifiers, and their faculty of inference stumbles over every fallacy. Try, for example, to advance the proposition discussed here, that for true sociability being agreeable is not enough: five indignant voices will exclaim, 'So you like disagreeable people!' A nicely articulated idea, neither conventional nor perverse, nor charged with ulterior motive, seems an unknown species *in society*—for every educated person must frequently meet one in his reading. In society, it may be surmised, everyone is made more delicate, fine-grained, and impressionable by the presence of others; and since impressions strike at random and exclude their rivals, each person is engulfed in the confusion of the senses, hence self-conscious rather than self-aware, oppressed by a surfeit of personality, his own and others'.

At other times, a vestige of the desire to not merely report but comment on life will produce the accepted substitutes for conversation—the anecdote of the raconteur and the quasi-lecture of the expert. Both may be, like any other thing, good or bad of their kind, but at their best they still are not conversation, even though either may be so much preferred by intellectual people to the usual small-talk-in-depth that they always invite a known 'entertainer' for the evening. Whatever the burden of his monologue, his presence implies the other guests' known inadequacy—especially if his words purport to inform or instruct. For conversation—as must be said of most good things in this infatuated age—is the antithesis of education. Before conversation begins, the participants must be finished and polished persons; what must be 'real' about them is the possession of their intellectual resources. They must know their own minds and have taken care to furnish them, deliberately, with tenable ideas—Yeats's 'matured convictions.' With opposing views they must deal briskly, lightly, and in evident pleasure—Yeats's gaiety of mind. The result is a spectacle the beauty of which is the subject of a famous passage in James's *Psychology*:

'When two minds of a high order, interested in kindred subjects, come together, their conversation is chiefly remarkable for the summariness of its allusions and the rapidity of its transitions. Before one of them is half through a sentence, the other knows his meaning and replies. Such genial play with such massive materials, such an easy flashing of light over far perspectives, such careless indifference to the dust and apparatus that ordinarily surround a subject and seem to pertain to its essence, make these conversations seem true feasts for gods to a listener who is educated enough to follow them at all. . . .

'But we need not go as far as the ways of genius. Ordinary social intercourse will do. There the charm of conversation is in direct proportion to the possibility of abridgment and elision and in inverse ratio to the need of explicit statement . . . some persons have a real mania for completeness, they must express every step. They are the most intolerable of companions, and although their mental energy must in its way be great, they always strike us as weak and second-rate. In short, the essence of plebeianism, that which separates vulgarity from aristocracy, is perhaps less a defect than an excess, the constant need to animadvert upon matters which for the aristocratic temperament do not exist.'[5]

If James is right in his terms as well as in his description, it is not surprising that democratic manners spoil conversation and make it the last resort of the socially marooned. But where he says 'aristocratic' he might more aptly say 'patrician,' for he is thinking of the nineteenth-century blend of lordly and upper bourgeois manners, and not of politics and the prerogatives of class. The aboriginal aristocrat is certainly not a *causeur*, much less an intellect; he is a fighter, not a reasoner. It was the high middle class that historically wedded knowledge and elegance, reasoning and *politesse*. This compromise excluded pedantry, on one side, and arrogance on the other, while retaining a pleasurable echo of both conflict and learning. From which it follows that the problem of manners for democratic societies—supposing that modern men and women desired conversation—would be to add the democrat's good will and brotherliness to the earlier ingredients without upsetting their balance within the ideal.

To do this, and find again a place for Intellect, the democratic heart would have to be purged of some of its other feelings. For, as James goes on to show: ' . . . the gentleman ignores considerations relative to conduct, sordid suspicions, fears, calculations, etc., which the vulgarian is fated to entertain; . . . he is silent where the vulgarian talks; . . . he gives nothing but results where the vulgarian is profuse of reasons; . . . he does not explain or apologize; . . . he uses one sentence instead of twenty; . . . in a word, there is an amount of *interstitial* thinking, so to call it, which it is quite impossible to get him to perform, but which is nearly all that the vulgarian mind performs at all. All this suppression of the secondary leaves the field *clear*—for higher flights should they choose to come.'[6]

These observations, made when class lines were not yet effaced, bring us back to the expedient of shuffling in our manners and its hindrance to free intellectual movement. Shuffling is not an individual fault, but an accepted solution to a general problem. Thus in the common round of committee meetings, it is necessary to differ, but also impossible. Manners therefore decree that one shall say: 'I may be all wrong, but—'; 'You'll correct me if I'm wrong'; 'I'm only thinking aloud'; 'It looks that way from where I sit—'; 'It's only a crazy notion that crossed my mind.' The lexicon of pussyfooting is familiar. On its title page should appear the motto: 'Never say, "I think," which is obsolete; always say, "I feel," as in, "I feel that the Treasurer has been dipping into the till"; then if you are wrong, you haven't said anything.' Though the shuffling vocabulary is all hypocrisy, it is a routine hypocrisy concealing a desperate wish to placate. Torn between the fear of error and the fear of being thought inhuman, hating to be misunderstood and hating even worse to be misliked, we verbally cast off self-confidence and throw ourselves on the mercy of the court, saying 'frankly' before every sentence and giving warning when we are going to be 'candid.'

The dominant feeling confronting its mate in these encounters is vanity and not pride. Vanity is a static thing. It puts its faith in what it has, and is easily wounded. Pride is active, and satisfied only with what it can do, hence accustomed not to feel small stings. The distinction, though not absolute, is highly suggestive. True, men have always been vain and the proud have not all died out. But if under democracy the effort to placate has eclipsed the art of pleasing, it is because democratic life exposes tender vanity more widely, and because increased numbers multiply the claimants to placation, that is, to being kept in good humor. Formerly, the crux of the art of pleasing was to 'shine,' which meant to flatter others' pride by a visible effort of mind, charm, wit—in short, by a gift of something more valuable than plain unvarnished self. Nowadays we coax rather than flatter and we do it by whittling down the self so as to spare vanity the smallest hurt. To shine would be egotistical, one must merely glow. This is of especial importance in the practical relations of life, or as we say, in public relations. Just as contradiction is taboo within doors, to avoid division, so any 'stern opinion'* is ruled out abroad, in deference to a vague self-interest: everybody senses that in the free agitation of so many human molecules anyone may become another's customer, relative, employer, employee, or 'opposite number.' One must guard against disaffection by being always smooth, lubricated, ready to talk and even to lunch. This is neither politeness nor servility but public relations.

The native critics of Western culture blame commercialism for this mind-destroying habit, as if trade by itself produced the wormlike stance. They fail to see that it is popular government which has made accountability universal and thus caused everybody to be forever 'selling himself' to everybody else. It is not commercial greed or any clear advantage that moves one government official to butter up another in a distant bureau: he is moved by the you-never-know which a society of unsure equals engenders. And to his mild apprehension, mixed with genuine fellow-feeling, the other responds. This mutual tenderness is the wellspring of all our philanthropies. Conversely, in a society that had little free movement but fixed ranks and set forms, the most rapacious merchant could go through life

---

*I borrow this useful phrase from a sketch of the life and character of the great American athlete, Rafer Johnson: 'Johnson never says anything controversial, has no stern opinions about anything, and is not generally regarded as "good copy" by track reporters. Yet everybody likes him. . . . A lot of kids,' adds the university coach, 'are shy and look away when they're talking to you. Not Rafer. He is literate.' *New York Times*, July 29, 1958.

without fawning and would not dare sell himself or anything else during social intercourse. He might represent as fitly as anyone the human dignity we talk about so much, seeing it so little.

To generalize, the main cause of our distress as social beings, a distress all the greater for being obscure, lies in the democratic rule of Everything for All. Distinction, discrimination, by which the intellect divides and reduces its burdens, mean for us only invidious distinction and unjust discrimination. We resist exclusions and accordingly do not even exclude ourselves but remain perpetually in competition with all our fellow men; we never give up, a priori, any of our pretensions, in consequence of which there is nothing to relieve us of being continually our own shock absorbers.

Meanwhile, this obsession with public relations injures Intellect by taking precedence over all other motives and interests—simplicity, independence, acquired rank and repute, and the force or fantasy of talent itself. The surrender is by no means a purely American weakness, or one affecting only the captive intellectuals of Madison Avenue. The world over, the demands of every profession now come second to the need of perpetual self-justification. To take a foreign example that is especially vivid by its contrast of then and now, consider the English stationmaster. Traditionally, he has been a man of strong character and quick intelligence, whose responsibilities, far heavier than those of his American counterpart, could only be shouldered after a long apprenticeship. Until recently, his dignity was signalized by the wearing of a top hat, dark clothes including pin-striped trousers, and often some decoration in the buttonhole. A modern 'profile' confirms the fact that 'of all railway functionaries the stationmaster is the most impressive,' and goes on to detail his nerve-racking generalship. Then comes the modern conclusion: 'But perhaps the most important qualification for the job is being able to get on with people—both his own staff and the public. The pleasantries exchanged with passengers on the platform, the views he expresses as a member of the Newbury Chamber of Commerce, his weekly visit to the cattle market to discuss the day's traffic with the local farmers, play a vital part in keeping British Railways in touch with its customers.'[7]

In the accompanying illustration, the stationmaster new style wears a sack suit and cap. As his technical duties have yielded first place to public relations, he has become informal, casual, 'human.' But the rational necessity for this is worth noting: the public must not be allowed to forget so inconspicuous an institution as the railways; must be made to love them *via* the stationmaster and his pleasantries. Which suggests that if man ever conquers space, a competent staff will be needed to keep the public favorably reminded of the existence of the sun and moon.

The extent to which the difficulties inherent in framing a code of democratic manners have been aggravated by the spread of literary emotions is still imperfectly appreciated. This is true even though modern art has portrayed the shuffler in all his poses, and proved again and again that the maze of his feelings is superior to the rectilinear intellect. From the many fictional models everyone has learned that 'the other' to whom all manners are directed is, like oneself, sensitive and a psychologizer. He is watchful, anxious, and vain where patrician pride would scorn 'sordid suspicions, fears, and calculations.' What ensues among the educated is a game of forestalling and reassurance by self-depreciation, which is shuffling intellectualized. Its manifestations are so familiar that we cease noticing how they destroy good sense—as, for instance, in this circular from a research institute: 'Despite some difficulties undoubtedly traceable to the recession (the term has possibly been replaced by another, equally inadequate and confusing word by the time these lines reach you). . . . ' Or again, in a column about books: 'We are not the one to tell you about the virtues of one dictionary as against another. We hardly know anything about them and we have never quite believed in them. They disquiet us. . . . Nevertheless . . . '

What is the double play here? A does not want us to think he believes the recession is an entity or an excuse, while he actually does what he deprecates. B does not want us to think he is a high-brow familiar with dictionaries, or that he is about to say what in fact he does say after his 'Nevertheless.' This wanting to and not wanting to seem to, because one knows how others will gloat or blame or laugh, has been exquisitely described by a distinguished essayist and writer of short stories who is a connoisseur in self-consciousness. He tells of going into a bookstore in Athens to buy the supposedly dirty book, Nabokov's *Lolita*: 'I . . . held it in my hands . . . while a lady clerk, very clean and genteel, stood smirking beside me. . . . Perhaps I only imagined it, but she seemed so clearly to condescend to me, so unmistakably to consider it beneath her station to engage in such transactions (she had to make a living, of course, and she did not hold it against me *personally*) that I left finally without buying the book.

'If I could only have said or done something to make it clear that I was not just another provincial American professor on a moral toot (after all, I was precisely a provincial American profes-sor), but a reader who has relished for a long time Nabokov's oblique, unidiomatic war on our culture, and who—it would not really have been the point, even if I could have said it. Either way, it is a trap.'[8]

The description is ironic, of course—what statement these days is not?—but modern irony includes literalism, and we can take this *marivaudage*, this dizzying interplay of 'insights' (plus irony), as the formula of the suspicions, fears, and calculations that make up sophisticated shuffling. In reason, all these formulas and episodes are indefensible. Simple reflection says to the researcher: use the word that everyone uses or find a better, only come to the point; and to the critic: in a column about books why hesitate to speak of dictionaries? Do it, we expect it; only, forget yourself and omit apologies. As for the professor and the lady clerk, their tangled emo-tions would require a revolution to dissever.

But in tracing the trouble to its source, reflection picks out of the recital the reference to the novelist Nabokov's 'oblique war on our culture.' For the phrase gives a clue to the tortuous relation between the shuffling manners of democracy and the modern artist's oblique thrust at society. Where have intellectuals learned, together with their anti-intellectualism, these diffident gestures of the spirit? The answer is: in the novel. The novel from its beginnings in *Don Quixote* and *Tom Jones* has persistently made war on two things—our culture and the heroic.* Unlike tragedy voluminous and explicit, the novel, depicting life with cruel educational intent, has been the textbook of increasingly plain manners, a manual of resentful self-consciousness. Again unlike tragedy, in which everyone is in the right, the novel is a melodrama in which everyone is in the wrong. The novel knows no magnanimity or logic and makes the most trivial traits indicative. The inflection of a voice, the angle at which a head is carried, the coarse hairs that grow on the back of a hand—at some time or other, every physical accident has served a novelist to characterize the victim or the instrument of a moral lesson. Two centuries of geniuses have shown us that every moral attitude betrays an immoral urge, every virtue its complementary vice, every institution the evil it is meant to restrict. No wonder modern man has grown suspicious of himself and others, devious, ironic.

And now our scientific determinism reinforces the novelist's habit of reading back from sign to soul. Owing to this psychological license, the same manners which ignore birth, position, speech, and deportment, fasten on a man's complexion and habitus with the avowed endeavor to 'see what makes him tick.' The upshot is to reduce ticking to near-inaudibility. Everyone muffles his soul for fear

*We speak indeed of the 'hero of a novel' and continue to regard Don Quixote, Tom Jones, Julien Sorel, Pierre Bezuhov, and Dmitri Karamazov as figures larger than life. But their careers and that of their equals show chiefly their weakness even as they imply the wrongness of society. The ultimate models of this joint inadequacy are Flaubert's Frédéric Moreau and Joyce's Bloom. Only Scott and his disciple Balzac attempted to portray heroic heroes.

he shall be deemed one who thinks well of himself, a seeker after power.

But evasion is useless: the novelist's point of fire is never still and there is no pleasing him. He will blame his puppets for not being or doing something which, if they attempted it, he would brand as affectation and would kill with ridicule. This double standard the intellectual part of society learns from him and so acquires the knack of captiousness: nothing, no one, is ever quite good enough. Better to carp at all who stand up in public than turn magnanimous and overlook inevitable flaws, for skepticism is a better guard against power than admiration. This temper affects the judgment of lives, including one's own. Biography, which has borrowed from the novel the guerrilla technique, derides ambition as pretentious and absurd, though it also blames thinkers and doers for not having converted the world and made it perfect. From these failures, miscalled 'tragedies,' the reader learns the futility of taking risks, and studies to be small.

Behind these literary lessons lies the fear of power, to which I have often referred. Why is this fear so pervasive as to seem obvious wisdom? One reason is that, historically, democracy has followed the libertarian ideal, which asserted itself slowly and painfully at the expense of monarchical and aristocratic power. The long struggle has left us the tradition that power as such is evil; power is something that need not be and that no good man would want, for whoever seeks evil must be evil. Since the world cannot subsist without some visible concentrations of power, the *world* is evil. And it follows that the acts and attitudes suggestive of powerlessness constitute the definition of virtue. The effusions of philanthropy, the self-abnegation of science, the unworldliness of art, seem the models of the good life. Like the history of liberty, the history of art is used as a Golden Legend full of pious examples. The naughty world, triumphant over genius, proves the artist a martyr, not a doer, and hence superior to the power that destroys him.

The increasing zeal for art thus re-enforces the hatred of power, quite as if artistic geniuses were not in fact the embodiment of ruthless power, fanatically bent on exercising sway outside art as well as within it. The truth is that when great artists go under, it is not as slaughtered lambs but as the vanquished in the struggle for power. Yet even when a modern critic perceives this, the moral drawn from it is that art must renounce the struggle 'in the court of kings' and search for its rightful place 'in the castle of God.'⁹ Though Western art as a whole teaches no such lesson, modern artists have not resisted, but abetted, our century's obsession about power, often with a lack of humor which will divert posterity. Not until our time, as Diana Trilling pointed out, had anyone enacted Mozart's Don Juan as a victim of his impulses, innocent of the lust for power, simply a dilettante carried away, presumably, by the possibilities of public relations.¹⁰

This other-worldliness of our day necessarily fears and shuns Intellect. Discipline is too close to power, logic too far from philanthropy. Rather, the relaxed will associated with art and with its many surrogates called 'creative' appears as the only goal for the intelligent. Men no longer speak of careers, they disavow ambition; they are rebels without a cause. Formerly, the goal of a rebel was to destroy in order to *do*. On his way, he would bend the least possible under pressure, he schooled himself to yield without losing integrity. But for this kind of success one must be an integer to start with. A man can resist, a little more each day, along a self-set course, until he masters his soul, his work, perhaps his age. Though often beaten, his intellect and his conscience help keep each other clear. But the disintegrated, dis-intellected intellectual of today, whether simon-pure bohemian or turned commercial in his own despite, fights sullenly and shuffles his way out of any possible exercise of power. His excuse to himself rests on the postulate that unless he can set the whole world right, he can do nothing. And thus the doctrine of a universal, unconquerable evil feeds itself.

Abdicating power generates the taste for organized inaction and the pursuit of pseudo-work: I refer to redundant talk, broody sittings of committees and proliferating plans and reports fore and aft of nonexisting accomplishments. It is not exaggerating to say that ritual gathering has by now become a polite form of debauch. I have before me a pressing request to attend one of these consultations without fee: 'Our meetings so far have been so stimulating that I can't imagine you would be bored. We're full of ideas and anxious to bring to these ideas the best . . . the most. . . . Could you come to lunch [with six others] at which time you could give us some invaluable . . . which should . . . most serious consideration?'

In these conferrings, of course, anything resembling direct assertion and the maintenance of intellectual order is forbidden by the manners and vocabulary of good-fellowship, and this insures at once the orgiastic effect and its prolongation. But we are left with a puzzling fact. Some of the participants in meetings of this sort feel penitent. Why have they come? It is of course part of the ritual to protest against the waste of time, but some few mean what they say. Why do they not decline? I would not impute to them the desire of the guilty to corrupt others. Rather, they give in as the drunkard does when urged by his cronies: he does not want to be pointed at. That the haunter of committee rooms has forgotten the strain of genuine intellectual work is evidenced by his long loose reports. His endurance is reserved for 'work-type' activities—telephoning, dictating, scheduling, and lunching creatively. He and his kind are caught in a tight web of these obligations, which must be discharged day by day under pain of chaos and reprisals. The executive aim becomes the subduing of 'arrears,' whereby all are overoccupied and underworked.

Critics who observe this entrapment of the able generally ascribe it to 'organization' and the authority of the group, which are in turn attributed to the inertia of the 'mass man' and the strength of his unanimous desires.* This view implies that it is the weight of the characterless millions which oppresses a stoutly resisting intellectual class of individualists, after robbing each of the dignity and pleasure of work in solitude. But the behavior of intellectuals in living

*E.g., most recently by Mr. Aldous Huxley in an interview with Mike Wallace, published by the Fund for the Republic in the series *Survival and Freedom*, No. 4, p. 12.

rooms, editorial rooms, and committee rooms does not support that generalization.* True, intellectuals often think of themselves as individualists, because of their dislike of concerted action; but this lack of cohesiveness is not necessarily the mark of a self-aware, self-confident individual. It may be, rather, the disease of a bewildered group-seeker. It is noticeable that in circles where one would expect quick responses to common difficulties—say, in educational or medical administration—'individualistic' diversity in words is enormous. But this often expresses little more than a stubborn whimsicality of impression and utterance.

Again, nothing is more common than to attend a forum or conference on social or artistic 'problems' and to hear, after a few hours of guarded meandering, a growing majority declare that a consensus is impossible. The next remark is that this is another symptom of the contemporary chaos. Soon, a ghostly yearning for the thirteenth century is seen to emerge from the wainscoting. Despair seems the only tenable conclusion. The truth is that the twenty or thirty gentlemen who are thus ready to give back their tickets are extraordinarily alike in outlook, as they are also in training and temperament. They have once more said the familiar things that enlivened many another three-day conference. But the repeated failure to join issue, the perverse wish to remain misunderstood and put upon, and the decay of certain intellectual powers, including the faculty of analogy, have left them unskilled in the art of concurring. They cannot translate what they hear into what they think; they jib at incidentals and misconceive the main points. They are reminded of the wrong instances and they humor themselves in the nursing of abstract grudges. In a word, they lack the high purposefulness of intellectual passion.

*An uncommon sociological study tells us that villager and townsman form their image of themselves after the models which come to them from large-scale journalism and broadcasting. If so, the influence is not up from the mass but down from the articulate, who transmit, with their own antiheroism, the next-to-latest conceptions of high art and literature. *Small Town in Mass Society* by A. J. Vidich and J. Bensman, Princeton University Press, 1958, 101–105.

Yet they are not free of self-distrust, and since this is with them a habit rather than a judgment, it helps to create the ill-success they regularly meet. From that self-imprisonment they then choose a vicarious rescue: they idealize youth. If this is Intellect at work, they say, if reason and discussion produce only this irritable shadow-boxing, then let us have the prattle of babes. With this added cause for resignation goes the hope that youth will bring to the conduct of life an energy that manners have sapped in their elders. We saw an expression of that despair and that hope in *The Family of Man*. One is reminded that the earliest dithyrambs on youth as saviors occurred in Germany in the 1880's, when Langbehn and others, who were waging an oblique war on their culture, were demanding 'an age of art' and, soon afterward, 'a youth movement for adults.' Their love of innocence and art was hatred for the present that neglected them and a vengeful appeal to the future. In our century, the worshipers of innocence have similarly laid on the future the task of repairing all their mistakes. But forgetting that innocence petted and prolonged can only make dupes and cynics, they have produced conditions in which strength other than physical cannot grow. The notion that 'free growth' and 'integrity' in the young requires the absence of formal manners—no thanks and no subordination, no regard for time or fitness, no patience with difficulty or distaste, no feelings of reverence or pride, and in many 'excellent' households, no respect for objects and no constraint of cleanliness—that anarchical notion seems curious only till we see it as a first step in liberation from power and its attendant responsibility. Those who are reared in this permissive atmosphere seem embarrassed by, almost afraid of, human respect. They try hard to earn the opposite by affecting a slovenliness of dress and a lack of reliability which are so *outré* as to prove casualness a branch of study. That this pose is not merely to shock the public appears from the fact that the young unshaven, half-shod, intellectual beachcomber does not exhibit himself differently to his best—I mean, his only—girl. The behavior at least shows thoroughness: having nothing, claiming nothing, he knows nothing can be required or reproved. What is odd is the expectation that such a mode of life should produce individuals, that is, persons distinguishable from one another.

Even when the pose is only a passing phase in the adolescent intellectual, its drawback is that it allows but two lines of retreat: anger and resignation. The ego is hemmed in and cannot disport itself. It swings dissatisfied between antagonism and conformity, out of which one can fashion but few objects of delight: one imagines with difficulty a life's work wholly devoted to expressing rage or listlessness. What is left for private or social purposes is a kind of moral vagrant, who projects upon his surroundings the menace of his own indiscipline. I can think of a case in point, that of an intelligent young man of twenty-five, with all the makings of a good painter. He works at his art, but by dint of brooding about his aims and talents he has concluded that 'to be himself' he must show rudeness and hostility to all who approach him, including the teacher he has himself chosen. His easygoing parents are to him as Oriental despots. They have promised to support him in his artistic career if he will go to college—a sinister attempt to clamp him in a mold and turn him into a 'square.' Their evident goodness barely shackles his hostility, which he turns on others with a virulence close to delinquency.

Delinquency itself is usually thought to be a mirror image of 'the dreadful world in which we live.' But the truth of the explanation depends on which dreadful world is meant, public or domestic. The delinquents from suburban families* who seem to want risk and a barrier to push against, find it only in the rival gang or the police, now that the paternal power, which is youth's proper and useful antagonist, has abdicated.† The young also are underworked and deprived of the outlet that intellectual effort and polemic with peers offer to aggressive energy.

*The United Nations report on juvenile delinquency notes that in the United States this type of crime 'thrives in communities and families where standards of living are relatively high.' *New York Times*, August 3, 1958.
†A California psychiatrist, Dr. Milton Wexler, detects the virtue of energy in the 'horror of juvenile delinquency,' and prefers it, as I do, to 'apathy, tranquilizers, and inspirational psychologies.' *New York Times*, May 19, 1958.

Everywhere, the void left by the suppression of mind and ambition is filled by improvised generalship and conflict. Battle is joined, more or less openly, whenever a group of children invade a public vehicle. It lurks in the notorious behavior of undergraduates at a certain college where, it is said, guest lecturers are systematically heckled while the faculty looks on helplessly. And it was unmistakable in recent events at a large university, where an undergraduate grievance growing out of restrictions on receiving girls in dormitories was made clear by throwing eggs at the president and dean, the rebel leader being the son of a faculty member. This is not animal spirits or the traditional prank: it is an oblique war on our culture in order to find out whether there are not, somewhere, some angry old men. And intellectually speaking, it is the effort to replace a torturing self-consciousness by a self-aware reason for living.

For in the straight wars against culture, those waged from strength and not weakness, the fount of power is Intellect. By it, the enemy is singled out from the rest and the strategy devised. When the war is over, it is deemed just or unjust by its intellectual rightness. Nowadays, on the contrary, it is assumed that all attacks on culture are equal in virtue, and that attacking society, because it is society, is the one aim and test of genius.* The young therefore enlist and fight; without asking of the ugly world they have inherited whether anybody ever received it fresh, perfect, and beautiful. Their intellect does not stretch so far as to criticize, with whatever *furor adolescentium*; it condemns, vaguely yet vehemently, as one would expect from the sentimental education they have received. Just so did the unfortunate Smerdyakov, whom his half-brother Ivan Karamazov, a thorough intellectual, had tried to awaken:

---

*The assumption is well expressed in a comment on Samuel Beckett who, according to Mr. Rexroth, 'is so significant, or so great, because he has said the final word to date [*sic*] in the long indictment of industrial and commercial civilization. . . . Now this is not only the main stream of what the squares call Western European culture, by which they mean the culture of the capitalist era: it is really all the stream there is.' *The Nation*, April 14, 1956.

'He had encouraged him to talk to him, although he had always wondered at a certain incoherence, or rather restlessness in his mind, and could not understand what it was that so continually and insistently worked upon the brain of "the contemplative." They discussed philosophical questions . . . but Ivan soon saw that . . . Smerdyakov . . . was looking for something altogether different. In one way or another, he began to betray a boundless vanity, and a wounded vanity, too. . . . There was in fact something surprising in the illogicality and incoherence of some of his desires, accidentally betrayed and always vaguely expressed.'

It would be foolish to imagine that a whole generation could be composed of Smerdyakovs. The young in this country or elsewhere do not all make up for raw manners and lax discipline by truculence, much less delinquency. The 'abolitionism' of our leading prophets under thirty is indicative of only one, and the most arid, tendency. The majority of college graduates with some pretensions to education deal otherwise with their innocence and the horrors they are asked to contemplate. Many conceive themselves as modestly contributing, through some organization, to the general good. Practical philanthropy gives them, perhaps for the first time, ideas linked by purpose, and a guarantee besides: it must be good to do good— though often they suffer intervals of bewilderment and are beset by problems that only intellect could solve. For example, some forty graduates of an Eastern woman's college, now living in a Western city, not long ago addressed to their alma mater a piteous but not untypical request. They wanted help, undefined, to get themselves established as young wives in a new community, so that they might in turn help their college in some way, through meetings, teas, lectures, publicity—anything desired. They wanted (in their own words) someone to inspire them and co-ordinate their efforts, to 'indoctrinate' them.

The college of course publishes the usual illustrated bulletin, which is full of applicable suggestions, and provides a traveling representative to aid local clubs. This person found the young wives 'eager to work though they did not know how or for what.' Now comes the oddest part of the story. The traveling delegate's recommendation was that not only the forty lost sheep, but many others throughout the land, should periodically be brought back to the college 'to renew contact and inspiration, help them in their lives and make them feel part of the group. . . . I speak,' added the reporter, 'from a feeling of osmosis.'

Obvious points could be made about the apparent uselessness of the written word and a college training, and about the hidden costs of higher education, but what concerns manners is the acute self-consciousness which paralyzed the group and created this 'problem.' The desire for special ministrations viewed as 'help,' the need to be directed, the urge to hold meetings without object, the longing to come home to the sheltering herd—these are the unexpected fruits of 'free, individual growth,' coupled with the cult of informality and the refusal of power. It can hardly be coincidence that, shortly before, these young wives were among the undergraduates for whom recitations and laboratories could not be scheduled on Monday mornings or Friday afternoons, because they would be cut, and who had to be subjected to biweekly room inspections to maintain in the dormitories the semblance of civilized life.

Bewildered or sullen or defiant, the young who are wise enough to conclude that meetings are no substitute for careers, nor publicity for power, gravitate toward the last institution that promises rest from evil and uncertainty—the self-centered family. Having started an exclusive courtship in childhood, John marries Jane as soon as practicable, for only she means peace, goodness, and truth—that is, until little Jonathans come to share the exclusive virtue and interest of John and Jane. The self-centered family competes with study, politics, and social life, and makes them show cause why they should interfere with individualism *à deux*. To put it another way, this latest substitute for status and privilege gains strength by domesticating everything—love, study, pleasure, ambition, liberality, and the broken remnants of intellectual curiosity and conversation. By reducing all these to its appetite, the self-centered family is a small fortress against the monsters outside—the huge institutions, the anonymous mass, the agitated world. The self-centered family is not an institution, it is a cocoon. Warm and small, it matches the other reductions of size and scope we are witnessing: the tiny house, the tiny car, the tiny stature of humanity on the bluish window through which, cozily, in the dark, the family views some of the strange events outside.*

What I have been describing does not of course imply the physical isolation of the young family, nor does it contradict their elders' gregariousness or their own. Rather, it shows in another setting the social quest which we defined at the outset as the search for essences. The search occurs between families in an attempt to reproduce the intimacy of the home, the warmth (rather than the affection) brought into our lives by (as we say) our *personal* friends. They are known by their ability to be no different at home and in company, and their easy, informal behavior is the model for strangers who want to join the circle. We know what they must do. They must divest themselves of their last names, as would the men of their coats and ties on a hot day and the women of their shoes at almost any time. And they must have a sense of humor.

For since we decline to meet as minds or characters, and cannot boast a multitude of pals, we need humor to provide a moral holiday. Constraints dissolve and something like self-assertiveness can sally forth when cloaked in humor. This is why humor is so overused in our meetings and greetings. The term humor, indeed, is here a courtesy title, for most of the laughter and the words that arouse it are mechanical and we are not amused. At home or in the course of business, the jokes express self-depreciation or make fun of the routine duties and accidents of life, loudly burying our false shames. After everyone is seated and holds a glass, the laughs and grins (as in newspaper photography) shield our vacuity and make

*Life imitates art: when Mr. Cyril Connolly made his witty remark about anxious man's desire for 'a womb with a view,' television had not become the fulfillment of that wish.

plain that the danger of falling into a Roman *gravitas* is permanently at bay.

At times, too, one suspects that the forms of this humorless humor stand for the lost forms of the drama of intellect in true conversation. This is noticeable in everyone's heavy irony and in the special, noisy overemphasis affected by women to pass off triviality or dullness: the abnormal drawl, the contorted features, the limbs and torso acting out some unfathomable anecdote of dustpan and brush, give us a glimpse of the abyss and reconcile us to the large, anonymous cocktail party which, for all its toll on the five senses, often serves moral decency like a curtain.

That it is impossible to talk or hear at a cocktail party does not lower much the amount of successful 'exchange of ideas' in a society. A more potent influence is the state of the language. The erosion of the mother tongue will occupy us on a later page. Here it is enough to point to the fact that our manners do not favor highly organized speech. The desire to be inconspicuous, that is, to take on the color of one's surroundings, encourages the use of vogue words and phrases, which, being for the most part inexpressive, have to be helped out by grimaces, interjections, and test borings into the listener's receptivity. All this augments agitation and decreases attention which, even among the articulate, is strained by the great number of professional jargons and ready-made conversations—the cant of political, psychological, and artistic coteries. The upshot is that where these groups mix and also where they remain apart, there is no society.

One can readily understand why such groups might prefer separateness. Intuitive and self-conscious, they too seek a family in which to exchange warmth and share anxieties. Comfort takes precedence of curiosity, the comfort of quaking by the same hearthstone. How often do they not say of the passing event, 'It is frightening!' But each group finds a different cause for the fright that unites them, and the last virtue displayed or desired is equanimity. It would seem even more arrogant than lacking in sensitiveness, a breach of the equality based on common suffering, and hence a sign of superiority.

To this it might of course be answered that the implied claim is not against others but against oneself, and that those who claim nothing of themselves have nothing to give.

But to continue on this theme would be to propose new, unheard-of manners, which is beyond my present purpose. It only remains to point out that it is the manners of the powerless, and not outside forces, that bring about the invasions of our privacy. If we must all suffer, agree, worry, partake, in unison, under pain of reproof, then the world is no longer a stage peopled by distinguishable actors, and the living room vanishes with the individual—there is only a tribe milling under a tent. To this image, some reply that the modern world being full of concentration camps it is absurd to hope anywhere for individualism and privacy. But the intellect is not deceived by this fallacious argument from horror: the fact that under necessity some detestable thing happens is no reason why it has to be everywhere reproduced and accepted.

The fallacy is more consequential than it looks, for it is generally the same 'thoughtful' propounder of the concentration camp analogy who at other times indicts 'our culture' for violating the dignity of man. But how does he resist encroachment on his own privacy and dignity from day to day? We have had no statistical survey on this point, but an incident for which I can vouch throws light on the question. One of the world's leading photographers concludes his session with a sitter by requesting a favor: will the sitter jump for him? The artist explains by bringing out a stack of photographs of the world's leading notables taken in the act of jumping. Fists clenched, faces taut, feet off the ground, they are on view—prime ministers and presidential candidates, noted jurists and princes of the royal blood, lady novelists and Nobel Prize winners. If an unprepossessing rictus casts a doubt on their identity, the photographer dispels the doubt in the course of his running commentary on what the photograph reveals of the jumper's character. This one is a coward; that other, jumping with his wife and looking at her, is obviously ruled by her; the next is a pompous fool, and so on. *Now* will you jump for me? According to the artist himself, only two of his subjects have refused. Each time he asked for their reasons. Whether both mentioned the supreme informality of the pose, the impudent overdose of candor, or the rancid flavor of amateur psychologizing, the photographer is too offended to remember.

IV

Education Without Instruction

Clearly, the blame for much that is lacking or painful in our manners can be laid upon our education, individual and collective. The same cause will also explain what is wrong with our politics and ways of business, with our press and public opinion. Indeed, whatever is wrong is the fault of the schools, for is it not there that we learn to become what we are? This common indictment overlooks but one point, which is that the schools are run by adults—and run to suit other adults in political, intellectual, or business life. The schools are thus as fully the product of our politics, business, and public opinion as these are the products of our schools. It is because the link is so close that the schools are so hard to change.

They are, for the same reason, hard to describe, showing as they do the diversity and elusiveness of culture itself. Because it is thought of as a sheltered place invaded by worldlings, the school is often forgiven for resembling the world; it is always possible to say, 'That is society's doing, not the school's.' But this only proves that the best of schools can be no more than half-innocent. They work with spoiled materials: teachers marred by the ugly world and children already stamped with the defects that their parents condone by habit or foster on principle.

From these facts one great truth emerges: there is, there can be, no such thing as a good school.

The conclusion is repellent to our desire of perfection, but it is inescapable. It does not mean that all schools are bad: some are better than others; but none will do what in our naïve fancy we liken to the work of an instrument of precision functioning independently of its makers. Any school has a system, and its action is therefore that of a cookie cutter carelessly handled. Schools that repudiate system as harsh and unjust turn out anarchical and more unjust. That is why the profoundest theorist of modern education, Rousseau, limited his scheme to one child and a tutor. Rousseau begins by pointing out that the story of Emile is not a model, but an ideal case that suggests new intentions rather than new practices. It is not imitable, if only because the tutor is a genius who devotes all his time and thought to a pupil who is unnaturally responsive.

Today, the Western world is at the other extreme from this situation. It is headed toward mass schooling, the European half of that world making the attempt some sixty years after the United States. Our current discussion of education in America is thus of peculiar interest, because we, dissatisfied with our handiwork, are seeking to change just at the time when England, France, and Germany are courageously starting to repeat our mistakes.* Our words and acts are doubly important because we are the pioneers others copy or listen to.

Ours is surely the most remarkable of educational systems in that it is the only one to deal with anything like the same numbers with so much liberality and persistence. We offer education from infancy

---

*For a sample of foreign discussions, see in *The Listener* the protracted controversy on 'The Child-Centered School' from April, 1957 to February, 1958; also in the Supplements to the German weekly *Das Parlament* for January 22 and 29, an essay of over fifty pages by Einrich Weinstock on the responsibility of the schools in an age of democracy and technology. Finally,

to—I was about to say 'the grave.' Education in the United States is a passion and a paradox. Millions want it and commend it, and are busy about it, at the same time as they are willing to degrade it by trying to get it free of charge and free of work. Education with us has managed to reconcile the contradictory extremes of being a duty and a diversion, and to elude intellectual control so completely that it can become an empty ritual without arousing protest.

Not that we have ever been satisfied with our schools. Long before the postwar self-searching, thousands of meetings and millions of words were being spent each year in debating improvements. But our characteristic softness then and now invests the whole attempt and reduces it for the most part to abstract worry and repetitious piety. The *doyen* of educational theorists in this country,* addressing in 1955 the Middle Atlantic States Philosophy of Education Association, opened his remarks with the words: 'There is urgent current need for a broader and more effective education.'[1] Last year, another critic, whose words make him representative of many others, expressed alarm at the insufficiency of present-day teaching in science. Did he suggest something to do, now or as soon as possible? No. He asked for a 'broad concept.' A third lecturer, a well-known businessman, who knows the general resistance to intellectual subjects, wants to turn the present outcry to use by strengthening the universities' public position. Excellent. But what does he, an expert in 'public relations,' set forth as his main point? Defining goals: 'The broad role of the institution must be defined.' He does after a bit speak of curriculum, higher faculty salaries, and new buildings; but he soon relapses into 'broad' ideas: 'Creative thinking and creative teachers must, it seems to me, be given primary importance in defining the goals of any institution.'[2] Read any segment of the press, lay or learned, and you will find that the angry protests

---

see the three issues of *Education in France* published by the Cultural Services of the French Embassy, New York, 1957–58.
*William H. Kilpatrick, Professor Emeritus of Education in Teachers College.

and anxious injunctions swing between what is broad and what is creative. A visitor from outer space would conclude that we had lost, or perhaps never formed, any communicable idea of the purpose of schools.

We did have such an idea until about 1900, when it began to yield to the indefiniteness of mass education. But that phrase alone is enough to quell our impatience. We can never forget the magnitude of the difficulties in what we then undertook. The worst faults of the schooling we now give are due to the large numbers of pupils relatively to the natural supply of true teachers. And most of the other faults are due to the unending task of acclimating the alien and native millions to increasingly complicated modes of life. If the high schools make dating and 'driver education' part of the curriculum in place of Latin and trigonometry, it is because 'preparing for life' means giving information that is of everyday use, fraught with social consequence, and that no one else will impart.*

But what of Intellect and its ancient nursery, the classical curriculum? The answer is soon given. Who would teach it? How many parents would approve of it? How would children respond to it? Suppose it magically restored, what gaps and failures in the common mind would immediately be deplored, unrelieved by scattered intellectual accomplishments that millions of citizens would rightly deem useless?

It is a proof of the low state of our Intellect that the present debate on education refers to 'our schools' at large, without marking off kinds and grades. People argue for 'more science' or 'the liberal arts' or 'better English' or 'a longer siege of American history,' without considering the conditions of teaching and study that now obtain. Nor is due attention given to the country's beliefs and acts regarding Intellect and its employment. No doubt the continual comparisons with 'Soviet education,' of which very few know any-

*I have paid my sincere respects to the principle of 'preparation for life,' and to the teachers who carry it out, in an essay entitled 'The Battle Over Brains in Democratic Education' (*University of Toronto Quarterly,* January, 1954). In the present chapter I take the point for granted and go on to discuss our schooling in its relation to Intellect.

thing reliable, have upset us; and so has the image of the 'tidal wave' of youth expected by 1970. This prospect in turn leads to agitation about the educational use of television and other machinery, again in the belief that multiplying voices, rooms, and seats to the right number will bring 'education' to the newcomers. Whether the educating that now goes on face to face will remain the same when put on the screen is a question seldom raised. Hardly anyone knows what does go on, nor is there agreement about what should go on and does not.

The confusion is not ours alone. Most of Europe is recasting its old systems, also in the dark. According to one survey, some forty nations of the world are short of teachers and engaged in school reform. Considering how dreary educational discussion is, the number of people now being bored with it must exceed any previous maximum. What is especially distressing is that our own brand of theory and practice is now reaching to the antipodes and threatening to eclipse there the demands of Intellect. From Tasmania, for instance, comes an official pamphlet entitled 'Learning Is Living,' which details the island's adult education program. The title by itself reveals what a congenial error overtakes modern states on the threshold of mass education.

It is the error of supposing that because under popular government all good things are for everybody, it follows that all things whatever are interfused and all distinctions are false. This is the belief that we saw at work in journalism and publishing, and again in democratic manners. If it is indeed true that 'learning is living,' then the school loses its institutional—its properly artificial—character, and soon people forget that learning requires attention and assiduity. They end by repudiating the school and entrust to some sort of pseudo-schooling, some 'life-like' contrivance, the task of teaching.

Yes, but what is wrong with life? Do we not say: 'experience teaches,' 'suffering educates'? That is just the trouble. We do, and we mean, or should mean, something indefinite quite remote from schooling. Meanwhile the strange pantheism which finds learning and living identical comes from these shores: 'I learn what I live,' says Dr. Kilpatrick,[3] 'and I learn it as I accept it . . . I learn it in the degree that I live it. . . . I learn what I live. What is learned is the inner object of the verb to live. We learn the content of our living and learn this content as we accept consciously to live it.' This incantation is powerful—the seat of learning is the liver.

The fallacy is buried in the damnable word 'education,' from which all this wordplay started, and which we now find emblazoned in all the mansions of life. Besides all the educating for health, character, happiness, and pedestrian safety, we now have driver education and alcohol education,* cancer education and sex education—just as next to the *Education of Henry Adams* we have *The Education of a Poker Player.*† The advertisers educate us to the fact that a new detergent is afloat and an old oil company has changed its name.‡ A thousand and one leagues have 'campaigns of education,' which means occupying space in the papers and teaching us by correspondence their pressing need of cash. The YMCAs and evening schools, the Sunrise Semesters and Midnight Colleges§ all profess to educate 'in' something—business English or the Australian crawl: never was so much sharing of crafts and powers carried on with such good will and so little uneasiness of mind.

The word 'education' should accordingly be reserved for all this, which it has conquered, and absolutely banned from discussions of *schooling* and *instruction,* which in an evil day it replaced.‖ 'Education' sounds 'broad,' a richer, more philanthropic gift than 'instruc-

*Cf. the handbook by Joseph Hirsch.
†By the late Herbert O. Yardley, the distinguished cryptologist and poker player.
‡See the report on the Calso 'educational campaign' to implant the 'complicated idea' that its name has changed. *New York Times*, May 23, 1958.
§Sunrise Semester, the first television course offered for credit, by New York University; Midnight College, a comparable undertaking by Fairleigh Dickinson College in New Jersey; Continental Classroom, a national and co-operative form of the same.
‖When the French schools became less competitive and took on more welfare activities in the mid-1920s, the Ministry of Public Instruction turned into the Ministry of National Education—the change is a description in itself.

tion.' There is less of superior-to-inferior in it, hence egalitarian manners prefer it—we are all educating ourselves together; and—cheerful thought!—education is never done, whereas in instruction there is a point (or should be) at which one knows how to read, count, write, speak German, and understand physics. Education also suggests—rightly so—the diversity of men's minds and talents, which seek different ends; it is thus the more democratic and liberal word. The modern vision of endless creativity, the love of art and the relish for indefinite inwardness also call for 'education,' the all-inclusive. Finally, science in the form of psychology and 'guidance' has transformed teaching and learning into 'the educational pro-cess' and made teaching and instruction seem dry and mean. Edu-cate, educator, educationist—the names permit a humble profession, armed with method, to permeate our life with its confident pre-tensions.

These things being so, we must, if we really intend to change our schools, forget the language, and especially the slogans, of mass education. They betray the user as well as the listener. 'Keeping the schools democratic,' preventing them from 'producing an elite,' insisting on 'giving all our children the same education' would not satisfy the very people who fight for these 'principles,' if 'education' were omitted and the other words replaced by honestly descriptive ones: shall all children receive *instruction* in the same subjects through high school, whether they or their parents want the same or not? We say we need research scientists and engineers: does the choice of these careers require different instruction from hotel-keeping and shorthand and typewriting, or does it not? Does train-ing a group of scientists at public expense in high schools and state universities create an elite likely to lord it over hotel managers and stenographers? Or more generally, does social equality depend on the possession of identical knowledge? This question of different training clearly applies as well to scholars in the humanities and the social sciences (who, it seems, are also wanted men) and to lawyers, doctors, accountants, and other professionals.

As for keeping the schools 'democratic' in the sense of ignoring differences of ability and 'giving' a college career to all who ask for it, this is the scheme which has just broken down and brought many people to the realization that it is wasteful, dangerous, and unjust. Ability and achievement are too important to the country to be any longer trifled with, as has been done by maintaining that failure is something a child must invariably be shielded from, lest he take a dislike to learning.* True, every reproof must be accompanied by encouragement, and error should not be represented to youth as irrevocable. But none of this means that to fail is one way of succeeding. The analogy of athletics must be pressed until all recognize that in the exertions of Intellect those who lack the muscles, co-ordination, and will power can claim no place at the training table, let alone on the playing field.

Why did we ever think otherwise? Part of the answer has been given in earlier chapters dealing with democratic manners and opinion, but there is so far something peculiarly American about the institution of the child-centered school. Americans began by loving youth, and now, out of adult self-pity they worship it. At the same time, in all their institutions, they do not merely desire, but work for the widest sociability. The American atmosphere requires that everybody present shall participate, have a good time, share the good things, and help maintain the universal good-fellowship. This outlook may recall by inherited memory the brotherhood of the humble transplanted from Europe, or it may spring from the more bourgeois doctrine of equality. However it may be, in such a moral climate it was inevitable that our schools should aim at social adjustment first, even if practical needs had not made this convenient. On the one hand, 'adjustment' helps to assimilate the for-

---

*To quote Dr. Kilpatrick again: 'Suppose a teacher scolds a boy for failure at fractions. That boy may next time study harder as the teacher hoped and intended. But the boy is likely to react inwardly against the scolding with some feelings against the teacher, and against some other boys who snickered at his scolding, and against fractions, and arithmetic, and school. Also he may be feeling that he is a comparative failure. . . . The older education seldom took account of such learnings except as it tried by advice and reproof to build them into the young.' *Op. cit.*, 289.

eigner and the poor; on the other, it respects the resistance of the
majority to intellectual work and makes teachers of many with no
special talents.*

When, therefore, critics from the universities attack our public
schools for anti-intellectualism, on the assumption that it would take
only a high resolve and a changed curriculum to make them seminar-
ies of Intellect, the attack falls harmlessly against the solid barrier of
facts: we cannot make intellectuals out of two million pupils—too
many are incapable of the effort even a modestly bookish education
requires; too many have the good sense to know that they want instead
some vocational training that will be immediately marketable.†

The only answer is the selection and special schooling of those
with a talent for abstraction, articulateness, and the pursuit of ideas
in books. This selection need not mean a new kind of segregation:
many classes can be shared by all the children in a school, special
classes will speed the intellectually strong toward their goals. Recent
attempts to 'adjust' in this new way have proved to school authori-
ties that the heavens do not fall at this differentiation and—what
they feared even more than divine wrath—that parents do not
protest, but accept philosophically the accident of brains. It seems as
if after sixty years of rugged trial American education were making
its way out of the lowlands. We could be cheerful about this if it
were not for two handicaps: the coming 'tidal wave,' which will
strain school funds and obscure recent gains, and the almost total
lack of intellectual attachments among those who think they lead
our schools.

That in a given public school there should be overcrowding and

---

*An English observer of his country's social revolution ascribes to working-
class tolerance the entire absence of standards. See *The Uses of Literacy,* by
Richard Hoggart, London, 1957.
†I agree with Mr. Conant and disagree with Mr. Mortimer Adler about the
latter's intention to provide the liberal arts for all. (See Mr. Adler's articles
in the Chicago *Sun-Times* for January 19, 1958.) For sidelights from the
German scene, see the articles by Helmut Becker on the need for a new
education in *Das Parlament,* 3: January 22, 1958, 5; and by Helmut Schel-
sky on vocational training in *Die Zeit,* October, 1957, Feuilleton page.

poor teaching by ill-trained substitutes is bad but understandable; the shocking thing is that in a better-served community, or in a private school proud of its selection of pupils and teachers, one should find deep hostility to Intellect (despite lip service to it) and solemn fooling professing to be science. The high-placed theorists in teachers' colleges, the experts in departments of psychology and centers of social research, have taught that the purpose of the school is not alone to 'prepare for life' by teaching vocational or other subjects of use to the greater number, not alone to insure the child's getting along with his fellows and finding contentment in schoolwork, but also to achieve a 'broad' program of private and social progress toward perfection. This overshadows all other purposes: 'From the kindergarten through the college, there is the general aim . . . that each pupil-student shall, in order to meet the needs of life, build an inclusive character, an informed and intelligent character, a constructive and responsible character, a character really adequate to meet the needs of life.'

Besides this are some 'specific aims': 'to help each pupil-student increasingly to develop as a well-balanced intelligent individual, that he may achieve the finest feasible best that in him lies. On this depends democracy and freedom and real life. . . . [to help him also] as an increasingly effective member of society with positive commitment to the support of the common good, each as an effective democratic citizen of his community, his state, our nation, and the one world.' Another 125 words enjoin 'help' to make the student 'increasingly' helpful to his family, 'sensitive' to the rights of others, 'especially minority groups,' and equipped with an 'increasing over-all moral commitment.'[4] Not one direct word about the mind, Intellect, or knowledge. And all this is a mere preamble to the question 'How Should Teachers Be Educated?' Obviously, the education needed to carry out this predominantly moral program, which has moreover to be made congenial to the young organism and its tender emotions, leaves the teacher little time to acquire clear and distinct ideas on any academic subject.

• • •

How, it may be asked, did a small group of such timid creatures as psychologists and pedagogues ever foist these visionary plans on a hundred million fathers and mothers, who are also practical Americans—housewives, businessmen, farmers, bus drivers, politicians?

The answer has been implied in the description. The prestige successively acquired in our century by science and art has seconded philanthropy, and together they have overcome the public's small awareness of Intellect. By now the alliance of Intellect's three great enemies in our educational practice is complete. You cannot tell where one ends and the other begins. Each is an irrefutable argument against the critic, for who today would risk being taken for an opponent of that trinity? Formerly one could at least count on the Philistine to resist art, but art has become a power in the land, serving diplomacy and national interests as well as private pleasure and vanity. As such it has turned into the third irreproachable Good.

We know the name it takes in school affairs: it is 'creativity.' The curriculum may pay no greater attention than formerly to painting and music, though in many schools today these arts figure importantly. The 'artistic' element which informs school 'creativity' enters rather as the awe-struck acceptance of the pupil's ways and opinions as if these were the symptom or promise of genius. The teacher's response to any liveliness of mind, any curiosity and imagination, has become so respectful that it generally excludes criticism, and often omits any demand for accuracy and logic as too likely to chill ardor. The young unformed mind is treated like that of a sage, which for us means the mind of an artist. We must never press it for an exact accounting, for it draws on mysterious sources of 'insight.' Is it not true, besides, that in the study of literature, history, and the humanities generally, insight and 'empathy' are more valuable than knowledge? To understand is a 'creative' act which some have not hesitated to compare to the original creation of the work of art. Hence in the school the perpetual adoration of the Magi before the infant expression of 'original views' on everything but the multiplication table.

The cult explains what is observable at the end of the sixteen long years of an ordinary education: young men and women of unquestionable gifts, energy, and zest, whose fine intelligence is not matched by strength of intellect. Freshness of taste and openness to novelty, yes; even refinement of sensibility, sometimes prematurely delicate. But no knowledge that is precise and firm, no ability to do intellectual work with thoroughness and dispatch. Though here are college graduates, many of them cannot read accurately or write clearly, cannot do fractions or percentages without travail and doubt, cannot utter their thoughts with fluency or force, can rarely show a handwriting that would pass for adult, let alone legible, cannot trust themselves to use the foreign language they have studied for eight years, and can no more range conversationally over a modest gamut of intellectual topics than they can address their peers consecutively on one of the subjects they have studied.

Any one or two of these abilities that they possess will generally be found to result from special circumstances, which include the urge to excel despite schools and teachers. But this is one place where favored exceptions mean nothing: it is the average of those selected for intellectual training that matters; and this group nowadays is intellectually underfed. Educationists keep talking of the 'tools' and 'skills' which they think they impart to the young with one hand, while the other cultivates the civic and cultural virtues; but this is mere brag. The tools have dull edges, and it is clear that when 'skills' came in skill went out. An example from my own experience will illustrate the degree of incompetence now current and tolerated among the intelligent: a class of 170 first-year graduate students in history was asked to explain the meaning of twenty of the commonest abbreviations found in ordinary books—e.g., i.e., N.B., B.C., A.D., *ibid.*, and the like, including one date in Roman numerals. Of these 170 hand-picked college graduates only one understood all twenty abbreviations; only 10 per cent of the class— 17 out of 170—understood fifteen or more; about half the class understood no more than four, and none in that half could read the date 1659 expressed in Roman numerals. Most of those whose score was low thought that e.g. and i.e. were synonymous, and of those who conferred with me about their failure, nearly all said that they 'sensed' a difference between e.g. and i.e. but could not put it into words.

It is easy to think this fiasco as small as the abbreviations it concerns. But that judgment itself needs revising in the light of what Intellect presupposes. In the first place, these small marks are part of the language and embody familiar and important ideas: B.C. is *not* A.D. What lack of mere bulk of reading is disclosed by the incomprehension of these signs—or else what inattention! If context failed to explain the marks, dictionaries, which are abundantly and expensively supplied, could be consulted. In any case, the mind of an aspiring intellectual—a *graduate* student, a would-be *scholar*, and a future or actual *teacher*—*could not help* learning and retaining these things, had it been properly taught. In the second place, how discouraging that able minds, sensing a difference between two symbols, should be unable to give themselves an idea of the cause. Without the power to articulate there can be no sustained thought. And finally, what a commentary on so-called preparation for graduate study that these trifles (if you insist) should not have been mastered long since. In a word, what wasted opportunities! Indeed, after listening to parents, to conscientious teachers, as well as to young scholars and professional men, one is tempted to conclude that our present 'approach' (for it is not a system) turns out with certainty only two products—complaints and cripples.

This failure to make boys and girls literate is not all for the sake of art. 'Creativity' is but the latest justification and embellishment of practices that grew out of philanthropy, I mean the liberal doctrine that school children have rights to freedom and individuality, that school should accordingly cease to be a prison governed by a tyrant, and that subject matter should correspond to the changing capacities of the pupil, rather than to the hardened interests of adults.

Few would quarrel with these maxims, which go back to Rabelais and Montaigne through the amplifications of Rousseau and John Dewey. The intellectual objection is not to the principle but to the interpretation and carrying out. One notes, to begin with, that these philosophers and the lesser ones who promoted school reform throughout the nineteenth century were men of intellect.* They intended that schools should impart knowledge more efficiently, with less of the unnecessary pain or pointless drudgery that alienates young minds. But one will not find in Dewey, or his predecessors, any repudiation of literacy and mental power in favor of gregariousness, conformity to group opinion, love of praise, and the nurturing of self-deception. The only reason these feelings concern pedagogy is that they may affect the acquisition of knowledge. Modern theory inverts this relation and makes of subject matter a device for correcting what the teacher thinks wrong in a child's temperament.† I quote from a recent and representative document published by a school noted for its particular interest in gifted children:

'The educational aim is that the child acquire the clear perception and decisiveness of adulthood without losing the free creative imagination of childhood; that he be able to go out after what he needs, wants, and believes in; that he be able to initiate action in creative [again!] and realistic ways [meaning?], organize and plan toward achievement of his ends, and persist if they can be accomplished. The free implementation of the child's vitality and healthy growth of it necessitate a large deposit of love on the part of parents and other adults. Once aware of the child's need to increasingly

*The contemporary assumption that a century ago or more no one had sound ideas about teaching children, that no one was kind or applied 'method' about his own subject, is part of that colossal ignorance and conceit which make modern 'experts' impervious to criticism.
†Those of us who care for art in its original guise and undiluted strength must watch that it does not succumb to that formula and become only a therapeutic device. The signs are that between the school, the mental hospital, and the Department of State, art will be stripped of both power and grace.

originate contact, a parent need never question originating it himself.'[5]

'Contact,' it should be explained, means here the conveying of feeling through some exchange of words or gestures. The author believes this should be frequent between teacher and child—at least once every fifteen minutes—and he offers this interesting reason: 'Some children spend much of the day without asking for contact: *they focus on the matter at hand,* or fantasy, or withdraw . . . Although they appear very independent, they too need much adult-originated contact before *they really can enjoy people.* . . . A teacher's ability to convey real care and involvement is tremendously important, although, to be helpful, it must be devoted to developing the child's own vitalities.'*

Now we know what a teacher is for. In all the six pages of the article drawn from a long 'research paper,' not one word has to do with the teacher's own subject, which is geography. When performance is mentioned, it is in relation to the child's self-esteem or to a vague thing called reality: 'A forgiving and forbearing atmosphere, in which each child feels his uniqueness appreciated, is best.' This is where we pass from creativity to philanthropy, though in the next sentence we are told about this incubator atmosphere that 'it can stifle however.' Hence the teacher may offer criticism, in order to 'help the child understand himself and reality better . . . helping him grow up, mature into a strong free individual.'[6]

The revealing word in this as in all other contemporary 'research' on schools is 'help.' The notion of helping a child has in the United States displaced that of teaching him. Anyone who tries to preserve the distinction is obviously unhelpful, and is at once known for a declared enemy of youth. The truth is that even apart from its hostility to Intellect, systematic coddling is as dangerous as it is impertinent.

The first possibility is that the maternalistic teacher does not know what he is doing. It is worth noting that when the schools of Portland,

*Italics added.

Oregon, put bright pupils in fast classes under the best teachers, some of the problem children became good citizens. It is a likely supposition that they had simply been bored. For boredom is not the trivial, harmless experience that common speech assumes: it is a violent assault on the self which it cannot or dare not resist. In bored children the animal spirits seek and usually find an indirect revenge. Other children, it may also be supposed, are already fairly 'free and strong individuals' at ten or twelve and they resent being interrupted every fifteen minutes for 'contact' when they want to 'focus on the matter at hand.' Conversation with the young shows that they often regard the mental and bodily agitation of the modern school as coercive and unjust, for all its assured love. Meanwhile their fidgets have been cultivated upon theory. As for 'fantasy' (which is always being subdued to 'reality,' as if it were easy to tell which is which), the true guardians of art, who know that fantasy is the food from which genius *makes* reality, should swear out a warrant against its blithe interrupters.

We see here the final inversion of purpose characteristic of the self-conscious curriculum: it assumes in each pupil the supremely gifted mind, which must not be tampered with, and the defective personality, which the school must remodel. Its incessant desire is to round off edges, to work to moral specifications—in short, to manipulate the young into a semblance of the harmonious committee, in accordance with the statistics of child development. This is the wickedness of the philanthropists, that they invoke the force of the group, on top of their own, to achieve something that no one has given them license to attempt. One may say that their tampering with the child's personality is saved from guilt because their goal remains vague and their effort largely unsuccessful. But imagine an explicit program, political or religious, and a corps of teachers more than gushingly dedicated to it, and you would have an irresistible machine for warping both mind and character.

It would of course take genuine intellectuals to organize the work while concealing their hand. At present, our 'liberal' teachers' college products show but the bare makings of a totalitarian force—

the zeal for inducing 'the right attitude'; a thick-skinned intolerance toward all who doubt or criticize so much goodness; and a special language, a flatulent Newspeak, which combines self-righteousness with permanent fog, so that its users are invulnerable—others abide our question, they are free.

The politics of the adjustment curriculum, at any rate, are clear: it is manipulation by sentiment and dubious authority, exercised by the least educated and the most vapid minds of the nation. The manipulators view themselves as a vanguard of liberal thought, and after thirty years of supremacy still believe that they are bold. The historic position of liberalism is in fact one with which they have no sympathy, for it is intellectual. It gives freedom of opinion—subject to keeping the peace—and thereby licenses, not playing with souls, but playing with ideas—debate and contradiction, the very opposite of that moralistic putting into Coventry which is the regular tactics of the educationist against criticism or heresy. The contrast was restated not long ago by a teacher of philosophy, in words so happily uncommon as to be unmistakable:

'Our concern as a profession is with the liquidation of ignorance. . . . If, as pedagogue, I allow myself to become professionally involved in the fact that persons are diseasable, or capable of bad will, or mortal, I am soon . . . beyond my depth. My business is with the liquidation of ignorance, not the liquidation of those other matters. I have an interest in them, to be sure; but this interest does not define me professionally.'*

That interest in 'those other matters' is the interest of anyone who finds obstacles in his path and tries to remove them. The teacher of the very young child, like his parents, does what he can to prevent interference with the child's natural desire to learn, while seeing to it that the child is not overtaxed or maltreated. But this solicitude is not an end in itself, however much some teachers prefer

---

*Professor Alburey Castell, of the University of Oregon, from an unpublished address.

its protective glow to the dull task of drilling the alphabet.* 'Adjustment' at that stage is purely for the sake of implanting fundamental knowledge and good learning habits. To try to adjust the undeveloped inner self to an equally indefinite outer world is presumption. And to do so at the expense of intellectual subject matter is simply to ignore one's own business as teacher and 'helper.' For Intellect is also a means of adjustment. It is adjustment at any point in life to understand what another is saying, to recognize clearly a complex demand, and to gather one's wits so as to respond to it exactly and promptly.

I shall be told that fear and confusion so often act as barriers to understanding and response that 'mere' intellectual facility is worthless. True, but why assume a mere substitution of intellect for poise? And what if the lack of intellectual power acts in turn as a cause of fear and confusion? This is what happens in the simple case of fuzzy reading in one's own language or inaccurate and speechless acquaintance with a foreign tongue. The theorists of teaching are always reminding us of the great truth that mind and feeling are not disjoined. Why then should the traffic of good influence go only one way, from feeling to mind? And why should the exclusivists of adjustment project upon their critics their own one-sidedness? Their assumption is that the school straightens out the 'real person' by 'contact'—wanted or unwanted; by forbearance—probably resented as soon as detected; by praise—worthless when doled out like medicine. Then, when these nostrums have cleared the brain, at some time unspecified, intellectual desire is expected to flow in of itself, from natural curiosity and 'motivation' and 'felt needs.' These needs

---

*It is widely believed that since the scientific observation of children has discovered norms of development, these should determine the time and the way any subject is taught. Yet also according to the experts, each child should set his own pace. This is blowing hot and cold. No statistical norm embraces the exceptions, and the exceptionally intelligent have the highest claim on a good teacher, as being rare and valuable. Theory first coerces the exception, then turns around and coerces the teacher into letting each pupil progress independently—as if this could be done in a class of more than ten or twelve and with a subject of any complexity.

when they come can indeed be strongly felt, but they should have been anticipated. By the time scholastic curiosity rages, it is about adult things. The drudgery of fundamental discipline seems unbearable, not to say insulting—as my students intimated after the test on abbreviations: they wanted to discuss Hegel's theory of history, not learn to read Roman numerals.

It is thus that our intelligent cripples are made, though they themselves, their relatives, and their employers wonder how the miscarriage occurred. The philosopher whom I quoted in rebuttal of the educationist states another truth rich in meanings: 'In general it is not up to pedagogues to decide what areas of ignorance shall be liquidated.' One of the meanings is that Intellect, as part of civilization, makes its own irresistible claims upon certain individuals—claims as important as those of sociability and private happiness. The duty of the school is not to make one or other prevail, but to discern good minds and instruct them without overlooking the common demands of life upon the person. I imagine that in using the term 'pedagogue' throughout the sensible remarks I have quoted, our philosopher meant to remind us gently of the role of plain instruction, and to mark the difference between the teacher, whose aim is the liquidating of ignorance, and the Dr. Pangloss who, setting up as a molder of character, is, in the language of Shaw's famous aphorism, an abortionist.

So much for theory. Setting aside the supposed influence of 'contact' and 'deposits of love' on the child's 'vitalities,' what does the practice of 'enlightened' schooling come to? A few pages earlier I used the word 'fooling' in speaking of the primary curriculum. I meant it descriptively and continue to use it so. Fooling is not alien to Intellect, and in the first years of school life it is the appropriate introduction to objects and ideas that might not engage a child's attention in any other way. But if a school is ever to teach, there must come a time when kindergarten and first-grade make-believe turns into the exercises of serious work. I find an unintended reference to this needed transition in the memoirs of Mr. James Farley, at one time a member of Franklin Roosevelt's cabinet: 'My schooling,' says Mr. Farley, 'began at the age of five in the Grassy Point Grammar School, which I attended to the seventh grade, when I transferred to the Stony Point Grammar School. I graduated from the Stony Point High School after two and a half years.'[7] Our present habit is to keep the young at Grassy Point forever. Their path is never stony, certainly not in high school, rarely in college, and just as rarely in graduate schools other than those subject to the control of professional boards, such as medicine, architecture, and law.

On the climb upward to high school the ways of kindergarten naturally change in appearance, but their principle is protracted until teachers themselves no longer see any difference between fooling and work. This is the corruption of the pedagogic advice of Montaigne and Rousseau. 'Teach the very young with the aid of real things,' they said (like Aristotle earlier), 'let children learn by doing.' They thought of the curriculum of Latin declensions and figures of logic, and wanted a little open-air life and bodily activity to relieve it. But the interpretation of object lessons by a modern elementary school is this: weekly 'shop' in the second grade entails 'a junket to Staten Island,' after which 'the children built a class-size ferry boat—main deck, topside, wheel, bell, and all, as a part of the regular curriculum'—meaning that this was not recreation. 'When the youngsters took their first imaginary voyage, the teacher explained the benefits: "It gives them the basis of their social study." '[8]

In that typical situation, it is the teacher we should worry about; and also the parents who hear of comparable junkets from their children grade after grade, and condone the habit; and the philanthropic people, who secretly want childhood to continue forever; and the 'thoughtful persons,' who are reading these lines and laugh at the example and think it too funny to be harmful. We have been laughing at the joke for a generation now, without seeing that what is progressive about it is its undermining of the intellect of the country.

To make the joke as unlaughable as it really is, I shall accumulate some examples showing the persistent avoidance of work. In the second-grade a 'real' ferry boat serves as 'the basis for social study.' In the next three grades the idea of an exhibit, a group project to carry thought or knowledge, takes the form of plays written and acted by the children to show what they know of Hindu or Egyptian or Greek life, with special reference to manners and customs— 'never mind names and dates.' In one school I can report that the teachers, highly trained as psychologists but educated only by what is found in their pupils' story books, mispronounce the commonest names of the Greek gods and heroes, and suggest that ancient Oriental or primitive customs are inevitably superior to ours—remembering, no doubt, the lessons in *The Family of Man*.

That rehearsals interfere with arithmetic and spelling classes, and that the casting, memorizing, and costume-making (at home) lead to emotional upsets more vivid than any information in the play, is never thought of. Children are fortunately resilient, and ten months later no trace is left of the Greek way of life. Should you mention *Agám-nenon* or *Themistóckeles*, the fact that they evoke but faint recognition and that the envious desire to play those roles is only an amused memory will reassure the most apprehensive parent.

But time has been wasted, and the waste continues. The year after, the make-believe invades the realm of abstract ideas. An assignment in 'science' reads: 'Name six persons whom *you* consider to be scientists. Name the places where they were born, their education, and the contribution of each which *you* believe to have most helped mankind.'

By this point, the joke has, I trust, lost all its humor. The pupil is eleven or twelve and capable of reasoning and judgment. Yet here is a question which defies all the canons of intellectual fitness, and for which, moreover, no preparation is made—no readings, no definitions or summaries given out in class, nothing but a 'free' discussion by the group to ascertain what a scientist is. The right answer is supposed to come out of pooled ignorance.

It comes, usually, out of the parents' dim recollections, aided by a search through the *Britannica*. This collaboration is expected, though it rather contradicts the boasted method of 'independent research.'* But that is as nothing compared to the rank stupidity of the assignment itself. What a child of eleven needs to learn about science is, among other things, the reason why he cannot offhand determine who is and is not a scientist; why he must know a great deal more than he does before he can say which scientific discoveries have been important. The children in their answers naturally put down Edison and Salk next to Newton and Pasteur, and the teachers, too busy with soul-probing to do any probing into ideas, handle the question out of their own shallow resources. They do not explain the difference between a scientist and an inventor, a theorist and a technician: they may recognize the distinction, but it is no more habitual to them than to the children. The result, twenty years later, is that only a handful in the nation understand the necessity for untrammeled theoretical research: the government contracts in aid of science are written by legislators and bureaucrats to whom Edison and Einstein are the same sort of wonderworkers, the edge being given to Edison as the more versatile and practical-like.

This shortcircuit between a child's assignment and a great national problem illustrates the origin and outcome of one type of intellectual deficiency among us: we are frivolously vague about clear-cut matters of Intellect and priggishly self-assured about the imponderables of the soul.

This 'method' applies throughout. Whenever possible the menace of drudgery, that is, of work, must be replaced by an 'activity.' To be ingenious about devising activities is the mark of the 'imaginative' teacher. In the 'living-museum' class (elementary biology) for example, the eleven-year-olds are divided into two groups. Those in one group draw and color a picture of a microscope, paste

---

*A natural philosopher of my acquaintance, a house painter by trade, greeted me one morning as I was taking my young daughter to school: 'Say, are you familiar with the modern homework?'—'Why, yes. What are you thinking of especially?'—'It's for the parents!'

it on a piece of cardboard, and cut it up into a jigsaw puzzle for the others to put together. Meanwhile, few in the group learn to focus the 'living' microscope; it takes practice and concentration and is not a rousing activity.

The best activities are of course those that bring into one 'project' the entire group, for then noise and agitation can reach their educative peak. The intention, one may suppose, is to inure the young to the ways of collective journalism, though it would be supposing too much to assume that all children are destined for it. Another purpose is to make the children self-governing. They decide what to do, how to do it, and who does which part. This looks like good practice for young democrats, but all it seems to develop is a taste for committees as a substitute for work, while teaching the identity of committee meetings with undirected thought and small achievement. No pupil, for instance, is shown how to lead a committee to discover its own best opinion—a difficult feat which the teacher herself does not demonstrate.

Indeed, the teacher remains purposely passive, believing, as we saw, that this is to give young minds full scope for 'creativity.' Though there is much 'contact' for emotional reasons, Intellect is not vividly there, on a platform, to be seen in action and imitated, consciously and unconsciously. Rather, personality, without which a teacher is as null as would be an actor, goes into hiding behind theory and amid the confusion of group activity.

Under this scheme, the outcome most desired is a problem, or rather an obstruction, to whatever might otherwise turn into normal classwork. The curriculum then begins to provide 'life situations.' To this end, 'gimmicks' must be found. Thus in a high school class one teacher, concerned about the split between the humanities and the sciences, assigned a project as follows:* 'It could be anything—written, oral, structural, or whatever—but it must show the influence of something learned in science on some-

---

*I reproduce verbatim the description given approvingly by a distinguished scientist at one of our leading universities. He thought the idea well worth considering for college use.

thing learned in another course.' Now prizes had been offered for the best projects, yet most of the class could not rise to the challenge—a sign, one hopes, of youth's unconquerable mind! Still, one boy won first prize by 'composing a piece of music which expressed his view of gravity.' At once, of course, a delightful problem arose, a veritable life situation: the teacher could not read music and neither could most of the class. A meeting was held, at which it was resolved that the composer would try to render his piece on the harmonica. The class listened and by a vote agreed that it faithfully represented the pull on a space ship trying to leave the earth.

The fact that the winning project did not meet the specifications (the influence of one piece of knowledge of a certain kind upon another of another kind) escaped notice. So did the absurdity of discussing an individual 'view' of gravity; and of course no music teacher was asked about the alleged representation. In short, no single idea or principle emerged from the experience—which one must confess is very lifelike.

I have dealt with science teaching in various grades because of the recent dismay at its shaky foundations, and also to suggest that merely increasing the dose of such sugar pills will change nothing. The gimmickry must change first and throughout. Consider study itself. For the sake of every subject matter educated parents have worried about their children's reading habits, or the lack of them. They need not wonder when some of the 'real-life' exercises in English consist in cutting out of a Sunday review of books 'all the reviews that would make you want to read the book' and pasting them in a scrapbook. At the end of the month these collections are then marked, on what basis, no one knows: Excellent, Good, Fair, and Unsatisfactory.

This is of course not the only assignment. The literary mind of our best teachers goes a bit farther.* A thirteen-year-old with a more than average liking for books is asked by the English teacher to

---

*I repeat that my examples bear upon the best—the dozen or so schools, public and private, Eastern and Western, of which I have knowledge from children (my own and others, some now grown up) and from parents whose reports I have reason to trust.

write—for the first time—a book report on some work read in social studies (a notable gimmick: cross-fertilization of fields, interdisciplinary integration). The pupil, whose associations with book reviewing are scissors and paste, asks what the difference is between a book report and a book review. The answer is muddled, as well it might be, and leaves in the child's mind the phrase 'more of a critique,' which is also not explained. The inquiry ends with the teacher's saying that the difference does not matter.

To assist in these exercises, the teacher recommends that the children buy two paperback volumes, one a college dictionary, the other a pocket edition of *Roget's Thesaurus*. This is sensible, except that the meaning of 'thesaurus' and the use of the book are not explained in class, nor in the book itself. When two or three of the pupils, who have left their copies at home, consult the school librarian, it turns out that the arrangement of the large, original Roget differs from that of the pocket version. The librarian, who confesses to never having used a thesaurus, can only puzzle over it and thus give the children an object lesson in the difficulties of research.

Who then 'liquidates ignorance'? Not the teacher, who knows about each 'age group' all its 'reactions' and 'social urges' and 'growth factors' ahead of time, but cannot give clear assignments, instructions, or answers.* The 'help' which is explanation comes from elsewhere. For example, the offices of foreign consuls and our own travel agencies take up the slack in geography and world politics, through their beautiful publications, which the pupil collects and hands in for credit. The pupil who is incautious enough to mention that his parents have a friend in some specially picturesque occupation—roentgenology or coffee importing—is told to 'consult' him about it and write a report. The child is in fact lucky if he is not summoned to arrange a 'field trip' for the whole class. If

---

*That this is well recognized can be inferred from the Wilson Teacher-Appraisal Scale, which asks pupils and supervisors, among other questions: '*Assignments*: I would say the teacher in making assignments is—Always definite;—Definite;—Indefinite;—Very indefinite.'

he can do so, he is much valued—'one of our best pupils, very co-operative'—in proportion to the success and excitement of the outing.

No one apparently notices that this lack of sobriety about school-work hides an undemocratic assumption. These good but ill-cared-for young minds are treated as if all were in a position to rediscover everything unaided, or through the help of parents, friends, and connections. The schools say they do not teach an elite, but they tacitly rely on 'background' and 'advantages.' True, they do this ignorantly, but their neglect of intellectual discipline amounts to denying the young the benefits of the long collective effort of Intellect which is their birthright. Of what use to even an unusually bright pupil are all the visual aids, paperback books, field trips, documentary movies, special lectures, and 'opportunities for independent work' if he lacks the categories of thought and habits of study which would enable his impressions to cohere?

More than one school catalogue I have read begins by saying: 'At the ——— School, the first of our objectives is to encourage students to think for themselves.' The redundancy gives away the pretense: encourage them, equip them, to think, and much will have been done. Whoever thinks does it by himself and for himself. But to encourage the utterance of opinion unchecked—as in those 'social studies' classes where Supreme Court decisions are discussed in a free-for-all—does nothing to encourage thought. Rather, it strengthens the prejudice against thought, by persuading each child that everybody is entitled to his own opinion, 'especially me to mine.'

Similarly, the other free-for-all of physical activities often persuades the pupil that he or she has no aptitude for a given subject, simply because that subject has never been extracted from the pseudo-life which buzzes around it. I have taken down the words of a scientist who has visited many schools in an effort to help remedy the poor teaching of his subject. 'It is a rare thing,' said he, 'to find a teacher who will *name, describe,* and *explain* a natural phenomenon. I don't believe most of them can.' Considering what these teachers have been told their subject is, and what they have not been taught about it, this inarticulateness is not surprising. The mind slithers with the subjects which it is antieducational to call by their right names: not astronomy, geology, and physics, but 'Earth Science'; not English and French, or reading and writing, or speaking and reciting, but 'Language Arts'; not history and civics and economics, but 'Social Studies'; not psychology and sociology and anthropology, but 'Human Relations': it is a positive call for vagueness and trifling.

Vagueness is bound to prevail when the aim of the school is no longer instruction in subjects, but education in attitudes to meet the needs of life. From the premise that life demands other qualities than learning, which is true and important, we have come to the conclusion that in a school scholastic ability and scholastic subjects are indecent and ought to be disguised: I am conscious that in using the word 'pupil' in this chapter I sound archaic: the child is the real thing. While biology and algebra are made genteel, play-acting goes on with 'living predicaments,' 'panoramas,' 'junior town meetings,' and 'research projects,' all of which can be used in many directions, like a transfer on a busline. The dogma goes far: a year ago or so, a good parochial high school in the Middle West was taken off the accreditation list because it did not offer Home Economics and Industrial Arts.[9] These last-named subjects are no doubt important, and to some, who will shortly become wives and machinists, very important. But to argue that they are a necessary part of the curriculum to a community that does not want them shows the distance traveled since Jefferson's and Franklin's naïve belief that public schools were for spreading literacy.

Meanwhile, the simple but difficult arts of paying attention, copying accurately, following an argument, detecting an ambiguity or a false inference, testing guesses by summoning up contrary instances, organizing one's time and one's thoughts for study—all these arts, which cannot be taught in the air but only through the difficulties of a defined subject, which cannot be taught in one course or one year, but must be acquired gradually, in dozens of connections—these arts of the mind are believed to be miraculously added unto the child whose creativity has been released by asking his parents haphazard answers to impossible questions, and who has received praise for their joint effort in an atmosphere of contact and forbearance.

The outcome is that the educated young are self-educated, not only in the trite meaning of the phrase, but in the sense that at some point in their career they confront their nurtured incapacity, and with gritted teeth set out to repair one or more of the deficiencies—linguistic or mathematical—which we have come to regard as normal and even praiseworthy.

The fundamental role that language, or rather the neglect of language, plays in all these losses and failures, including the scientific, is a characteristic of democratic schooling to which I shall return. I mention language here, as at every relevant point, not only to show how frequently the reference is in order, but also to point out how the defect perpetuates itself: the unquenchable talk about education is useless because most of the speakers, having no regard for the implications of words, cannot criticize their own thought or discover its absence. The very 'test' of teachers which I quoted as a by-product of this orgy of looseness pays no attention to its own language and asks the hapless pupil to find a pair of nonexistent differences between the teacher who is (1) 'Always definite' and (2) 'Definite,' and again between the (3) 'Indefinite' and (4) 'Very indefinite.'

Themselves brought up in an atmosphere where words such as 'contact,' 'life,' and 'problem' are cloudily conceived and used for a limitless range of feeling and fact, the teacher and his oracle, the educationist, can obviously not give their charges a clarity of mind they themselves lack, cannot pass tenable judgments on any mind or any idea, cannot control their own work, and cannot tell the public or one another anything important about children or schools. The report cards are a notorious puzzle to parents and pupils alike, and the public pronouncements about 'objectives' and 'broad programs' would also be recognized as bewildering if thanks to a kind of thought-cliché they did not sound just as one expects. The great danger at this juncture, when the laity is aroused and ready for action, is that educators will at last demonstrate their unfitness to direct anything but infants, and tire out the nation's patience and good will.

V

Instruction Without Authority

At the same time as they foster the blurred mind, then, the elementary and secondary schools postpone and finally make unpalatable the ancient discipline of work. But it would be a mistake to suppose that college brings about a radical change. How could it? There are mountainous arrears of ignorance, and little habit of study to bring to bear upon them. And there are, besides, the collegiate forms of philanthropy, make-believe, and the desire to play. The best thing that has been found so far to remedy a part of the incompetence carried forward from high school is 'general education'—the attempt to show the young how abstract 'subjects' hang together to form the traditions by which the world lives. In good hands general education courses at least teach a youth how to read.

But no way has yet been found to teach him how to write. The sole magic that could make freshman composition succeed would be the belief on the part of both student and teacher that writing mattered, that the instructor was bored by dullness, offended by barbarisms, and outraged by nonsense. Then the student might begin to feel, through his written work, a moral responsibility for his intellectual acts. As things are, he writes in order to gain three credits, work off a degree requirement, and 'satisfy' the English department, which has been delegated by the rest of the faculty to demand payment of this debt of honor. Members of the other departments can apparently do without clear prose, though some ask for it, grumbling at its permanent scarcity. More often, they rely on powers of divination to glimpse historical or literary or scientific truth through the mists of adolescent incoherence, which they themselves would find it grievous and perplexing to correct.

This is not to say that the best liberal arts colleges do not achieve remarkable results as remedial institutions. In four years they often manage to reawaken the high school graduate narcotized by the special dullness of the eleventh and twelfth grades. The college, moreover, sometimes gives the able student a command of one of the elements—language, logic, or number—which have hitherto eluded him: the cripple is first given a crutch and then taught to walk without it.

But these cases must be rare in proportion to the total college population, or we should not hear the continual complaints of those who admit to the professional schools. Dean William C. Warren, of the Columbia University School of Law, tells us in his Report for 1955: 'We have found that few of our entering students, however carefully selected, possess these skills [reading and writing] to the extent needed for law study.'[1] In England, a recent outcry of the Medical Council after a reading of examination papers led Mr. Alex Atkinson to write for *Punch* a lively parody entitled 'How I Done My Research.'[2] Taken together with similar indications from France and Germany, this suggests a democratic phenomenon, the signs of which began to be noticed soon after the turn of the century.

But in the United States the condition is aggravated by that indifference to central subjects which colleges continue from the lower schools. Dean Erwin N. Griswold of Harvard complained some time ago of capable applicants to his Law School who offered college records showing no literature, mathematics, philosophy, physical science, or foreign languages, but consisting wholly of courses in Principles of Advertising Media, Office Management, Principles of Retailing, Stage and Costume Design, and Methods in Minor Sports.[3]

'Real life,' it would seem, has crept in and ousted academic subjects, that is to say, not only those which are best for furnishing the mind and giving order to thought, but those which are alone capable of being taught theoretically. This fundamental distinction, elementary to the trained intellect, is virtually forgotten in the zeal of educators to 'offer' as a course whatever is a namable activity of man. This willingness matches the student's penchant for avoiding hard conceptual work in genuine subjects and for playing at others, which depend on practice for their meaning and whose so-called principles are but platitudes or tautologies. For the intellectually lazy, Methods in Minor Sports is as far as thought can reach. The student's desire to prolong his earlier 'activity' is understandable, but its indulgence is in fact a fraud practiced upon him, for his courses will neither increase his literacy nor impress his prospective employers. Meantime the law school that accepts him because of his 'general intelligence' has the task of starting him on his ABCs.

Colleges whose main curriculum is academic are not thereby saved from another kind of make-believe, which frequently leads a student to drop philosophy or English for journalism or business administration. In a university college, these 'enlivening' subjects are taught by men from the marketplace, whereas the academic ones are taught by young graduate assistants (section men), who are subject to the professional's fallacy. They look upon college students as future specialists of their own kind and speak to them of nothing but the methods and minutiae of scholarship. For example, if the college offers an introductory course in the civilization of India, scholarly standards require that it be taught by a student of Sanskrit. This is reasonable, but experience shows that one would have to supply a keeper or a policeman before one could stop a young Sanskritist from spending class time on doubtful etymologies and disputed points in the literature. That his students cannot follow, and are bored and discouraged, does not deter him for many years. Meanwhile one understands why Milton said, 'I hate a pupil teacher.'

No doubt some graduate assistants and young instructors are capable of good teaching, but something is radically false in a 'philosophy' which says that the college student should receive a general and liberal education, and which makes its teachers the living refutation of that ideal.

There is worse. The majority of assistants teaching in our universities are neither born scholars nor aspiring to be educated men. They are caught in a maze—preoccupied with their own studies and examinations, with their young families and the cost of living. For all but the best, the main responsibility in research and teaching consists in amassing facts and avoiding factual error. What they do in the 'third hour' of the course is try to correct the wrong impressions gathered from the textbook or the lectures of the senior professor—in short, coach the group to pass with a gentlemanly C the monthly quizzes and final examinations. The whole tendency of the arrangement is to enthrone the thought-cliché, to give it value as a passport, to convince the student that this facsimile is what learning and Intellect consist of.

Occasionally—for we must not forget the large number of intelligent people studying and teaching in any college—an embryo of intellectual discussion comes into being; fledgling ideas begin to fly about. But the young instructor, and sometimes the senior man, are not able to keep the collective thought alive. Where would any of them have acquired the art or the manners for it? The students have no skill in making their ideas clear or in meeting a point. One or two speak too much and too fast; a few others struggle with a weak vocabulary and faulty grammar to give body to phantom thoughts; while the dumb majority are confirmed in their suspicion of Intellect as directionless quibble. At best, the instructor straightens out the group on matters of fact and the accepted generalities of the subject. He almost never imparts principles for the conduct of the understanding, and he certainly does nothing that would spontaneously kindle in his students a bias in favor of Intellect.*

It is these underprivileged minds which in the last two years of college are expected to 'specialize,' do research, write an honors thesis. This is an attractive change from sitting, taking notes, and giving back in writing a faint approximation of memories associated with boredom and pain. At this point, surely, some men begin to receive intellectual training. But just as often, perhaps, the misdirection only grows worse. The instructor is an able specialist himself, and he puts his pride in treating his charges as fellow scholars. This means that he never dreams of telling them how to use a library or write a sentence. 'Maturity' and high scholarship alike require that all such trivia be glossed over, and the time reserved for the issues arising out of the assigned topic. The good student has long been accustomed to having opinions on issues, but he flounders among the technicalities of research and devices of expression which alone would make those opinions tenable. Details become more and more unmentionable as the tutorial hours grow loftier in contents. The students expect nothing but 'suggestions'—and praise. I remember a very able young lady, a graduate *magna cum laude* from one of our leading university colleges, and who burst into tears when she received from me her third failing grade in a row for her weekly papers in historiography. Conversation brought out the fact that she had worked in college with two distinguished scholars and had never received less than A– on her written work. She added very candidly: 'Of course, they made comments like yours in the margins, but they

---

*When the lack of this bias in public opinion is deplored, it should be remembered that the remedy cannot be given by preaching. Respect for Intellect, if not born in the home, must be aroused in school and college by a sight of the teacher's ordinary attitudes toward ideas, minds, books, words and their fit use. When one reads in the press of Paris and New York of the willful damage caused by college students to public library books during information contests, one concludes that college everywhere leaves the barbarian as it found him.

never marked me down for it.' The moral of this liberality is not hard to draw, and a clever student draws it almost unconsciously: grades and critical comments are part of the ritual she has been familiar with since infancy. It does not mean anything. What really matters, more than ever, is 'independent thought,' an 'original' point of view, creativity. Has she not reached the stage of higher education? Outwardly, yes, but who could say higher than what?— the phrase has the indefinite suggestion of 'the better hotels.'

Although college teachers are out of touch with high school teachers—inexcusably so—and university people are at war with educationists, the culture sees to it that the organic looseness of the lower schools infects the higher. Students are after all but pupils grown taller, and their bad habits become unspoken demands to which, owing to the sensitivity of our manners, teachers and institutions respond.*

This lack of strain begins with the 'flexibility' which colleges irrationally make their principal boast. All their rules, they announce, are made to be broken, and their curriculum adapts itself to the meanest understanding. Each institution offers hundreds of courses in case someone should want them. They are made attractive—and flexible in substance—by 'imaginative' titles, e.g., 'Drama and Dreams,' 'Evil and the State Since 1900.' The response to this offering is also flexible; it fluctuates, there is a perpetual boom-and-bust in subject matter. Now Russian is the rage and thousands are taking it who will never progress beyond bungling; at times economics is up and government down; at other times, it is the reverse. English and psychology maintain their lead, based, regrettably, on their relative ease. Behind this show, and influencing the participants, is a series of unexamined beliefs: Psychology helps you get along; En-

*The great Shakespeare scholar and keen observer of educational systems, Wolfgang Clemen, of the University of Munich, has noted the phenomenon in an article, 'The Avalanche of the Masses Falls on the University,' the subtitle of which is: 'The Level of the Teachers Sinks with That of the Students.' *Die Zeit*, March 20, 1958.

glish prepares for delightful jobs in publishing; economics leads to executive posts, and government to being employed by international agencies—the vocational urge is strong, but seldom enlightened. For these courses are quite properly not training courses, and they rarely mesh together to form a reasonably complete theory of the subject. They are just departmental electives, some of which the department hopes will be popular. Any four or six or eight will make a 'major'; and once the semester examination is passed, the knowledge acquired is sealed off from whence it came. No one other than the student has any right to ask for it again.

While this absence of a curriculum properly so called costs the college increasing amounts of money in staffing, record-keeping, and counseling, educators spend their no less expensive time asking what a liberal education is. Thus a former United States Commissioner of Education, who now heads a five-million-dollar institute for educational research, sends out a circular in which he says apropos of liberal education that 'a more descriptive definition in terms of human behavior is needed for our times,' and he asks his correspondents to 'draw up a list of such intellectual, attitudinal, and spiritual qualities which you believe represent the results of a liberating education—if I may use a term which is not as ambiguous and emotionally colored as Liberal Education.'

Meanwhile the student, whom one would suppose fully liberated, virtually licensed, chooses his 'work' as best he can. If not guided by the thought of a job, he is likely to be moved by some interest in the present; the lower schools have given him the taste for the contemporary. Being thought more marketable, 'more real,' the smell of the present almost takes the curse off learning. Woe to the teacher or textbook that refuses to be up to date, either by holding lessons for today or by leading up authoritatively to the events of last week. The truth is that dealing with the contemporary prepares the mind poorly for a thoughtful life, shortening judgment and distorting perspective. The contemporary, moreover, is extremely difficult to assess and teach, though dealing with it makes

the teacher popular. His references to the living satisfy in students
the illusion of being at last in the know. Colleges feed that craving
by engaging resident artists, poets, musicians, and statesmen, and
combining their courses with 'informal conferences.' For once
again, the best way lies through comfort, and comfort is happy confusion, mental promiscuity, or as is said in the Hebrides, 'all
through ither.'

In addition to this costly liberating, the college follows the
schools in their posture of wooing. When under democracy education ceases to be a privilege and becomes a right, the student's
motive and attitude change. The class turns into a clientele to be
satisfied, and a skeptical one: teach me if you can.* The mood follows naturally upon the child-rearing experts' demonstration that
'lock-step teaching' is hurtful to the very young, because their
development is uneven. They must be ready or feel a need. By
extension, there is now no point outside the professional schools at
which the student is told: *this* you must know, now and forever.
The enlightening belief that some kinds of ignorance are culpable is
gone.

In the sciences the notion of cumulative, indispensable knowledge has survived, and with it, in many places, an instructive sever-
ity. Yet there are ways of 'taking' and 'passing' mathematics or
physics which 'satisfy' high school and college instructors without
visible gain in knowledge. When this is true, in science or other subjects, it is not always due to the teacher's incompetence in the
abstract. More often it comes from his relation to the student,
which is no longer one of a legitimate authority met by willing submission, but one of popularity-seeking met by patronizing tolerance. Where formerly the student who did not like or admire his

---

*The cliché is current in colleges that students who came or returned under
Veterans' benefits after the recent wars were uniformly eager and enterpris-
ing in their studies. My experience suggests that this impression was vivid
but not uniform. I found many excellent students, and as many who sat on
their federal haunches, resisting what they had come to get.

teacher might feel hatred, he now feels a friendly sort of contempt. And though the modern student may like without contempt, he is not apt to admire: the feeling is not in our manners and therefore not in his emotional vocabulary. A teacher is liked because he is a 'good guy'; and he and his colleagues are 'just people,' as books on the subject keep reminding us.* A faculty of good guys would make the ideal college, one of friendly and informal equals, warm as a family.

Free fraternizing between teacher and taught is in fact recognized as one of the great advantages of the small college.† Students can visit their instructors at home, 'size up' their wives and children, and ascertain that they are all 'human.' The more human, the less likely that the demands in course will be heavy or strictly adhered to. For under our manners it is not conceivable that a man should break bread with you, call you by your first name, and without anger or unpleasantness, exact the fulfillment of your obligation. There would be in it no love of human error, no mercy: it would be rank justice.

The drive for popularity is, on the teacher's part at least, quite unconscious; and so is the inequity that results from being human at every turn. The special permissions, arrangements, and extensions of time that stretch academic rules into meaninglessness are not seen as doing an injustice to those who observe these rules, because students are not seen as competing with one another, nor indeed as engaged in work which belongs to the life of grown men.‡ These three notions—competition, work, and the life of men—are obscured by the pervasive democratic ideas of individual goals, self-development, and liberating education. In college, though life is

*'Teachers Are Persons—And So Are Pupils, says Educator in Witty New Book.' Circular from Henry Holt and Company about Charles H. Wilson's *A Teacher Is a Person*, New York, 1956.
†The first fraternizer, however, is said to have been an instructor in chemistry at Harvard, in the late seventies, Charles E. Munroe (1849–1938).
‡It is noteworthy that, like their elders, who are to one another 'the boys' and 'the girls,' the modern college man is a boy.

near and the present beckons, the appropriate life-likeness of performance and failure is largely absent. The institutional aim is rather to push through as many as possible. If a grade is required for an honor or a privilege, a student who misses that grade stands a fair chance of getting it nevertheless by appealing to his instructor in the name of all that hangs on his success.

So alien are justice and competitive effort to the academic world that recently a leading university abolished the requirement of high standing for scholarship students, on the ground that it made these students nervous and put them in a different academic category from the rest, who can pass with a low C. It is amusing to reflect that in Russia, where capitalism is cursed for its competitiveness, competition in schools is the norm, whereas in the capitalistic West it has all but disappeared.* When an American teacher awakens to his duty and fails the incompetent, there is an outcry. Students, parents, and often other teachers, object—no doubt correctly—that it is 'out of line.'

What is *in* line is the abdication of the teaching power. The claim itself is given up in an ambiguous cliché, regrettably echoed by Mr. William Faulkner when he was about to serve at Princeton: 'Nobody can really teach anybody else anything.'[4] If this means that there must be an active learner, it is true; but if it means that all teaching is self-teaching, then schools are wasting even more of the country's money than I suspect.

The question resolves itself again into that of work, and except for self-support, work is not inevitably associated with college studies. Periodically, the faculty utters the wish that students would 'read more on their own' and were 'capable of independent work' but they do not enforce their will. Taking notes on lectures that duplicate the text, or reading the text, or last-minute cramming from so-

*A conversation with an educational official from behind the Iron Curtain informs me, since the sentence above was written, that Soviet mass education has not been so competitive as the West believes, but has been plagued by many of the same defects as American education. For the earlier view, see Jules Moch, *Les U.R.S.S. les yeux ouverts*, Paris, 1955.

called review books suffices for most courses. But is not this work? No, it is at best industry, a virtue not to be despised, but lacking the essential element of work, which is passion. It is passion in work and for work that gives it its dramatic quality, that makes the outcome a possession of the worker, that becomes habit-forming and indeed obsessional. Of all the deprivations that modern life imposes on intellectual man, the abandonment of work is the cruelest, for all other occupations kill time and drain the spirit, whereas work fills both, and in the doing satisfies at once love and aggression. That is the sense in which work is 'fun,' with an irresistible appeal to man's love of difficulty conquered—a pleasure altogether different from that for which educators have turned school subjects into activities and play. Under the habit of play, drudgery, when it comes, remains drudgery, instead of an accepted purgatory close to the heaven of work. No man who works in the sense I mean can despise himself, even if the work is below his deserts, or its perfection short of his ideal.

An inkling of these truths is doubtless behind the talk of creativity which I may seem to be inconsistent in decrying. I do so because (as I said earlier) the word has become another excuse for caprice, for nonwork; and because I still attach importance to the word 'creation.' Industry is not work, and work is not creation. If by what is already a metaphor we call Michelangelo a creator, if we say that Poe created the short story, if we may even say that a new dress from Paris is a creation, then we must not say that Sally's finger-painting and the college boy's short story and the homemade costumes of amateur theatricals are creations. I am not worried about the effect of the misnomer on Michelangelo; I am worried about its effect on students and their parents, who will have been deprived by philanthropy of yet another intellectual awareness. Pitted only against their own capacities in school, denied the stimulus of failure by a world seemingly hungry for their crumbs of creativity, the talented young remain innocently conceited and hurtfully ignorant of both the range of common achievement and the quality of genius. I have talked with many brilliant students who could scarcely believe that their work was not readily publishable, at any length and without the alteration of a comma. Had they not always been known as gifted? Had they not won prizes? All they needed was a word from me to an editor: influence must aid achievement. They also considered it unjust that it should take ten or a dozen years of not especially agreeable work to prove oneself in a profession. A nurtured subjectivism about their own creativity made the thought of unrecognized effort as revolting as the statement that their work did not as yet equal the best. For the verbiage of 'self-evaluation' in school had encouraged their critical discontent only about others; their own aims, measured by sheltered ambitions, had never failed except from extraneous cause.* And that is how, when a whole society concurs in mistaking and miscalling the varieties of work, the notion of excellence departs.†

To judge by words, the academic world is very much alive to the desirability of maintaining standards. Not a minute passes without some reference to this sacred duty. Carrying it out is another thing. Here again few are incompetent or dishonest in the abstract; but the lack of clear notions and express demands produces the same

---

*A group of young writers not long ago circularized sympathetic friends, asking help to overcome a situation they described as follows: ' . . . the average first novelist thinks he has made the big move once he is published, only to find that the day after the reviews are printed, he is once more an anonymous figure. . . . We believe that one of the [reasons] is pure economics. . . . '
†This is surely the result of spurring the critical spirit while leaving it undirected, of 'thinking for oneself' without encountering the objections of a better thinker. I once had occasion to tell a group of graduate students that any of them would be lucky to achieve the fifth or sixth rank among historians. The remark was prompted by their dissatisfaction with all they knew: Gibbon was a bore, Macaulay a stuffed shirt, Hegel and Michelet were fools, Carlyle and Buckle frauds—this from students who could not write ten pages of readable and properly documented narrative. Pointing out that even second-and third-rate men, such as Milman, Bancroft, or Grote, were the superiors of these students' own instructors, who were by definition superior to the students themselves, was a sobering thought quite foreign to their experience.

effect as incompetence and dishonesty. The very customs of the academic grove militate against standards. The system of credits turns attention away from substance. The student amasses points in order to advance, as in the game of parchesi, but strange to say in the land of practicality, to ask what he can do is an invasion of privacy. As one student remarked when rebuked for an illegible scrawl, 'Well, it's *my* handwriting, isn't it?' At other times, on other subjects, the attitude is: 'It's no good, I know, but whose is any better?' Examinations are in bad repute, and some teachers boast that they do not take them seriously. Whenever possible they substitute exercises believed to be more 'genuine'—a report on the reading of three books, a long term paper, a set of questions worked on at home. Sometimes these do disclose ability, a general brightness coupled with responsible behavior. But we knew that our young in college were intelligent and nice; the question is, why are they there?

It is an unchallenged commonplace that what you learn in college does not matter. What does matter is not agreed upon: some say 'contacts'; others 'atmosphere.' College is 'broadening,' 'liberating,' 'stimulating.' How? Lectures, it appears, are no longer in favor; hence lecturers do not take the trouble they once did to organize, dramatize, and deliver, though they still address hundreds, sometimes in scattered colonies viewing closed-circuit television. Small classes *are* in favor, but I suspect more for 'human' than for intellectual reasons. In small classes more reading is done, perhaps, and more 'participating,' but somehow not much more instruction. There often is about the small class something of the illusion of work one finds in the committee meeting. It can be an agreeable chat. In general, the net worth of the time and energy spent in college would seem to be a residue of miscellaneous experience. The contents and coherence of the work the degree stands for are secondary; otherwise it would not be possible to do what so many are praised for doing—combine a fatiguing part-time job with athletic or other activities while giving a token performance in class. These sturdy campus heroes by common consent receive for their moral and physical endurance the kind of honoring that properly belongs to scholastic achievement.

The observer is driven to conclude that under democratic conditions of equality mixed with envy, the college degree is the last remaining mark of class. Any doubt that this generality applies in other than the American democracy is dispelled by the tone of such arguments as the following, taken from the usually sagacious English journal, *The Economist*: 'Are the universities—Redbrick obediently following Oxford and Cambridge—going to continue to regard themselves as existing only to turn out an elite of highly trained, urbanely specialized race of men and women, and to gear their whole approach and teaching methods to endlessly reproducing dons and higher civil servants? Or are they going to accept the logic of expanding higher education—which is . . . also to make the mass of people now just below "university standard" more educated than they are? . . . The universities and technical colleges together should be engaged in training the talents and broadening the lives of the top tenth of the nation's intelligence . . . and thereafter the whole first quartile should be regarded as collegeworthy. When that happens it cannot possibly be maintained that the methods evolved for dealing with the top five per cent should be applied to everyone. Everything must change—the varieties of degree, the methods of selection, and, above all, the idea that ordinary . . . graduates are merely a menial by-product of the universities' main task of producing firsts in arts and science for top jobs.'[5]

In the United States it is certainly social desire that presses the demand for more colleges to accommodate the new generations. Except among academics themselves the vivid awareness of a need to train the nation's talents comes only as an afterthought-cliché. Indeed, even the best-informed part of the public has no accurate idea of the merits of various colleges. Its opinions are fifteen years behind the times—except as to social ranking. But snobbery apart, the dividing line of the college degree is now part of the economic system as well as of accepted manners.* Someone has computed that seventy-one occupations require a B.A. When what is euphemistically called a noncollege graduate succeeds as a business executive making twenty-thousand dollars a year it is news.[6] I have known three or four persons of ability and education who, for lack of a diploma, had great difficulty obtaining employment corresponding to their unquestioned talents. No wonder that once a young person has a foot in college, he (or his parents if he is unconcerned) will do anything to reach the goal. For the great majority the name of the college matters no more than its curriculum, faculty, or standards.

Mass education, in short, has rediscovered the convenient badge of the English 'pass degree.' Does the present unrest mean that we are about to install a true 'honors degree'?† Some think that this is unnecessary because our many kinds of graduate schools choose the best minds and give them, at long last, the genuine higher learning. This is inexact. A few leading law and medical schools are able to guess at who may be the ablest and subject them to a discipline. But the rest, including the non-professional graduate schools, lack the opportunity and often the desire. As at every earlier step in schooling, graduate admissions have regard to promise rather than achievement; they are the gambles of a futurist on students whose

---

*One need not take seriously the demand for 'Girls with Doctorates,' which a hotel in Las Vegas advertised in January, 1957, presumably for a floor show. But an unpublished series of interviews with adult students taking evening classes at a large university supports the generality about degrees and snobbery. One woman, married to a doctor, answered the question, 'Did you ever feel handicapped without a college degree?' by saying, 'No, not at that time.' She went on to explain that at the army camp where her husband was stationed, 'there wasn't any way one couple could be said to be better off than another,' but by discovering that she had no college degree, 'they had me placed and down I went in the esteem of everybody. . . . It made me want to go to college.' She also found that her husband, who had told her she was 'so bright she didn't need to go to college,' represented her to others as a graduate of the institution she was only beginning to attend.

†Mr. Conant has suggested that high school diplomas should indicate rank and quality by carrying on their backs the student's full record. He thinks it unjust that there should be a dual standard, high and low, for obtaining the same certificate. *New York Times*, July 17, 1958.

ability and knowledge are incommensurable. Hence the student body is mixed and the training uncertain. Outside the professional schools, graduate instruction follows the routines of an apprentice system designed eighty years ago, when numbers were small and scholars were dedicated beings.

In some ways, indeed, it is in the modern graduate school that the falsity which permeates our schooling is most flagrant and seemingly least remediable. We have seen one aspect of the fraud in describing the teaching of undergraduates by harassed and unprepared graduate students. The same disparity between ends and means is reproduced in such accepted practices as giving promotion for research to men appointed and salaried for teaching. Research worth having can only be hoped for, not commanded; yet in the best schools teaching is deemed inferior to it and a nuisance. This judgment is expressed in the coveted research professorships, and even more vividly in the inducements recently held out by the wealthier state universities to the members of poor ancient ones: the distinguished man is offered a high salary, frequent leaves of absence, funds for research, and no duties. The highest prize of the teaching profession is: no teaching. For the first time in history, apparently, scholars want no disciples. And perhaps, seeing those that come forward, they are right. In any case, they accept sterilization at a high fee, while the funds voted by legislatures and foundations to 'increase facilities' serve in fact to remove the best minds from the classroom.

By the lore of graduate schools, to publish what is 'new' is the only accepted way to contribute to knowledge. It follows that originality is sought also in the work of graduates, whose general information is lacking or recently acquired, whose technical training, if they are fortunate, dates from a senior thesis, and whose ability to write a page—let alone a book—has never been developed by suitable exercises. As in college, the pretense is that 'mature persons' having free choice can educate themselves by following lecture courses which are assumed to be 'advanced' and which may be taken in any order and combination. After a suitable number of lectures and one or two seminars, in which students read papers haltingly in front of their uninterested peers, the comprehensive oral examination suddenly looms, demanding of the candidate a breadth and depth of knowledge equal to the sum of the same in the heads of his half-dozen examiners. In most subjects, few attempts are made to educe principles from ever larger masses of facts and to relegate detail to handbooks. The sum total of many specialities is required of the student, no matter how many years of his adult life are swallowed up in the preparation. Many give up. The rest go in for cramming, which after the strain of the vomition leaves a man reflecting that there was one week in his life when he knew a great deal.

The institution built on these assumptions crowns them all with the affectation of having nothing to do with the preparation of teachers. It would consider itself disgraced if it gave courses in pedagogy or in the history of education. It knows and wants to know nothing of the verified facts about learning, memory, and habit; about temperamental differences in verbal and visual powers; about anything that might prepare its graduates for the age-old difficulties in imparting knowledge. It sends out 'masters' and 'doctors' in the humanities—the academic study of literature, music, and the plastic arts—who have not an inkling of the psychology of perception—just as if Helmholtz and William James had never lived. And these cripples, many of whom have taught undergraduates while earning a license to teach, are seldom enabled to correct their own patent deficiencies as speakers, writers, and judges of work. Though it is upon them as inspirers of the next generation in college that the continuity of scholarship depends, no opportunity exists to tell them of such elementary faults as mumbling, disjointed utterance, and unorganized thought. In short, the graduate school reproduces on a lofty plane the errors of omission chargeable at every stage since the fifth grade.

No exertions by isolated teachers in college or graduate school can make up for the prevailing lack of the rudiments. The very mixing of those who can with those who fumble or grope destroys morale and turns every advance into a perpetual rebeginning. The net result is a general spoilage of the native ability which should be exploited from its earliest appearance. But to find and exploit talent as we exploit our other natural resources presupposes a body of schoolteachers who are at least intellectualized. This we almost certainly lack. We cannot be sure until we release our present teachers from professional superstitions, irrelevant duties, economic cares, and social oppression.

This seems a large order, yet much of it could be carried out by the simple expedient of letting teachers alone in winter and making them read books in summer. Their minds are today the least of their assets, in everyone's estimation including their own. Teachers have been the victims—often the willing victims—of that longing for a happy world which not only has made the school an anti-intellectual hothouse, but designed the Parent-Teachers' Association as a vestibule to utopia. There the teachers have given the last of their energies to justifying themselves by projecting impossible goals and pretending to enjoy with their audience's offspring a most unnatural bliss. In these public relations with the parents any respectable notion of teaching sank under the hypocrisies of the well-intentioned.

This subduing of intellect to pedagoguery and the cash nexus is so consequential for the discussion of money in a later chapter that it must be noticed here with the aid of an example. Since teachers in the public schools are presumably in no position to resist their masters, the taxpayers, I shall cite recent events at an old-established private preparatory school. The headmaster, not an educationist, invited a number of influential parents for a discussion of the school and its needs, chiefly financial. The first error imposed by our manners was that the headmaster must be mealy-mouthed, and pretend that what the school needed was not money so much as parental criticism and advice. The second error was that the parents naïvely believed this transparent lie and acted on it. After the week-end in question, typical remarks were transcribed and circulated. Amid ordinary good sense, one read the following:

'The parents have a feeling of not being wanted. They need a tip as to how to act. . . . ' Another complained: 'We've seen a good bit of the housemaster, but we haven't seen the teachers because we've felt they've been too busy. . . . ' Another: 'Your communications from the school tend to be formal and cold . . . it would be better if you went on to say that of course housemasters and teachers are interested and available for discussion, etc.'

'Available for discussion, etc.'—togetherness!* That is the summit we have reached after three thousand years of arduous *paideia*. 'A key point to the role of the parents,' the school report goes on, 'is to develop their understanding of the *why* behind the policies, programs, desires, and needs of the school.' To parents who want such a role it would be useless to explain that teaching is not an agglutinative principle but a separating, a detaching principle. Teaching is to get rid of the pupils, not to inherit their parents.

When parents begin to meddle in the direction of schools, the teachers' defense of 'the educational process' calls forth a jargon which is in good part responsible for the general decline in literacy—for how can we expect children to think and speak clearly when their elders in talking of school do neither? In order to suggest a perpetually gay adventure, everyone refers not to difficulties but to 'challenges'—the challenge of or to our schools; each new class is a challenge to the school; when the P.T.A. convenes, the division of home economics 'prepares to meet the parents' challenge' by furnishing coffee and cake and explaining how a new scheme was tried out (indeed, a 'research experiment') with results that were 'exciting.'

Contrary to the common experience, a teacher's excitement

---

*As one can see daily in the press, schemes are numerous for bringing parents and children together in the same classroom, e.g., 'Parents Joining Children in Art.' *New York Times*, July 8, 1957. This is another manifestation of the self-centered family, the sanctuary of innocence and incest combined.

seems never to stop. Yet, on sober reflection, a teacher who is free of false zeal should feel no more challenged by a new class (and no less) than any good craftsman by a familiar task; and should feel no more excitement in the classroom (and no less) than a surgeon at the operating table. Nor have parents any business challenging schools and teachers in another sense, as if here were policies to mistrust and candidates to elect. Notwithstanding, the political mixture of inquest and boasting continues, in the superlative mood of the advertiser and the mass media. A childish idea of wonder and surprise, of rescue and giant-killing, informs this agitation and colors it with megalomania.

What makes the pretense of dramatic thrills all the more absurd is that the practitioners lay claim, through another set of jargon words, to the results of a science called 'educational research.' There is, as a matter of fact, no such science. The results are vitiated in advance by the nonexistence of the entities they refer to. No doubt the children observed, the events counted, the test papers scored, are genuine objects in the world of experience; but the generalities inferred from them are either tendentious or tautological. They tell us over again in polysyllables what does not need saying, or they command us to foster in children certain motives or attitudes arbitrarily chosen, rather than others that are equally 'natural' and therefore equally 'found' by psychology. To the extent that psychology is a science, it prescribes nothing but merely describes. If our social bias did not lead us to prefer, say, co-operation and creativity, psychology could find excellent natural motives driving the young to hostility and imitation, on which an admirable system of repression could be built. Human capacity is more varied than educational researchers know, though their methods insure that they shall never find this out.

This simple intellectual point would be better appreciated than it is if that other creature of educational research, the hircocervus buzzing in a void, did not distract us with its capacity for dispelling sense. Try for example to think of any practical judgments that could be based on the answers to the questions I shall quote from a so-called 'evaluation study' of a small liberal arts college. The few I have chosen were among those called 'major' by the expert, who produced upward of a thousand. The remainder required the students, faculty members, and trustees to 'measure' degrees of importance, intensity, and the like by writing 1, 2, or 3 as part of their answers; that is how 'science' came into the inquiry. But the 'major questions' required no 'measurement':

'What is the major assumption underlying the program? What are the educational objectives of the students and the faculty? What is the relation of these objectives to the major assumptions? What evidence now exists to show the extent to which the objectives are now being attained?'

Let me interrupt here to make sure that the familiar sound of the words does not produce the illusion of meaning. The major assumption of any program is that it is good. The educational objective of any sane student is to be taught and receive a certificate of work done. The relation of the objective to the assumption is that if the assumption is true—i.e., the program (including its execution) is good—the objective will be reached more often than not, i.e., more students will learn and profit than fail. As for evidence that the whole thing works, it exists in the common consent to have things continue as they are. All I have said is of course truism; none of it differs from one school to the next; none of it is worth saying or asking—unless you want an answer like this: 'The major assumption of our distinctive program is that a balanced and enriched curriculum, broad in concept but carefully adjusted to the growing needs and motivations of the individual student, will help in the development of the whole person through the liberating influence of the arts and sciences considered as a contribution not only to personal well-being but to future service as a member of a democratic community.'

The 'self-evaluation' I have used does not dwell in abstractions throughout. But its concreteness is typically 'educational' in presupposing a godlike knowledge of human character. Thus: 'What is the nature of the faculty-student relationship? What is the value of these relations? Can an instructor who is a poor counselor at first become

a good one? Do creative writing majors get an increased appreciation of the work of others? Do science students know as many facts
as they should?' And—very apt for a girls' college: 'Do students who
apply and are accepted have irregular profiles?'*

It would be difficult to demonstrate the absurdity of these questions to anyone who lives in the atmosphere in which they sound
genuine. But that would only be because of the gap between words
and experience in the dream world of professional educators. He
who can read and understand other writers—philosophers, poets,
political theorists, scientists—is, after comparison, entitled to say
that the language of educational research does not point to the
common experience of teaching and ignores the rules of common
discourse.

This last conclusion is confirmed when one receives from a professor of higher education at a great university a printed inquiry such
as this, which I reproduce entire:

> Would you like to have a comparable overview of an impor-
> tant book in higher education on your desk periodically? A
> card is enclosed for your response.

Or again, when one reads in the paper that 'Paul V. Gump and
Jacob S. Kounin, of Wayne State University, noted that a "high firmness correction" such as a proper reprimand accompanied by leading
the child by the hand or looking at him pointedly had a salutary
effect on other misbehavior-bent children in the group. They
observed that "high clarity" statements, such as "Don't take the
blocks away when Johnny's using them" were more effective than
"low-clarity" statements such as "Stop it!" '[7]

This 'experiment' seems to have rediscovered that infants
respond to the intellectual virtue of explicitness. But when year after
year schoolteachers are told that to be an educator means remem-

---

*A technical reference to the graph representing test results in several
subjects.

bering the Gump-Kounin principle of high firmness correction, their minds acquire a, so to say, permanent dampness factor which extinguishes any spark of intellect in them or those committed to their care.

To be sure, the country still numbers a great many excellent teachers who know their own minds and speak them clearly. They are the ones who, when the book salesman comes around with blurbs and study aids for what he calls the language arts, rebuke him by saying: 'I am a teacher of English.' Without such teachers, spreading their light from the first grade to the last, there would be no hope for the host of intelligent youth, and we who teach in the upper years would never encounter the able and intellectual student, as we periodically do. But the self-aware and defiant minority of teachers who teach is overborne by the weight of school administrators, of a diffident or defeatist public opinion, and of an atmosphere heavy-laden with the science of nonthought.

Its opposite, the power of articulate thought, is obviously the only force that can penetrate and dissolve this pall that hangs over and darkens our schools. In another system than ours we might have hoped that textbooks would counteract the weakness of teachers, for textbook writers are usually university men with some energy of mind and a special talent for exposition. But this is not always so, and in a country where leading scholars will not condescend to review textbooks, where in fact, most textbooks are not reviewed at all, the miasma of the teachers' college and the P.T.A. often beclouds the printed page.

Besides, the writing of a text is no longer in the sole hands of the author, who in any case is often tempted to give up his principles by the great pecuniary rewards held out to him. In the 'processing' (the publisher's term), a textbook is submitted to a dozen or more teachers 'in the field.' The field refers not merely to the subject matter but to the field of action, the classroom, where local prejudices and sacred illiteracies obtain. Against these, the textbook writer must defend his words and views, squaring his mind with those of anonymous critics who are often his inferiors in learning and sense. His vocabulary at any rate cannot go beyond what 'science' says is right for the 'age group.' Frequency lists rule the mind of America and see that it remains average. For high schools, no text can describe New England's colonial trade as lucrative; it must read: 'profitable.' The word hegemony is unknown, and there is apparently only one adjective in common use to qualify strife, resentment, controversy, quarrel, and enmity—the adjective 'bitter.'

To offset this aridity, the modern textbook is magnificently illustrated and printed. At no time in the history of schools, I imagine, have children been given such beautiful maps, such interesting pictures of contemporary objects and persons, such clear scientific diagrams and fine typography, in short so perfect a page to study from. To those who have brought about this revolution, all thanks and honor are due. But their pride in show is a hindrance to other efforts. Textbook publishers do not sell to their readers but to the middlemen, the school administrators who order by the hundred thousand for groups of states. This lucrative, nay profitable, outlet justifies the expense of producing richly illustrated books, for it is patent that the buyers believe to a man in the supreme merit of visible attractions. What buyers and sellers cannot see is the great gap in quality between the visual and the conceptual matter they thrust on the pupil. They know from nineteenth-century psychology that imagination and memory do not work alike in everyone, some being visual, some auditory, some muscular. But they forget the two limitations of visual aid—let alone the interests of the 'muscular' memorizers. Pictures by themselves say little, or are ambiguous. To teach 'social problems' with photographs of domestic situations and then ask, 'What problems of human relations does the picture suggest?' and 'What seems to be happening in the picture?'* is to confirm the pupil in thought-clichés rather than add to his knowledge and give it complexity.

*A new method for teachers' colleges, according to the *New York Times*, September 20, 1956.

Moreover, it is evident that visual memory and the power to summon up ideas are not the same. Unless the student learns to turn a verbal account into the right vividness in his mind's eye, and conversely to frame his imaginings in words, he always remains something of an infant, a barbarian dependent on a diagram.

The power to summon up image-with-word and word-with-image is in truth the most completely undeveloped in our schooling. We keep it weak by the very means we think most advanced. Perhaps the abandonment of grammar, which has come about in the wake of the new 'scientific' linguistics, is too negative to be called a means, but it fitly represents the flight from articulateness. Meanwhile, the lavish use of things to see has turned pointing from bad manners to the lazy teacher's secret of success. Finally, in the universal use of the so-called objective test, both influences are wedded. Taking an objective test is simply pointing. It calls for the least effort of mind above that of keeping awake: recognition. And it is recognition without a shock, for to a veteran of twelve years old, the traditional four choices for each question fall into a soothing rhythm. No tumult of surprise followed by a rallying generalship and concentration, as in facing an essay question; no fresh unfolding of the subject under unexpected demand, but the routine sorting out of the absurd from the trivial, or the completing of dull sentences by word- or thought-clichés.* No other single practice explains as fully the intellectual defects of our students up to and through

*The first discussion, so far as I know, of objective tests regarded from the intellectual point of view (as against that of convenience for handling large numbers) is an article in *The American Scholar* (Spring, 1959) by Mr. Banesh Hoffmann, Professor of Mathematics in Queens College. It begins with an illustration of the penchant of objective-test makers for the thought-cliché: '*Emperor* is the name of (a) a string quartet (b) a piano concerto (c) a violin sonata.' The answer (b) is correct, but so is (a), one of Haydn's quartets being also the 'Emperor,' though not as widely known. Mr. Hoffmann goes on to point out the imprecisions of wording, errors of fact, and inconsistencies of expectation that characterize current aptitude and subject-matter tests, notably in the sciences. From a longer, unpublished study, Mr. Hoffmann has kindly allowed me to publish a few pages as an added note to this chapter. (See p. 273.)

graduate school than their ingrained association of knowledge and thought with the scratching down of check marks on dotted lines.

With mass education this so-called 'technique of educational measurement' is spreading. The Educational Testing Service announces a 'Project in Malaya to Train Specialists,'[8] while the American public is fobbed off with reassuring references to 'test reliability studies,' the 'translation of educational goals into behavioral terms,' and similar apings of the genuine tests and conversion formulas of physical science. The making of a single objective test costs about twenty thousand dollars and takes two years' work by a squad of experts. When it is made and used it is then necessary to warn college admissions officers not to compare the various test scores of applicants: 'The phenomenon of statistical regression . . . would tend to penalize students with high SCAT scores and give an advantage to those with low SCAT scores. If the SCAT is being used as the selection test, it should be administered to *all* applicants.'[9] Whether such tests and their comparisons are deemed scientific or not, the inexactitude of science as regards the individual is a subject that deserves the attention of all who understand what is meant by the rights of the person and the obligations of intellectual rigor. These are doubtless what Sir Alfred Zimmern had in mind when he called 'the two unmentionable letters,' I.Q., 'those deadly enemies of self-respect.'[10]

In theory and practice alike, then, and from top to bottom, American education serves other ends than Intellect. This state of fact, which has just begun to draw critical fire from various quarters is, as I said at the outset, the logical result of what we think and feel as a massive egalitarian democracy. The schools are made of our flesh and bone, our thoughts and emotions, which means that if we want to cut away any part and reshape others, we must be willing to bleed and feel pain. No amount of reshuffling within the present curriculum and rebaptizing of 'objectives' in the catalogues will accomplish anything. More will than we have ever used about 'education' is needed to make the least of our hopes into a deed.

And the first step to willing is the intellectual one of saying what we mean and meaning what we say. The philanthropy I have assigned as one cause of futility in our schooling connotes much more than kindness to the child. The debate is not on that point. Nobody wants to return to the school run like a bad prison, by terror and flogging. The question is not about kindness but about instruction: Is the school a place of teaching or of psychologizing? Is it to prolong vicariously the parents' love of innocence and act out their dream of a good society, or is it to impart literacy? And are we to wait till *after* the Ph.D. to get it?* When, finally, is the school to sort out types of mind and, assuming that all can read, write, and count, enable each kind to acquire the facts and principles relevant to their calling and their tastes?

To encompass such ends the school must know what it wants, not in the form of vague private or public virtues, but in the form of intellectual powers. It must stop blathering about sensitivity to the needs of others, and increasing responsibility for bringing about one world, and say instead: 'I want a pupil who can read Burke's "Speech on Conciliation" and solve problems in trigonometry. I want young men and women who can read French prose and write English. I want academic high school graduates who can remember what the Missouri Compromise had to do with the Civil War, and who will carry over into college their familiarity with logarithms and the techniques of the chemistry laboratory.' And having said these or similar things after due consideration, the school must enforce what it has said. It must pass judgment on performance and let accomplishment be known, quite as if it had the importance of a record in a track meet.†

---

*Many a man now teaching has learned to write by seeing his thesis rewritten under his eyes, one word at a time, by his sponsor.

†It is hardly more than a year ago that the College Entrance Examination Board consented to 'bare' the test takers' scores—at the insistence, be it noted, of the pupils themselves. But when one reads that the director of science in the New York City schools was appointed to his post after failing the qualifying examination a first and then a second time, passing it on his third try, though others achieved the feat the first time, one can hardly wonder that people think 'exams are the bunk.' *New York Times*, August 14, 1958.

Education with us has too long been a device for equalizing merit. Thinking of education as the open door to economic and social advancement, we have made schooling, or the token of it, available to all. Let us, we have said, favor the young who work their way through college, and make allowances for a poor showing; let the city spend half a million on retarded children but not a cent on the intelligent, for that would again widen the gap; and let us not make the bachelor's degree stand for anything exaggerated in the way of brains. The equal opportunity it affords *after* college cannot be widespread if we are strict about getting into college and staying there.

Once this reasoning is perceived, the puzzles about mass education disappear. The system of credits and electives permits an education to be made out of interchangeable parts; everybody fashions the same B.A. out of subjects variously difficult: Spanish as well as Greek, elementary geology as well as quantitative chemistry, will 'satisfy' the ostensibly stern requirement of a science and a foreign language. And for other 'prescribed' subjects the 'blind-spot' excuse will bring a waiver and a substitution.

The bookkeeping system has another democratic advantage: it conceals the fact that there may be a relation between Intellect and ancestry. This is a delicate question to raise, but sooner or later someone will have to bell the cat. The connection I speak of may or may not be found in heredity; its farthest cause does not matter so long as the obvious influence of domestic habit is known and seen to be cumulative after two or more generations. There is no mystery about it: the child who is familiar with books, ideas, conversation— the ways and means of the intellectual life—before he begins school, indeed, before he begins consciously to think, has a marked advantage. He is at home in the House of Intellect just as the stableboy is at home among horses or the child of actors on the stage. Medical schools recognize this truth when they give preference to applicants who are children of physicians. Sometimes, it is true, the specialty of the house causes rebellion and revulsion. But when it does not, it produces what we want in able minds—concentrated power. This does not preclude the genius or great scholar from being born on the farm or in the blacksmith shop; there is nothing fated about the harvest of talents. But it is historically true that two of the prime elements of intellect, continuity and concentration, go together. One has only to think of the long list of distinguished men that have sprung, in England and in Germany, from the Protestant clergy.

The generation born just after the wars of nationalism, between 1860 and 1880, retained traditions of intellect and presumably could have transmitted them, not intact, perhaps, which no tradition can ever be, but unimpaired. That generation fathered one of intellectual cripples by being itself emotionally lamed. Circumstances blighted its hopes—in the disillusion of the First World War, the failure of Parliamentary liberalism east of the Rhine, the Great Depression and the Second World War, each seeming a disproof of the power of reason. But the intellectuals of that era also took a hand in their own maiming. Their manners betrayed them, as we know, and they yielded the point of reason while pursuing their liberal, democratic aims. In creating public schools they refused to sort out of the crowd those most capable of learning. In turning individual militant liberalism into socially protective liberalism, they idealized all downtrodden minorities, including children, and instead of 'liquidating ignorance' hunted down Intellect as an ogre to destroy. Complacency did the rest by making them forget the economics of kindness: give-and-take was replaced by give-and-give, known in child-rearing as the permissive system, though better described as 'All for Love.' So defined, the formula of liberal philanthropy and science has come to mean: 'Nothing for Mind.'

Yet no secret formula or special device is needed to make the most of our inherited wealth of intellect; simply do not penalize it as is now done in deference to theory, whether political, social, or psychological. Do not assume, for instance, that the child of professional parents who shows this natural advantage has been pushed or forced and must be saved from neuroticism by 'contact' and group activities that bore him. His boredom is, I agree, a dangerous sign in a future committee member, but if we want his other talents, as scientist, scholar, linguist, poet, or mathematician, we must not let him lose his advantage; we must maintain his impetus. If he does not 'develop evenly' let the sociable side of him delay its flowering, instead of adjusting it at the expense of his possibly unique powers: that too would be kindness, democracy, and opportunity. Let him throughout his schooling share classes with all the rest and get used, without priggishness, to the prevalence of slow wits. But do not wait till college or middle life to let him be the intellectual that nature and domestic circumstance prepared; that is, do not hold back the hare till near the end of the race to spare the feelings of the tortoise: the notion that she won is a fable.

VI

❧❀❧

The Case Against Intellect

'But intellect isn't everything!' Of course not. Nothing is. Only in a century that patterns its feelings on those of children, the primitive, the weak, and the unworldly, would intelligent people so readily believe that whatever is represented as good must be a panacea. Compared to food, love, and medicine, the good that Intellect brings to life is small. It still may be indispensable, but its advantages are limited; and since like any other limitation this implies cost, the advantages may be bought too high. For example, Intellect is known to be connected with emotion, and is generally suspected of spoiling or chilling it—at least when emotion is not accused of warping Intellect. Everybody at any rate agrees that Intellect is a power that can destroy; which is why (some point out) it can protect. These uncertainties suggest that no reasonable man, least of all an intellectual, should permit himself to advance the claims of Intellect without first becoming familiar with its perils and limitations. He should be just as eager to keep Intellect out of places where it does not belong as to uphold it where it does.*

*To take a trivial example, it is absurd that latterly the contest for female beauty which leads to the choice of a Miss America should have been made to include conversation—and even recitations—by each contestant, to

Intellectual work is often thought a difficult task reserved for the few, but it is in fact easier than keeping Intellect alive yet within bounds. For society is one vast concourse and whatever is strong enough to affect one part permeates the rest. That any such influence will lose its character in so doing does not reduce the harm to society or make prudence less necessary. Thus the greatest danger to a democratic state is probably the contamination of its politics by Intellect. At the same time, the sound instinct which keeps apart the work of Intellect and the work of government can turn into an anti-intellectualism that is equally dangerous to both.

It seems at first sight a paradox that political life should be better off without Intellect. The common supposition is that democratic government depends on 'free trade in ideas'; that parties, which are the bulwark of that government, are formed around clusters of ideas called programs or platforms. The educated voter is expected to study issues, so that he may choose programs rather than men. And it is clear that if he continues to develop his political ideas he is but a step away from intellectualizing politics. Where in all this is the menace? It lies in the possibility that, for him and others, ideas will come to seem more important than public service and social peace. The scrimmage of politics is for the purpose of determining who shall transact the government's business. If in the struggle the desire to accomplish one's purpose turns into a desire to annihilate one's opponent, the outcome is civil war. Historically, this desire to annihilate finds its support and justification in Intellect, in ideas, for ideas are clear-cut and divide. Material interests can be compromised, principles cannot. A man who sensibly will not fight his neighbor over depredations in his garden will fight him over being called a liar. The intangible idea is sharper, more potent than the physical damage. Intellect, which makes distinctions, separates forever what

---

impress the judges with Aphrodite's intellect. Again, and equally misplaced, was the recent complaint against the British royal family that its members did not participate enough in the cultural and intellectual life of the nation—as if their job were not grievous enough as it is.

it has distinguished. The parts cannot be rejoined, the wound is never healed. War comes because of man's unconquerable mind.

The threat of 'great ideas' to the peaceful conduct of ordinary life is plain: compromise, bargains, tolerance, the salutary neglect of trivial acts—all these are at once ruled out. Intellect is rigid and allows no oversight. The wars of ideas have always been the most fanatical and needlessly prolonged of all wars. It took Europe a hundred and fifty years to work the ideas of the Reformation out of its blood, by shedding it often and copiously in the name of abstract ideas—transubstantiation, prevenient grace, or communion in both kinds. This is not to say that coarser motives did not help perpetuate the fighting; but the ideas are what kept the antagonism vivid and strong. Conscious of 'your' idea and 'his' idea you can remember who your enemy is: he believes in justification by faith—or states' rights. You need not fully know what either entails, but you know it is monstrous and threatening to your dearest beliefs. Idealism springs from deep feelings, but feelings are nothing without the formulated idea that keeps them whole. Indeed, the force of abstraction, which is part of the concentrating force of Intellect, does not exert itself only in war or other great crises. In any assembly, the simplest way to stop the transacting of business and split the ranks is to appeal to a principle: 'This, gentlemen, would mean nothing less than discrimination.' Or: 'I do not see how we can tolerate this compromise with our stated aims'; 'I am shocked and surprised that my friend across the room can entertain for a moment the possibility of yielding on an issue as clear-cut as this one: it is not the money, it is the, etc.'

Modern committee work, as I said on an earlier page, does not often use this rhetoric, but in larger groups old habits return, revivified by a word or an incident. In certain nations, the conduct of politics is as regularly hampered by Intellect as ours may be by its absence. For example, the countries of Latin America pride themselves on their educated governing classes and feel superior to stupid, 'pragmatic' North Americans. Yet the interference of ideas with good government in South America is a patent and distressing fact.

In those countries it is not the supposedly volatile and inflammable emotions that cause division and war; it is the responsiveness of the mind to ideas, it is the energy that drives everyone to work upon ideas instead of practical arrangements.

The model of this political activity is well known: it is France. The thought-cliché about France is that its people are logical—born so. No evidence has ever been adduced for this, and it is likely that none exists, logic being as rare in one population as in another. But certain intellectual habits that are conspicuous—articulateness, quick recognition and comparison of ideas, a repertory of formulas for all the vicissitudes of discussion—such things can be widely diffused by schooling, and as the mark of the educated class will give a stamp to a whole culture. France in the earlier Middle Ages was not a country especially noted for its intellectual temper; it became so in late medieval and early modern times. The Schoolmen and the Jesuits, the Napoleonic and the Republican schools codified the arguments and phrases which give French social life its lively tone, but which also denature politics and hinder government. Not that all Frenchmen are intellectual. The majority of the nation is cautious, unassuming, and as reluctant to innovate as anyone could wish for purposes of stability. But the leading part of the nation is articulate and has a passion for entertaining ideas. It is this pleasure, this sport—the opposite of British fox-hunting or bird-watching—which gives the appearance of logic to public affairs in France, and makes responsible men think it more imperative to score a point by showing up an inconsistency than to grope toward a conclusion and try it in action.

Walter Bagehot, who observed the French government from the eve of the Second Empire, and had it always before his eyes when studying the British, has profound things to say about the small place that Intellect should occupy in any regime. Being himself a thinker enamored of the play of mind, he cannot be suspected of ulterior motives in deprecating Intellect:

'A really practical people,' he points out, 'will work in political business almost the absurdest, the feeblest, the most inconsistent set of imaginable regulations. Similarly, or rather reversely, the best institutions will not keep right a nation that *will* go wrong. . . . I fear you will laugh when I tell you what I conceive to be about the most essential quality for a free people, whose liberty is to be progressive, permanent, and on a large scale; it is much *stupidity*. . . . I need not say that, in real sound stupidity, the English are unrivalled. . . . In fact, what we opprobriously call stupidity, though not an enlivening quality in common society, is nature's favourite resource for preserving steadiness of conduct and consistency of opinion.'[1]

Unfortunately for themselves, Bagehot goes on, the French value the qualities exactly opposed to 'stupidity' and give them power over their collective life—'the keenest tact in social politeness, the most consummate skill in the details of action and administration . . . an amazing readiness in catching new ideas and maintaining new theories, a versatility of mind which enters into and comprehends everything as it passes, a concentration in what occurs, so as to use it for every purpose of illustration.' And the result? Too much cleverness and too many principles for action in common when time presses and interests diverge: 'No deliberative assembly can exist with every member wishing to lead, and no one wishing to follow. Not the meanest Act of Parliament could be carried without more compromise than even the best French statesmen were willing to use on the most important and critical affairs of their country. Rigorous reasoning would not manage a parish vestry, much less a great nation.'[2]

A people under representative government had therefore better avoid making a fetish of Intellect. In particular, a country as large as the United States, whose local interests are bound to differ widely, should avoid intellectualizing its politics. Rather, it should congratulate itself on maintaining two large parties which can both accommodate inner contradictions. To introduce strictness and rigor into the politics of adaptation, variety, and pluralism would be to give birth at once to a dozen groups of eternal enemies. The more firmly each group was 'dedicated to an idea' the less it could allow the others to live, the more each would fear for its life, and the more the life of the population would become a battle, of words first and then of arms. On the one great occasion when an idea and its concomitants aroused the American people, it cut a chasm between North and South which a million corpses did not suffice to fill.

I speak of an idea and its concomitants, for ideas have mutual implications that fill the mind and attach to themselves the strongest feelings. With or without logic, ideas form systems, and systems absorb lives. A believer in a system, or as we say today, an ideology, supports it with all his gregarious instincts—he is no longer alone in his struggle against the world; with his sense of liberation from uncertainty— he has found answers to many perplexing questions; with his pride of learning—the 'science' he has mastered is difficult; with his moral conceit—the idea or cause he has adopted makes him superior to those who pursue only crass advantage. Compared to the man who is moved only by scattered and changeable interests—an oil well here, a bank or a factory there—the man of ideas is like a force always marshaled for action. Disciplined as only Intellect can make him, he stands in relation to the mere man of interests as a trained soldier to a recruit.

In any country and at all times intellectuals feel a natural affinity for the ideologies that arise at home or make a noise abroad; each seems at once a challenge and an opportunity. For it is plausible that Intellect, which inquires so assiduously, should believe in the existence of answers. The intellectual has fortitude but also wants to be saved—by ideas. This is shown in our secular times by the religious revival of the last twenty-five years; and in that revival it is shown even better by the addiction to mere religiosity than by the conversions that entirely reshape life and character. For religiosity makes plain the attraction that systems as such have for the intellectual. By playing with religious definitions and symbols, with the subtleties of theology and the learned details of ritual, the searching mind is arrested and fulfilled even if devoid of moral or spiritual fervor. The excitation of the intellect and the membership in a chosen brotherhood suffice.

But when the cultural historian wants to gauge the force of system and intellectual passion in modern life, there is an example close at hand which is more massive and moving than that of the religious revival, a tragedy more violent and unresolved than that of the American Civil War. I mean the example of Marxism. True, the hold that Marx's ideas have on the populations of the world extends farther than Intellect can claim devotees. There is the Marxism of hunger and anger. But this does not affect the value of the example. No encounter between men and ideas during the last half-century shows so clearly as the Marxist fever the weakness and the strength of Intellect abstractly considered. Indeed, the rise and fall of the movement among the laity of the West presents a series of object lessons that the student of Intellect as an institution ignores at his peril.

The first success of Marx's formulas occurred in Europe in the nineties, about a generation after he had framed them. They bore, as everyone knows, the character of German academic scholarship, and as such were the reverse of alluring. Marx's chief works are ill organized and ponderous without being complete or consistent, and this was early remarked upon. The later spread of the doctrine among the educated classes of the Continent and, in our day, to England and the United States, therefore argues special susceptibility rather than the inherent charm of Marx's thought. In the 1930's, the most educated part of the middle class, half of it turned toward literature and the arts, the other half toward science and scholarship, found in Marxism a vocabulary that brought them in touch with each other and with concerns they had neglected. Contemporary events—war, Fascism, revolution, and depression—favored the shift to new preoccupations that seemed urgent and overwhelming. The merit of the ideology was that it gave the desultory mind, the insouciant intelligence, a chance to become 'committed' and stake out a claim in the realm of ideas. To learn scholastic terms and propositions, to know the traps of the system and the means of extrication, to subordinate common life to the demands of a 'study group,' to argue the finer points left obscure by the great inditer—all this seemed like a wondrous re-education fostering a new professional pride. It fed the taste for pedantry—a democratic taste par excellence—and it satisfied a long-ignored appetite for order in the mind.

Some of these attractions also drew many who were already professionals of the word and who might have been expected to find jargon and gigantism repellent. What they found instead was the challenge of making the doctrine harmonious, complete, and invulnerable, while acting as mentors to new converts. To be sure, they also believed that the doctrine was true and historically necessary. They were moved by the thought that this new politics, unlike the old, made use of the intellect and would be run by intellectuals. In the United States of thirty years ago the men who took up Marx were handicapped by a long indifference to political life and an ignorance of history that allowed them to believe Socialism and Marxism synonymous. Prejudiced in favor of Europe by reason of their exile from it or in it, they were confident that they were bringing to America an element of culture it had too long done without. What they actually taught the country was that intellectual politics not only follows the common rule of "Whoever is not with us is against us,' but also makes the choice of sides irrevocable. Principle never forgives and its logic is to kill. How, under Marxism, could there be any overlooking of individual error by the majestic force of history? What chance had anyone to change his mind and seek reconciliation with a dialectical march which embraced all mankind? The individual was lost in the unfolding conflict of categories. And this was in truth the greatest inducement to joining the side destined to survive.

But after a dozen years, when the struggle proved not to go according to plan, leading only to cruel retaliation by forces history was supposed to have swept away, the ideologues were heard to wail that the witch hunt was directed at ideas, and that the persecutors were moved by hatred of Intellect. This was having it both ways—complaining, first, that Americans were culpably indifferent to ideas, that their political parties were brainless, and that material success had extinguished in the people the power of speculative thought;

then suddenly crying out that philosophic ideas were being taken too much in earnest—as when a man lost his livelihood or his friends, when colleges were attacked for alleged subversion, and when the two big parties themselves started to accuse each other of harboring 'ideas.'

In an intellectually alert society, protection against the particular form the self-delusion took would have come from three sources: the history of ideas in Europe and America, the established criticism of Marx's thought, and a sense of the limits of Intellect. Certainly in the United States, the damnable consequences of intellectualizing public issues should not have been a new discovery. For three centuries earlier, when religion was strong in the state, it was a similar intellectualizing about faith and government that provoked the founding of the English colonies in America. Out of a doctrinaire deadlock over church authority, re-enacted here for four generations, came compromise and the growth of the tradition that deeds, not thoughts, are the test of man's loyalty to the state. Embodied in the law, this pragmatic test provides the best means so far devised to protect both persons and ideas. The Bill of Rights is the bulwark of the free Intellect because it provides for a *non*intellectual government; it says that ideas in the mind do not matter politically.

We know that they do matter and that it is a legal fiction to deny it. We know that political and religious ideas disturb men's minds and can lead to social disorder. Hence the convention to exclude these ideas from conversation, at least in times of stress. And hence also the recurrent exercise of social pressure and ostracism to do what the law forbids. In democracies, as Tocqueville perceived, the tyrant public opinion 'no longer says: "You shall think as I do or you shall die"; but he says: "You are free to think differently from me and to retain your life, your property, and all that you possess; but you are henceforth a stranger among your people. You may retain your civil rights, but they will be useless to you, for you will never be chosen by your fellow citizens if you solicit their votes; and they will affect to scorn you if you ask for their esteem. You will remain among men, but you will be deprived of the rights of mankind. Your fellow creatures will shun you like an impure being; and even those who believe in your innocence will abandon you, lest they should be shunned in their turn. Go in peace! I have given you your life, but it is an existence worse than death." '3

Against this silent sentencing by the herd the only safeguard is their leaders' developed sense of what ideas are. That this sense was lacking in the men and women who espoused Marxism is shown by their eager play with dogma and deviation, by their enthusiasm for a system and a future in which intellectual differences lead to the settlement called, with characteristic abstractness, liquidation. The fact, now evident, that these people did not vividly connect their talks and meetings and moral airs with the prospective death of their families, friends, and fellow citizens is a measure of their failure to understand what the Intellect owes to ideas. Ideas are at once more and less than the common view supposes. An idea prefigures action and as such may be menacing; but it is also a means of weighing actions before they happen, and as such an idea can be examined and neutralized or destroyed apart from its bearer.

The examining should have begun with the ideas of Marx himself. It ought to have sobered the recruits from the outset to know that the leading minds who looked into Marx's work at the turn of the century—men such as Shaw, Sorel, Croce, Bernstein, Veblen— had little regard for his formulas and apparatus. They might remain Socialists and even accept Marx as an important figure in the history of mankind's rebellion against want, but they were not taken in by the jargon and pseudoscience that were to capture and hold in fetters a good part of the Western world thirty years later. What saved these thinkers was that, though they valued Intellect, they never believed in its primacy. They knew that Intellect is a servant, and one to be held on a short leash. Intellect is not fit to lead, much less to dominate, for it knows only intermediate or contingent goals: 'If you want *this*,' it says, 'you must do *that*.' Or else it assembles instances to guide choices. What is wanted can be sought and adapted by the

Intellect, but cannot spring from its rules or operations. The Intellect, slave to the passions as Hume said it should be, sorts them out and brings them light. It directs but does not quell them.

That is why the demand frequently heard that democracy develop an intellectual system, an ideology with which to combat Communism and catch the minds of the wavering, is an absurd demand. If democracy means anything, it is diversity of ends. In that diversity it opposes all unitary systems, Communist or Fascist. Therefore a 'system of democracy' must be either a piece of empty verbalism or the plan of an imposed unity. In pointing this out, Intellect is doing its proper work; in cobbling together the proposed system it would be usurping the role of will and making itself a dangerous substitute for satisfactions which democracy denies. To put this more generally, the greatest danger of Intellect is that it so readily breeds intellectual*ism*.

The symptoms of this disease are unfortunately infinite. They cannot be catalogued. But its onset and fatal course can be illustrated, once again, by the late Marxist fever. Intellectualism has been a European, or more precisely, a Continental affliction, and it is from Europe that Americans who between the wars had acquired a taste for the cultural and intellectual life of the Continent brought the contagion over. For the American tradition is suspicious of ideas in politics and indifferent to theories of society. A new, prior faith in Intellect was thus required on the part of the would-be Marxists before they could accept even the first tenet. This was, in effect, the conspiracy theory of history, which Marx shares with his times and which he uses in two equally seductive ways: from his angry footnotes one learns that the bourgeois steadily conspire to gain their ends, so that no contemporary event is what it seems, but is rather a product of hidden malice. And from Marx's main text one learns that the conditions of economic life conspire with the rising class to usher in the new world. History will conspire with you if you give it a chance.

The two beliefs are variants of the commonest intellectualist error: having used the Intellect to make order among ideas, one then believes that the order has been discovered ready-made in the facts. This supposed discovery, first announced by the seer, becomes imperative truth, disbelieved at one's peril. Marx's mind was fiercely intellectualist from the start. In a letter written in his twenty-fifth year, long before his final dogmas were even sketched, the desire for them was stirring in him. 'We will not, then, oppose the world like doctrinaries with a new principle: "here is truth, kneel down here!" We expose new principles to the world out of the world itself. We do not tell it: "Give up your struggles, they are rubbish; we will show you the true warcry." We explain to the world only the real object for which it struggles, and consciousness of it is a thing it *must* acquire, even if it objects to it.'[4]

Marx's mature work showed the same passion to prove that his utterances were the very voice of reality. He repressed the evidences of Intellect so far that he would have none survive in history. Ideas, he maintained, played but an illusory role in human affairs; they masked sinister motives; they were flimsy constructions floating on the stream of material forces. With these assumptions behind the potent enough ideas of class war and coming revolution, Marx imposed a ruthless Victorian moralism upon his adherents' political emotions. After him, it proved easy to make the whole world familiar with the attitudes and the verbal pedantries of dialectic and devia-tion, spying and informing, betraying and purging—intellectualiz-ing, in short, the anti-intellectual goal of war. In this warfare and its dreary verbalisms we are still involved; the habits are in us, whether Fascism or Communism happens at the moment to be strong or at low ebb. And as the reader has doubtless worked out for himself, the two ways of naming the disease are equally valid: intellectualism and, consequently also, anti-intellectualism.

But how to define and enforce the proper limits of Intellect? The question is difficult, for it requires a double answer—one relating to the individual and one to society—and the two are in contradiction. What I have said in this book might itself be represented as blowing hot and cold: saying in the earlier chapters that for the general good, as well as his own, the educated man should cultivate Intellect far more than he does; and saying in the present chapter that, for its good and that of the individual, society should shun and discourage Intellect far more than it does. The paradox or rather, the antinomy, is not one of my creating. It is one that every state that calls itself free must live with. But since the practical difficulties are not new, modern societies need not despair.

The first step is to see as clearly and evenly the danger to be apprehended from Intellect as the defense it affords. In distinguishing between the critical, literal-minded work of Intellect and the overabstract, self-blinding work of intellectualism, I have tried to show the catastrophes of intellectualism as the result of going halfway with Intellect, of not turning it upon one's ideas or those that beckon from without. For the lure of system, and the adventures to which it tempts, do not resist the questioning of the mind that, by surveying both itself and the systems, has learned the limits of Intellect.*

But this is cold and cruel work and not likely to move mankind. On the contrary, the study of history suggests that, in Western civilization at least, all progress has come from the heretic, that is to say the man of ideas who believes them with intellectualist fierceness. Now, progress or not, heresy cannot be received with open arms, for not all heretics carry the true message, and time is needed for testing the new and adapting it to the old. This mode of change by agitation being always at the mercy of a determined tyrant, there grew up in modern times a code of behavior for governors and heretics—the Bill of Rights or its equivalent. This is a device which, as I said ear-

---

*The great example of this power is the one to which Matthew Arnold drew attention in the life of Burke who, having for many years been the foremost critic of the French Revolution, made at the end what Arnold calls a 'return upon himself' and was carried by sheer strength of Intellect to see that 'if a great change is to be made in human affairs, the minds of men will be fitted to it . . . and they who persist in opposing this mighty current . . . will appear rather to resist the decrees of Providence itself, than the mere designs of men.' The point lies not in any reconcilement of Burke to revolution but in the power that saw both the fraud and the rightness in a complex event. 'The Function of Criticism at the Present Time' in *Essays in Criticism*, 3rd ed., London, 1875, 17.

lier, charters the use of Intellect by both the heretic and his articulate opponent. Out of their debate comes the disturbance and reform of the whole society we call progress, though *progression* might be the humbler and better word. Here at last we seem to find, in licensed scrimmage, the practical limits of Intellect, the corrective to intellectualism.

But suppose the heretic arises against the code itself. Intellect then faces a second antinomy, the one exemplified by the nineteenth-century Catholic pamphleteer, Louis Veuillot, and repeated by the Communists. Addressing his anticlerical opponents Veuillot is reputed to have said: 'I demand freedom of expression because that is *your* principle; but I shall deny it to you when I am in power because that is *my* principle.' With a dim sense of the same duplicity, a group of state employees in California refused some years ago to post a copy of the Bill of Rights, on the pretext that it was 'a controversial document.' The Chief Justice, in a speech deploring the incident, said that 'thoughtful people' might well ask 'whether ratification of the Bill could be obtained today if we were faced squarely with the issue.'[5] His doubt is neither surprising nor of its time only, for intellectual freedom came out of political victory in the past, and victory means a party vanquished but not necessarily destroyed. It is precisely because the party lives on that a Bill of Rights is needed. Its threat compels a free state to be unwavering in its maintenance of the code for heresy. Deny its protection to your opponent and you have lost your *intellectual* means of defense against him: you must take up arms. There is no third way. We therefore call unquestionable and sacrosanct a document that guarantees endless controversy; we must call it unquestionable because many will always question it. 'And I am,' Pilate then asks in Shaw's words, 'to spare and encourage every heretic, every rebel, every lawbreaker, every rapscallion, lest he should turn out to be wiser than all the generations who made the Roman law and built the Roman Empire on it?' This is a poser, but Jesus has the last word: 'By their fruits ye shall know them. Beware how you kill a thought that is new to you . . . : I say to you Cast out fear.'[6]

This is the point where Intellect finally proves its advantage: it and it alone supplies the test by which to judge or predict the fruits. The roving intelligence of man will invent a hundred schemes that his energy will promote, as he thinks, to satisfy his passions. He may make this or that view prevail, this or that scheme carry the day. But only Intellect can pass on the merits or demerits of the case, the advantages and drawbacks of the scheme. When given the opportunity to do this speculatively, before the trial, the success of the test justifies the existence of a tradition of Intellect, and thereby also the claim of man to live not as the insect of a day but by the funded experience of the race.

Had the educated classes which gave Marx credence and renown been more accustomed to the cannibalism that should obtain among ideas, had they had an easy, professional grasp of the difference between abstractions and facts, had they habitually trusted themselves to think—instead of merely prospecting among ideas—they would not have been gulled by formulas and explanations reminiscent of Molière's doctors. If, for example, these ideologues had used their wits on the word 'science' as applied to Marxism, or had considered in the most elementary way the play on the word 'law,' which bestows on Marxian 'laws of history' the immutability attached to 'natural laws,' they would have spared themselves much superstitious anguish. Nor would the prolix theorizing upon state and society, art and society, man and society, ethics and dialectic, biology and dialectic, music and dialectic, language and socialism, socialism and realism, have received, in Russia and beyond, the solemn attention they did receive.* The unhappy projectors of these visions, some of whom were shortly to pay for their follies with their lives, at one time or another predicted the disappearance of self-interest, the family, and the state, of law, literature, and fine art—all replaced by Marxist substitutes in a future disinfected of humanity and idyllically motiveless.

---

*The Fascist and Nazi regimes produced, imitatively but in lesser quantity, the same sort of special scholarship, philosophy, and prophecy—an orgy of intellectualism.

Since here and there Intellect raised difficulties, the intellectualist will to preserve the system supplied ingenious answers. The dialectic movement of history, which had hitherto been interpreted as progress by conflict, could no longer be seen as perpetually violent where Communism ruled; so it was discovered that within the dialectic there were two kinds of contradiction, antagonistic and nonantagonistic, and it only remained to apply these labels properly. Again, it was a solid and desirable fact that the new Russian state did not look like withering away, as prophecy had foretold it should. Accordingly, 'any dialectical thinker,' said Stalin, 'must understand that in order eventually to wither away, the state must first grow stronger.' Later, Stalin discovered that the superstructure of ideas and beliefs, which Marx had declared ineffectual, was after all not a mirage thrown off by the conditions of material life, but a group of real elements working independently of the base. This return to a bourgeois faith in the efficacy of ideas was good logic in regimes that dictated to writers and called down musicians like schoolboys for writing tunes contrary to policy. But the successive postures gravely assumed by the dictators, the abject apologies of those dictated to, the semblance of intellectual operations, and their solemn mimicry outside the countries where they functioned existentially, would excuse any man who should now, after forty years of the buffoonery, declare himself sick of the very name of Intellect.

Yet that too would be the conclusion of an all-or-none temperament in a domain where antinomy, or the double view, is commanded by the facts. To know that the sharp, irremediable divisions of intellectual discourse have no correspondence in the realities of political and social life, is the first maxim of the self-aware Intellect. To know with confidence and modesty that the painfully learned rules of judgment remain true in the face of all intellectualist fireworks is the second. Nothing was more heartbreaking in the spectacle of the Hungarian revolt of November, 1956 than to see its brave intellectual leaders spell out haltingly the simple maxims they should never have forgotten: 'In the evolution of democracy,' wrote one of them on the eve of the uprising, 'the first step is this: citizens outside the Party, including writers, should not have to applaud things with which they do not agree. To make anyone do so is unfair and unworthy of man. But to force a writer to do so is to make him sick in spirit, for a writer's element, his *profession*, is to tell the truth. And if he does not tell the truth he is only a slave and a scribbler.'[7]

It is indeed noble to say this when violent death is sure to be the penalty. But where was this conviction, in the writer and his friends, during the long months before the revolt—indeed from the very outset of the darkness to which they all consented? What had these men learned from their national heroes of the liberal, Romantic age, from Kossuth and Deák, from their own mothers and fathers, from the experiences of their youth, from history?

Out of intellectual Poland, also in ferment, comes a volume of writings representing the new, liberated outlook.[8] One of the contributors, by way of freeing other minds, distinguishes 'Permanent and Transitory Aspects of Marxism.' The conclusion he wants to reach is that Marx is but one of many thinkers whose work has furthered the study and improvement of society. We can measure the depths of the intellectualism in which young Poland has sunk when we scan the twenty pages of preparation for this mild and platitudinous conclusion. Every step is a problem: 'We are thus faced with a question: if the sort of Marxism in which the doctrinal content was periodically established by the Office is now dead in the minds of the majority of intellectuals who considered themselves Marxists, has the concept of Marxism retained any meaning at all?'[9] And one of the 'meanings' taken up and weighed is this: 'One could, of course, agree on a convention to call all achievements of science and all scientific truths by the name of "Marxism." But in such a case we should have to consider as Marxist all discoveries in astrobotany, every new generalization in physiology, and every new theorem in topology. In this sense of the term, sometimes specifically postulated, the word "Marxism" is completely devoid of meaning and becomes a superfluous pseudonym for the word "truth" or "scientific knowledge." This pseudonym is not only superfluous but also mystifying, because it deviously suggests that all human knowledge is either inspired by

Karl Marx or progresses only thanks to the method formulated by him and uniquely characteristic of his scientific work. And this, obviously, is false.'[10]

What a winding road to the self-evident! The labor must argue a long paralysis of the Intellect, masked from the self and from others by an unremitting smoke screen of dishonest intellection. Perhaps this is the special danger that modern societies, made vulnerable by literacy and suddenly exposed to a glut of ideas, must incur—a relish for the work of Intellect with an imperfect grasp of its discipline. But no excuse for this weak frivolity will serve: one can withhold or disguise criticism during a common danger, one can lie out of fear or compassion, but if one has an Intellect one cannot knowingly and habitually produce nonsense and falsehood 'for a reason.' That reason fails as a reason. That impossibility is what having a mind means.

It is perhaps relevant that the history of the Russian church under the czars shows none of the intellectual activity that characterized the relations of Western popes and monarchs from the Middle Ages onward. The conflicts between church and state in the East were less bloody but also less articulate. In making up these arrears, Russia is teaching the lesson that Intellect needs aging before it is potable and safe. This thought makes the student of Intellect more prudent still in his use and advocacy of it, for today all populations are in a sense new. They are all born in literacy and lost to tradition. And though in the West (the Marxist debauch being almost forgotten) the majority are repelled by the rigors of Intellect, and are lured instead by the blandishments of art, they remain as susceptible as any other group to the temptations of intellectualism. For the disease, as we shall see, is but the virulent form of the pedantry endemic in the culture of science and technology.

The political indictment here drawn up against Intellect and its perversion, intellectualism, appears doubly formidable because emotionally charged with the force of an illustration that could hardly escape being used. In some other age between Luther and Marx, the same ideological evils might have seemed less menacing. But suppose the period to be that which began just before the French Revolution and continued after, then Intellect's capacity to cause political harm would be swallowed up in a still graver charge, the charge that Intellect is a threat to life itself.

As was made clear in the chapter defining the subject, the deep, universal distrust of Intellect rests upon its hostility to what is felt as the pulse of life. Common language records this opposition in a dozen ways: Life is warm, hot, glowing; Intellect is cold and dull. Life is its own mover, impetuous, heedless of reasons and obstacles, intent upon a few elemental goals which are not to be argued with—food, shelter, love, survival. Intellect is static, calculating, aimed at purpose clear to a few, but uncertain in their results, and vague or invisible to the multitude. Intellect observes rules of its own making that no one enforces, and is full of scruples in private, though in public it speaks confidently of itself and callously of life. The classic instance of Intellect's inhumanity is Voltaire's remark after he had asked why someone wrote bad books and was told that 'the poor man had to live': 'I do not see the necessity.' Intellect has apparently nothing to say to the predicaments and tragedies of life; it is a fair-weather friend, just as conversation, its highest social embodiment, is diversion for the idle and opulent. Whereas life is immediate and convinces by throbbing in your veins or panting in your face, Intellect stands on the margin of existence and convinces, if at all, by the roundabout road of argument—words in place of acts. Any pair of common images about the two shows them as antagonists—Intellect, stiff, angular, unchanging; life, flowing and adaptive. Intellect, the blade that carves and separates forever; life, a perpetual mixing and joining, fusion and confusion. Intellect the watcher, life the participant.

Even as a means to understanding, Intellect is severely limited. Since it deals only in the general, in abstractions and formulas, it can do no more than take notes on the unstoppable flux. Life does not 'deal with' at all, it *is* the flux felt as particular, flooding sensations. That is why problems of conduct can never be resolved by rule. Ethics that attempt to codify life and predetermine its options become casuistry. The moral man is one who feels what is right and acts on it before he can demonstrate it. Indeed, the ultimate perceptions of life are not only not demonstrable, they defy communication. If it were possible to talk to the unborn, one could never explain to them how it feels to be alive, for life is washed in the speechless real. And conversely, whoever checks the sense of life by always preferring ideas and words grows blind to realities. But it is also true that to drift on the stream of sensation without articulating a judgment would be to remain a baby or a mollusc, feeling life but ignorant of it. And this explains why Intellect, with all its shortcomings, does in the end know life and enhance it.

Yet there have been periods in the history of Western man when the elaborate structures that Intellect built on impulse and feeling became a carapace which threatened to crush the life out of the creature. Such a period was the eighteenth century, called the Age of Reason though 'reason' is a misnomer. For it was unreasonable to make such an abuse of intellect and to suppose that underneath the verbal elegance and accepted regularities all was well. Longings were felt for the irregular, for the solace of the irrational. By degrees Intellect gave way and styles changed: unspoiled nature, quaint superstition, wild poetry, Gothic architecture, and tearful sensibility came into favor. Finally, the cataclysm of revolution destroyed the old forms, made the old words and wigs obsolete, and opened a new era of art and thought called Romanticism.

It being the era which is now drawing to a close, its reformation of the Intellect is relevant to this inquiry. The just place of Intellect in civilization is not fixed, but always relative to other elements—politics, manners, literacy, social purpose—and especially to the presence or absence of an intellectual tradition in the immediate past. Popularly, the Romantics are said to have revolted against Intellect and avenged its crimes by substituting everywhere the heart for the head. This is untrue because impossible. Feeling cannot long subsist without thought (though the thought may be ill chosen), and thoughts, however dry, express feelings, however weak. The Romantics, brought up on the culture that they combated, were themselves men of thought. It was Intellect they used in order to define its limits and fuse once again particular ideas with the appropriate feelings from which they had been divorced. When Rousseau urged mothers to bring up their own children and dress them in clothes suitable for play, he was simply reconciling means and ends by the application of Intellect to a contrary and artificial custom. When Wordsworth introduced a tragic character study with the words, 'Let us suppose a young man of great intellectual powers yet without any solid principles of genuine benevolence,'* the poet was aiming at a contemporary type. He was acting as a thoughtful critic of his times like any modern observer who thinks 'our culture' in need of scrutiny and reform.

When, more generally, the Romantics argued the need to set the emotions free and let impulse flow, when they pointed to the reality and force of inspiration, and worshiped genius as the wisdom of the irrational, it was in order to discover what unknown ranges of experience would be disclosed by adventuring. If, as they believed, an excess of verbalism and classifying zeal in their forebears had cut off the sources of pleasure, knowledge, and power, the only appeal was to the container of all possibilities, life.

But 'life' being so inclusive, and its particulars so fugitive, it can serve but crudely the purposes of argument and reform. An opponent can reply that the dry-as-dust antiquarian, by the very fact that he exists, is as much part of life as the flaming poet; and a charlatan can claim revelations about life which he has only imagined. Consequently, the Romantic campaign to reconquer ground from Intellect was carried on in the name and through the medium of art. For art is both an extension of life by means of simulated and ordered experience, and a discipline and language subject to judgment. Art distills sensation and embodies it with enhanced meaning in memorable form—or else it is not art. And as the Romantics pointed out by shining examples, art has the power to instruct without the use of

*Opening of the Preface to *The Borderers* (1796–97). See *The Poetical Works of Wordsworth*, ed. Selincourt, I, 345.

words. These powers made art pre-eminent. And so strongly has it imparted the tendency to replace thought by sensation that the modern art of words itself strives for the inarticulate, deeming it superior.

Art thus swung to the other extreme from Intellect, which does not so much embody as anatomize. Intellect tends automatically to undermine or at least to counterbalance the effect of art: at the source, Intellect dismisses the concrete particular, reducing it to an instance of the general; and in the product—the work of art—Intellect either challenges with stubborn literalness its evocative and richly ambiguous assertions or, when baffled by the calm self-sufficiency of the object, it asks, as the philosopher did about the sonata, 'What does it prove?'

On the comprehension of art, therefore, depended what I have called the Romanticists' reformation of the Intellect. It is not too much to say that the chief cultural effort of the nineteenth and twentieth centuries has been to raise art and confound in a common ruin Intellect and Philistinism. For both the merchant and the professional intellect are marked by the exactitude with which they check extravagance. They want to know in what sense, precisely, the moon is queen of the night. The pair of insensitives thus has had to be repeatedly ridiculed and rebuked and finally ostracised.

These successful efforts did not merely benefit art; they renovated social life, religion, the sciences, and ultimately transformed the ordinary consciousness. For although Intellect has to be personified to be discussed, it exists not as a decanted essence but as a variable trait in men. They shape it by their weakness or strength and are afflicted by it in return. Accordingly, the battle of the artist against what he in turn personifies as society has been, for over a century, a battle for the possession of the common educated mind. And it has been won by showing, not the delights of art, but the dangers of Intellect. 'Save your soul alive' has been the watchcry: Intellect will harden your heart without damping its passions; it will blind your sympathies while using their energy and pertinacity. Most grievous, Intellect will destroy the wholeness of your self by throwing doubt on instinct and making habitual the arresting of impulse, until there is born within you a second man, nullifier of the first or inspirer of devious courses. In a word, Intellect, as Rousseau said with great precision, makes of man a depraved animal. Any ideas an animal has are likely to fit his needs or fail altogether—which it is to be, a few trials will decide; whereas man in civilization can entertain with blind persistence ideas that cripple him or cause his undoing. He develops a love for them as for inherited furniture—ugly, inconvenient, and ruinous to maintain, but 'unthinkable' to be without. To sum up, Intellect makes the fanatic through intellectualism, the Philistine through stunting the senses, the doubter through self-consciousness, the hypocrite through afterthought. Against such vested interests nothing less than the full force of native emotion, concentrated through art, stood any chance of winning.

The gains made in each Romantic generation at the expense of the classical spirit have at last become our culture, the culture of art, philanthropy, and science, which continues to marshal its ever-enlarging battalions against the old enemy. That the enemy is not reason or intelligence is shown by the place that education, art, and science occupy in our midst. Indeed, the march of mind itself has proved it true that art is the key to a knowledge of life. By the nineties psychology had shown that the mind in its secret operations was an unconscious artist. Anthropology then showed that social organization grew not by rational but by mythic and poetic ideas. Sociology and psychiatry showed that the relations of men followed the designs, not of intellectual purpose, but of irrational associations and ancestral compulsions. Finally in our day, art the great parent, using these disciplines which were its stepchildren, has turned still farther away from the deliverances of Intellect, in order to take up systematic anticerebration, sounding the depths of unconscious imagery, automatic writing, catatonic syntax, and shapes and sounds voided of associations.

The appropriateness of these signals is shown by the response they elicit from even the least instructed. The great merchant wins public acclaim as an aggressive patron of the arts while Intellect is not even a minority on the defensive. Many are found, moreover, who attend to art (and to the social sciences on which it leans) with an eye to finding warrant for their own confusions. These connoisseurs confirm their aliveness by contemplating objects which, like themselves, have fled the confining grasp of the enemy, Intellect.

Modern man is thus a product of art and hostile to Intellect because of an historical evolution whose rightness we must uphold. Where does this leave Intellect in relation to the inner life? And in this seeming deadlock between the claimants—life and art versus organized thought—which are we to choose, believe, follow?

First, we may take it that the Romantics knew what they were doing and that the antagonism which they brought out into the open is in the nature of things. We must live with it as we do with other antinomies, notably the political. But next, we must see that the precarious balance of the antinomy is always a temptation to fly from one exclusive attachment to the other. The swingabout, when it comes, is extreme and intolerant, and there is never any guarantee that in the upheaval either 'cause'—Intellect or art, thought or feeling—will retain its virtue. Great cultural changes begin in affectation and end in routine. This dead end is where we stand, now that the revolutionary purpose served by aesthetic feeling has lost its force and the aesthetic quality itself become merely consolatory. Art, in other words, is now reaction in spite of seeming to be innovation. The daring is now a system, the novelty but a certain stance which makes people say, 'Oh, yes, an experiment.' The object being in a gallery it must be a painting; if published it must be a novel. Meaning has evaporated because clear thought is no longer considered an important constituent of art. What the maker proffers is fantasy without direction. Paradoxically, art as 'advanced' as this protects the beholder from unwelcome discoveries, because it no longer claims attention for its clear meaning or its particular form, but simply for its general property of being art, which today means denouncing the universal wrong. The art lovers are now, as they never were, the world haters.

In other terms, meaning does not necessarily reside in art because in the Age of Reason it perished under excess of Intellect. There is thus a possibility that Intellect is the element now needed to restore energy to minds altogether too contented with their artistic diet. Their perceptions require a shock that art no longer gives, or gives without sequel. And as feeling was cramped and hidden but not lost in the classical age, so is Intellect today. It is consequently in the interests of art itself, of emotion and religion and science, that the observer of contemporary society should study the circumstances and test the vitality of Intellect. It may soon become our common task to restore its strength while protecting the feelings against its dominion, and deciding in which of our institutions the force of ideas is and is not required.

It is of course in the individual mind that—to use the largest terms—art and Intellect must first be rewedded, and by multiple instances of the same union, the culture revived. This does not mean that every artist must be a man of ideas, any more than every intellectual must be an artist. The mutual appreciation of each other's existence is enough, provided it goes with an awareness of the limits of the power each wields. For that sense of limits brings humility and may induce sober attention to one's complement. Intellectual power has certainly not spoiled any work of art that it helped construct, though nothing is so harmful to an artist as an idea which he carries about like a mithridate, to ward off worse poisoning; or again, which he shows off as a sign of superiority.* But if one of the chief functions of Intellect is to link desires and goals, its value to

---

*In Chapter IX I shall give examples of such 'ideas' drawn from science and philosophy by modern artists. But the notion which satisfies and misleads an unintellectual artist can be very simple, not to say childish. A memorable example is that of Mrs. Patrick Campbell, who let herself be persuaded by someone that the true, profound way to play Lady Macbeth in the sleepwalking scene was 'as seen through a sheet of glass.' Shaw says to this: 'I wish I had been there with a few bricks. . . . Why do you believe every ASS who talks nonsense to you, and bite everyone who talks skilled common sense?' *Bernard Shaw and Mrs. Patrick Campbell: Their Correspondence*, ed. Alan Dent, London, 1952, 217.

any man lies in the speed and strength with which it can help him to clarify his desire and to act or build according to its dictates.

After indicting Intellect as the poisoner of political life and the desiccator of feeling and art, and going on to discover the antinomies that make the conflict forever inconclusive, there remains to put in evidence the professional intellectual—the scholar, scientist, or publicist—who has survived all shifts in taste and politics and who, in Europe especially, gives Intellect its public aspect and character. It often seems as if the Continental tradition were political in the worst sense—the sense of betraying Intellect at large for a partisan cause that happens to be intellectual. Such a tradition is bound to be one of repression and death. The mood and tone are those of the mathematician David Hilbert, who once addressed a learned congress in these words: 'We are often told that pure and applied mathematics are hostile to each other. Pure and applied mathematics are not hostile to each other. Pure and applied mathematics have never been hostile to each other. Pure and applied mathematics will never be hostile to each other, because, in fact, there is absolutely nothing in common between them.'[11]

Not even if applied mathematics were some shady form of error would this tigerish contempt be admissible. By his act, meant to repudiate unworthy associations like one loudly disowning country cousins, the would-be champion of high and pure thought was subduing his own intellect to low and corrupt uses. His ostensibly lofty motive masked snobbery and self-praise.

This is the immorality of Intellect. It has grown worse since the scattering of the clerisy into a hundred complacent specialties, perhaps because each feels that unless it lauds itself the others will exhaust the public's small stock of regard. Besides, the overextended sensibility of the age makes for bad temper. The most self-absorbed suffer under a diffuse torture that never ends—too many people to respond to, directly or through recklessly improved communication; too many proliferating, ramifying ideas and objects, of which analysis (we think) tells more and more, until nothing is what it seems and the world is quicksand; a too finely divided self, frittered away by its impressionable delicacy, crazed by the accumulation of creeds and interpretations—in a word, the grating touch and voice of multitudinousness.

But one must not overdo the explanation by modernism. The blood lust among professionals is also a result of the very virtue of intellectual man. His devotion to something other than immediate self-interest makes him intransigent; his high-mindedness warrants in his eyes the expression of every animus. 'Bring the best wits together,' wrote Emerson in *The Natural History of Intellect,* 'and they are so impatient of each other, so vulgar, there is so much more than their wit—such follies, gluttonies, partialities . . . that you shall have no academy.'[12]

Intellect and feeling can even become split, each into two parts within one man, his two selves following alien courses in the world. Thus the sentimental poet A. E. Housman, who wept over the sadness of young love and sorrow, wrote, as classical scholar, book reviews that slew young hopes without remorse. Even aside from such perversions, the servant of truth seems always ready to kill: the mild scholar lives to destroy his colleague with a theory, and this fratricide is his duty and title to fame.

The method of science, it is sometimes thought, is less sanguinary, being an impersonal arbiter to whom all gracefully bow. But the reality under the ideal shows a history of violent words and rending of flesh. Wherefore the hiss of hate? What had the applied mathematicians done to David Hilbert? Is it because the intellectual's energies are concentrated in his mind and tongue that his is the fiercest species of gladiator? Is it something inherent in ideas, or is it merely vile manners and vicious habits in the possessor of ideas that account for the appalling anarchy which confronts the observer of the intellectual life? Go to any university campus and listen to the remarks of one division about another. Outside the university, listen to doctors speaking of dentists and psychiatrists; physicists referring to engineers; lawyers and musicians and poets and critics characterizing one another ex cathedra. The world gets used to this reciprocity of contempt and attaches no importance to it. But it cannot help poisoning the intellectual atmosphere and conveying the taint to the laity. The incivility of the layman when addressing writers and other public figures is partly an aping of the professionals.

But every good reason for damning intellectual behavior when we observe it, like Emerson, in its crude natural history, is but another argument for encouraging, strengthening, and disseminating Intellect in its regulated form. Intellect is not for all purposes and occasions. Man in his daily life must meet feeling with feeling, even stupidity with stupidity, and without growing proud of his tact, leave to others the pleasure of calling him humane and tolerant. Since by definition the place of the Intellect is at a distance from the helter-skelter of life; since the work of Intellect professes to be exact, considered, civilized; since the very purpose of Intellect is to make and keep order by channeling passion to its veritable objects, it follows that the ethics of the intellectual must be those, not of worldly habit, but of deliberate scruple. His only models are the Just Man and the Magnanimous Man. These are distinct technical terms which must not be taken as roughly synonymous with saint. They mean nothing more than what they say: the just man is he who puts his whole strength in seeing the object or idea as it would appear if he had omniscience; and the magnanimous man is he who puts his pride in declining mean advantage or easy victory.

These virtues cannot, of course, change the intrinsically militant character of the intellectual life, nor are they meant to. The new idea on which salvation depends will always bring not peace but a sword; the battle must remain a battle. But one must not forget that in so saying one speaks metaphorically. There is a radical distinction between vehemence and violence, even in debate. If one asks who was the greatest, most dauntless intellectual fighter of our century, the right answer is surely 'Bernard Shaw.' He jousted with thousands of people, prejudices, and vested interests, saying and writing words that millions thought noxious. But as his lifelong opponent, Chesterton, records, Shaw's strokes never left a festering wound. Shaw had found the art of being uncompromising and even outrageous without fouling the air or undermining the arena. We can measure the difference between his intellect and the common sort when we recall how his was interpreted by his peers: 'too intellectual—all head and no heart.' But he had heart enough never to forget that his antagonists were men and companions in thought; and his head always knew the degree to which, in the circumstance, an idea should enlist the passions. What many people missed in him was the gestures of the slugging match followed by the sentimentalities of remorse. But what they missed is the measure of their deficiency, and of his superiority, in Intellect.

This is not to say that in every intellectual dispute 'there is much to be said on both sides,' and that 'the truth probably lies somewhere in the middle.' These are but thought-clichés. The point is that a defeat or contumely suffered by intellectual effort is a defeat or contumely suffered by Intellect as a whole. The wrong done is to a discipline, that is, a set of self-imposed rules. The notion that such rules exist—not only for polemics, criticism, and journalism, but also for conversation, for remarks about the absent, and for the privacy of silent thought—is certainly foreign to our customs. Yet by scorning this hygiene of the mind the intellectual deprives himself of the benefits supposedly attached to his position. Intellect, far from being a cause of anxious agitation, should calm and compose the soul. It should preserve from the fatiguing indignation of the overpolitical and from the ideological drugs with which they repair exhaustion. Through its power to name and remember, it should safeguard the living minutes from the inanities of trumpery art. In dealing with would-be science, with education, with benevolent undertakings, with new religions and new thought, it should protect against facile enthusiasms, exaggerated estimates, and the disillusion to follow—no small advantage in a time when so much effort goes into furbishing ancient fraud and new foolishness with a modish glamour; and when excessive information gives everyone the gullibility of the learned, far more dangerous than the gullibility of the innocent. For the innocent see things in their nakedness and call them by the only names they know. In a word, Intellect is the broom with which to clear the mind of cant.*

It is of course much more. Intellect is the great binder of mind with itself and of minds with one another. In art it is Intellect, implicit or explicit, that raises the work from fineness or virtuosity to what posterity calls depth or greatness. In society, it is the conventions of Intellect that permit debate, instead of battle, reciprocity instead of childish self-will, and tradition instead of perpetual recommencement. At the juncture where we now stand, between ideology and Zen-Buddhism, between emancipated art and the seductive automatism of cybernetics, the repair of tradition—by which I mean nothing other than continuity of thought—is a pressing concern. For it is daily more evident that the loss of tradition in that sense is impeding the great peoples of the West in the furtherance of their aims. Even if Intellect had nothing to offer man as a political and domestic animal, or as a sociable and artistic sensibility, its need would still be felt as the builder of a stupendous edifice of knowledge. To maintain and raise it higher, money, energy, and good will are not enough. They are helpless, or worse, destructive, when the codes of discourse and judgment are missing. And that Intellect cannot be improvised or caught by contact goes with the meaning I assign to tradition. In the realm of money, public and private, to which I now turn, observation makes all too plain what comes of ignoring these maxims of the house.

*It is useful to recall that Johnson's definitive words on cant were preceded by Boswell's quick awareness of the egotism in the fault: 'Have you not been vexed by all the turbulence of this reign, and that absurd vote of the House of Commons, "That the influence of the Crown has increased . . . and ought to be diminished"? JOHNSON. Sir, I have never slept an hour less nor eat an ounce less meat. I would have knocked the factious dogs on the head, to be sure; but I was not *vexed*. BOSWELL. I declare, Sir, upon my honour, I did imagine I was vexed, and took a pride in it; but it *was*, perhaps, cant. . . . JOHNSON. My dear friend, clear your *mind* of cant. You may *talk* as other people do: you may say . . . "These are bad times; it is a melancholy thing to be reserved to such times." You don't mind the times. . . . You may *talk* in this manner; it is a mode of talking in Society: but don't *think* foolishly.' (May 15, 1783.)

The Folklore of Philanthropy

Valuable as Intellect may be to society, productive of pleasure, serenity, and wealth, its exercise has never been lucrative for the practitioners. This generality a reading of history will confirm. The scholar, the teacher, the scientist, the man of letters, is traditionally a poor man. That the exceptions are negligible is shown by the pride which the intellectual takes, or is supposed to take, in his poverty. The world complacently believes that the rewards of Intellect, though hidden from common view, are enough for the recipient. His life is, as we say, dedicated to higher things, and as no one can have everything, the lower, or material, side is expected to be wanting.

Higher or not, it is true that the pursuit of ideas is as great an obsession as the pursuit of money, and most men lack the energy to be obsessed by two objects at once. Moreover, the signs of a good idea are so different from the signs of a profitable bargain that it is rare for one mind to be expert in the judgment of both. When at times there has been a commercial demand for intellectual talents— the Sophists in ancient Greece are the stock example—history has always attached discredit to their fortune. Again, in the professions that pay well for the immediate services of intellect, such as law and medicine, the honors go to the masters of theory whose profit is small. And yet no one capable of judging has ever denied the immense economic and emotional advantages to mankind of the application of Intellect. People dimly know that civilization has been fashioned by intelligence and kept alive by Intellect, and they can see for themselves how many tradesmen make their living out of its products. A single copy of a book that is in demand for a century will, by passing from hand to hand, feed a dozen people more handsomely than its author. Euclid's theorems probably brought him no royalties, and the original adding machine was no source of income to Pascal. But the vendors of surveying equipment or school geometries and the stockholders of International Business Machines have over the years been fairly well paid for their trouble.

This ancient divorce between Idea and Cash rests on a conviction deep in Western culture that he who knows ought to give his knowledge away for nothing. When in the Middle Ages two educated Scotsmen landed on the Continent and offered their logic for hire, they were nearly stoned to death by the infuriated students.[1] A modern instance may be seen in the common attitude toward books: a friend who borrows a dollar or a handkerchief will punctiliously return it to you; but he will borrow a book worth five times as much, and possibly irreplaceable, with no thought that he holds any of your property. He will lose the book, deface it, give it away, or take it from your house without notice, honestly unconcerned whether it is his or yours. Indeed, if he cared, he might find on the flyleaf the name of a third party from whom you had purloined it on the same terms. By virtue of their relation to Intellect, books are felt to belong to the common stock; though they are objects, they seem as intangible as mind itself.

This intangibility, or rather this vivid difference from the physical that we noted earlier as affecting the judgment of intellectual ability, governs all the relations of Intellect to money. And when attempts are made to give concrete representations or equivalents of this intangible power, the results are unconvincing, vulgar, and harmful.

This is why it has always been so difficult to keep the men of intellect alive. Not only do they fail to keep money in the forefront of their minds, but others find it hard to imagine minds having needs. Intellect is a minority interest whose demands are rarely made vivid or studied with patience and system. When a self-aware intellect sets forth its own practical claims, an air of egotism—as of one bothering the public with a purely private concern or soliciting help while concealing assets—beclouds the outsider's vision. A philanthropist feels much more comfortable with the sick or insane, and secretly compares them to Intellect's disadvantage. Hence the rewards of Intellect are capricious, even in an economy of abundance.

To the worldly man's discomfort in the face of Intellect is added the resentful envy of the democrat. If the intellectual knows as much as he pretends, why does he come to the businessman, or to his attorney the legislator, for support? The businessman is struggling with his rivals and with the rising cost of materials. He has a weekly payroll to meet, and a note at the bank—and here comes a dreamer who despises him and his works, asking for subsidy. It is as if the man of Intellect wanted two shares of life—the good life of which he has the secret, and also the life of food and drink which he says in print is only fit for common men. The age-old penury of the intellectual is explicable, paradoxically, by mankind's envious respect for Intellect.

To offset this grudging behavior, the stratagem devised by Western civilization has been the marshaling of religious and ethical feelings behind intellectual work. Most conspicuous during the Middle Ages, this natural association of purposes had existed before, in the ancient world, where it took the form of the educated slave's teaching his master one of the philosophies in vogue. The worldling's desire for virtue or salvation, and sometimes for power, has been the main motive relied on by Intellect. We owe our college endowments to these desires—the secular mixed with the pious—so that Intellect today, though no longer a slave, is still a mendicant friar at the mercy of philanthropy or liberal goodness.

· · ·

The force of this philanthropy is undoubtedly greatest in contemporary America.* The largest fortunes, we know, turned into the largest foundations—Carnegie, Rockefeller, Ford—a triple image of the modern United States and its recent evolution. It was abstract greed and rivalry, organizing ability and mass production, blatant advertising and self-righteous individualism that amassed the wealth which now irrigates the realm of the intangible, the disinterested, the humanitarian, and the remotely practical—a realm whose boundaries are not those of the United States merely, but of the world.

In our amazement at this posthumous worship of the muses by three of the craggiest figures of power outside fiction, we must not forget the tradition that encouraged or induced their mellowing. The principles of American philanthropy were established on this continent by the most intellectual generation it has ever known. It was the Founding Fathers—the men of letters who wrote the Declaration of Independence and the *Federalist Papers*—who laid it down as axiomatic that schools, churches, and other institutions for welfare should be tax-free. They fastened the custom upon us like an immemorial law. Curiously, it was after 1825, under a more 'democratic' generation, less dominated by highbrows, that state legislatures began to pass bills allowing tax exemptions. Where such bills were not passed, the practice might be challenged, but it was not overthrown. The state of Virginia, for example, did not enact a law on the subject until 1869; the state of New Jersey not until 1947. Tax exemption is part of our inborn creed: in California, recently, a suit to deprive parochial schools of tax exemption was declared by the Court 'no substantial Federal question': the judges deemed the issue long since settled, and with such finality that they would not even rule upon it.

To be sure, the men who had settled it were following the more

---

*European foundations are few, and in the West, under the welfare state (which includes state art and state universities), there are few objects on which such private funds can be spent. In Denmark, for example, the leading foundation, based on brewery profits, has found only graduate students and unwed mothers in need of further benefits.

capricious precedent of royal charters and showing deference to church establishments. But most of the Founding Fathers were children of the secular, enlightened, rationalist eighteenth century; they belonged to the literary and scientific societies of Europe; they speculated on the rights of man; they believed that education given freely to all, and fully to 'the best geniuses,' would make mankind, if not wholly intellectual, at least wholly respectful of Intellect. Men would see its power to dispel brutishness, improve government, equalize conditions, and polish manners.

In one sense we have achieved the bulk of what that generation hoped for: our manners are smooth and our governors alive to our wants; education is ubiquitous and our ethical concern for our fellow man unexampled. If, as I maintain, Intellect is in disrepair and disrepute, it is—as I have tried to show—because the very passion of philanthropy which our forefathers kindled is now distorting judgment and superseding thought. It is an excess of good will, of fraternal love, of deep feeling for human life and its reflection in art, that is causing the neglect of mind. True, the Founding Fathers' legacy is still bringing great returns. Each year more and more money is drained off from private and corporate wealth to serve education, religion, and charity, and some of these ends presuppose Intellect.* And not content with setting free of taxes the land and buildings used for welfare purposes, the law on incomes, by permitting high deductions for philanthropic gifts, actually offers every citizen a bribe to support Intellect.† The list of the hundreds of tax-exempt foundations that give money for education and research fills a large book; it would take a shelf of books to list all the nonprofit establishments that foster art, science, teaching, and religion in this coun-

---

*Internal revenue figures for 1956 put deductions for charity at nearly five billion dollars, or about four percent of the reported income. Estimates for 1958 give seven billion as the total. *Philanthropic Digest*, January 7, 1959, I.
†This device is used in no other country except West Germany. Wealthy Europeans of other lands freely admit that they have 'better ways of avoiding taxes.'

try. The Founding Fathers built solidly. The question is whether we understand and carry out their full intention—or any better one of our own—in our private and public spending for Intellect.

The now characteristic behavior of the modern foundations was determined soon after they were established. One can readily imagine the awesome weight of responsibility that descended on the men who were first given millions of dollars with which to do something for the good of the nation. What should they do? What could they do? Everybody's eyes were on them, everybody's hand was stretched out. The beggar, one surmises, was ready as always to curse the professed Christian who passed him by. Does not the Christian depend for his salvation on the beggar? No beggars, no Christian charity. Does not the foundation depend on takers of money for its continued existence as a charitable institution? No applicants, no tax exemption. So from the outset the tendency of the foundation was to prefer large demands to small, clear social undertakings to dim private ones—in a word, projects to persons.

Holding in check any likelihood of indiscriminate largesse was the ever-present sense of responsibility. There was the annual report to think of, in which the grants would undergo public scrutiny. Even before the annual report, the relation of the executives to the trustees put a premium on projects with an attractive exterior. The trustees' review might go only a little deeper than the public's, but for that very reason, projects must be defensible from the surface outward. Their briefly stated aims and skeleton budgets must commend themselves to the average educated man of business.*

Among the applicants themselves the criticism of favored projects might be sharper, but this would not matter if impartiality seemed to rule the distribution—equal-handedness to North and

---

*A confiding official who kept using the phrase 'problem-oriented research' and was asked to define it began by saying: 'First of all, it is trustee ointment.'

South, to large and small institutions, to old and new, to home and foreign missions, to health, to education, and to welfare. It was important, also, not to compete with any going concern, especially commercial enterprises such as trade publishers of books and magazines; not to encroach on individual rights by anything like a contract requiring work for value received; and not to weaken initiative by helping those who would not help themselves. These motives led to rules which still govern foundation awards, irrespective of their effects on education and Intellect.

To particularize: 'impartiality' has meant the support of institutions ostensibly in a class with others, but actually weaker. The principle of concentrating resources has never been acknowledged or deliberately followed. If it has come into play at all, it is only because the leading institutions, embracing more units, could not help receiving more support. And this support, given to projects rather than to the institution, has nearly everywhere had the result of weakening the structure and scattering the intellectual forces of the establishment. Today, the chief beneficiaries are alarmed to see the damage done to their fabric. The levers of destruction were the matching grant and the short-term allowance for 'original' ideas, which I shall discuss farther on. As for the projects themselves, they were hampered by the rule that denies money for publishing. When their results are in hand, scholars must spend time and energy to secure commercial publication or beg a subsidy from some agency that can use the book or brochure for its own interested ends.

Finally, the show of freedom from obligation has been mutually deceptive. Projectors have known how desirable it is to be copious in the production of forecasts, interim reports, and summaries of results; and yet the foundations have never exercised any authority, such as their knowledge might warrant, to insist on even so elementary a need as the readability and compactness of the conclusions offered to the intellectual community. This negligence has meant that innumerable 'studies' have crowded the library shelves and enlightened only their makers. In short, abdication of power has occurred on both sides—the foundations wanting no responsibility and the researchers no audience. This was to be expected. The foundations have been great amplifiers of the dominant traits of our intellectual life, rather than artisans of a new conception of it.

As foundations grew in number, they tended to specialize, explicitly or by custom. But apart from this limitation and those implied by the rules I have described, access to the reservoirs of charity was kept entirely free. Anyone could apply for any purpose and would receive a courteous answer on thick paper. From being a public trust the foundations were soon forced into the position of a public office, which meant that they had to develop a bureaucracy.* The work of sorting out from the mass of plausible and mad projects the deserving cases devolved usually on young men drawn from academic life. They were first attracted to the grueling work by the importance of the trust and its influence for good, and secondarily, perhaps, by the executive mode of life, which seemed an improvement on the academic mode of shabby-genteel. The talent required consisted of administrative ability coupled with the diplomacy of the personnel manager, both of which implied interests broader than the specialist's.

Most of the traditions created by these tireless young men were unconscious adaptations of ideals current in the national life; a few were deliberate policies framed by the trustees out of their experience of business and public relations. For example, the practices that grew up about the framing and judging of projects reflected the common inclination toward the measurable, and this not in a crude sense, but on the contrary, a complex, often fantastic sense. Likewise, the lust for novelty, the 'creative' and the exotic found the dispensers of money ever sanguine, not to say progressively infatuated.

*The few European foundations, though wealthy, are ordinarily managed by one man and his clerk.

But the aesthetic attitude joined to the taste for the tangible produced a bias toward natural and social science, on the one hand, and toward the performing arts, on the other. The regard for humanistic scholarship was also high, but the scholar's needs, most characteristic of Intellect, seemed to defy the established order of thought. The humanities gave rise to no projects properly so called, were not expensive enough, and promised few social benefits. Their work remained invisible. To support it was like gambling sums too small to be exciting on horses altogether too dark.

The recipients of foundation grants naturally did not criticize these assumptions—only particular decisions under them—and to this day the general public has but a vague idea of foundation procedures and their effects. Indeed, it is but fair to add that the effects are only now becoming clear to the officials and petitioners themselves, though the new currency of terms such as 'projectism' shows a growing awareness.*

In trying here to make that awareness both deeper and more general, I am not, of course, aiming darts at any particular foundation or foundations, nor have I any of their officials in mind, save as Platonic archetypes. I have naturally disguised details while keeping strictly to the philosophic truth of the case.

It says much for the acceptance of foundation folklore that we all know what a project is: it is something neatly clamped in a folder, not too thin and not too bulky, and typed preferably on an electric typewriter. The last page consists of figures, headed 'Estimated Budget' and divided into three- or five-year slices. The project is in truth a literary form, like the Shakespearean sonnet, and its correct composition is an art not vouchsafed to everyone. There is a language

---

*The reader with a taste for intellectual history can reread with profit Swift's description of projectors in Gulliver's third voyage, to Laputa. It is not a coincidence that the satire aims at the recently established Royal Academy of Science, whose descendants now encompass every subject matter.

appropriate to projects, a tone which veils the diversity of minds, an indefinable fitness to the particular proposal and the promise it holds forth. Just as there is the love sonnet and the meditative sonnet, so there is the problem project and the survey project. Each must follow style and fashion; the idea must be turned in such a way that it shall make the project different from all others, yet 'in line with current programs' and at the same time 'widely applicable' if successful. Thus a psychologist who might like to know whether modern composers can actually hear the counterpoint they write would have to present his project either as a device for predicting future success in music students, or else as a measurement scale* for rating with precision the great contrapuntists of the past, thus 'making obsolete the crude, subjective criticism still in use.' If the example seems satirical, it is nevertheless true to the mythology of research and the desire for a universal submission to scientific method, both of which weigh heavily on all projects.

In every branch of learning and in every center of research, some persons are found capable of converting a thoughtful piece of curiosity into a project so that it will appear ideal—or, as is said, 'a natural'—for foundation support. Other people, also able but without this knack, must have their projects 'processed,' and still others learn the trick. The consequence is a strong urge in many a man to stultify himself at the expense of what used to be called intellectual honesty. The scholar or scientist salves his conscience with the thought that he will turn the proceeds to good use. He hopes to do 'his own work' behind the shelter of phrases denoting expected attitudes; to do fundamental research though proposing foundational research.

For he knows that if he does not use the accepted language his most commonplace ideas will seem wild or barren. They will shock and not be receivable. It would be rude, for instance, to say

---

*Not tautology, owing to the possibility of momentary confusion with a musical scale.

that you 'expect to finish the work in three years.' You must say: 'It is anticipated that the project will be satisfactorily completed within a three-year period.' It would be egotistical to suggest that 'an answer to the ancient and perplexing question, What are the rational principles of translation, must interest every scholar and educated reader, and I mean to have a try at it.' You must write: 'The project here submitted to the Modern Age Foundation is in line with similar projects which it has endorsed before in its valuable program of people-to-people understanding and co-operation, and it is hoped that by deploying on the crucial procedural focus of the translation problem the specialized competence and distinct approach of a team of experts from varied areas under the close supervision of the undersigned, a contribution may be made to a problem currently of urgent immediacy and global importance.'

Nothing, in effect, is closer to the stance of projectism than the attitude shown in the dedicatory epistles of earlier centuries, in which a patron was similarly wooed by flattery, circumlocution, and conventional promises. There is this difference, of course, that the flattery of the modern is not directed at a living person but at the effigy of itself that the particular foundation has hoisted aloft. And this impersonality is reciprocal. The foundation by its ethics takes no interest in the persons of the suppliants, but only in that self-same effigy. Princely patronage, in becoming institutionalized, has thus bred a centaur-like abstraction: a beggar on horseback, if you will, in which it is the horseback (so to say) that drives and chooses the road. This is why it is correct to speak of project*ism*, more powerful than beggars or bureaucracy.

At first sight, one might think that stated goals and a disregard of persons would best serve the great abstraction of Intellect. The fact is that intellectual ambition and power still reside in individuals and nowhere else. Teamwork may discover but not invent. The most characteristic, because the oldest, features of Intellect continue to occur in the subjects least susceptible to collectivization. It is in the foundations' gingerly handling of those subjects, notably the humanities and the highest type of theoretical science, that one sees how incompatible are foundation lore and Intellect. The foundations have been embarrassed in consequence. I have had visits from half a dozen representatives of foundations earnestly inquiring into the mystery: how to serve the humanities. These men were perturbed by what seemed to them irregular about pure scholarship and their distress is instructive. It shows, on the one hand, the desire to do right and serve all interests; and on the other, the oblivion that has overtaken the rules of Intellect. Although foundation officials tend to use their trustees much as in Dickens Mr. Spenlow used as an excuse for refusals his supposedly hardhearted partner Mr. Jorkins, whom no one ever saw, it is not the trustees by themselves who are to blame, nor even the influence of business habits. It is the temper of distrust toward persons, our refuge-seeking in the 'objective,' which is fostered by our schools and universities, our political institutions and public prints, our ideas of philanthrophy and our pride in the impersonality of science.

Fifty years ago, William James said that the social value of a college education was to tell a good man when you saw one. From the way he said it, one infers that this simple truth already seemed a paradox. It is now a heresy. You do not tell a good man when you see one: you ask him to fill out a blank. You ask him to collect letters of recommendation; you send out forms on which distrait persons put check marks opposite the names of qualities and virtues and guess at percentages of merit. The guesses help or hinder the applicant's chances and bear as little relation to life—let alone to objectivity or the nature of Intellect—as the inert heap of letters of recommendation. The truth of this is acknowledged in practice. Short of proved criminal tendencies or dementia praecox, every candidate turns out to be able, responsible, co-operative, and well trained. The astonishing variety of mankind nowhere appears in these documents; rather, the population of the country turns out to consist wholly of paragons,* for letters that hint of a defect are a species of death warrant and hence are seldom written.

Around leading personalities, it is true, judgments collect and create a reputation independent of the paper file. But this comes late in the day, usually when it is no longer needed; and reputation is hard to establish after middle life, especially if the person is not a native and yet already on the scene. I remember a foreign scholar, whose works were well known and whose residence in this country for some ten years had made him many distinguished admirers. He wanted after his retirement to finish a three-volume work in an important branch of philosophy. The combined efforts of a dozen or more high-placed American scholars were unavailing to obtain for this man the supplement to his pension which would have given him three or four years of peace of mind to finish his work. Every foundation was interested; innumerable letters were filed. But when it came to the disbursement of twelve thousand dollars, half a century's alienation from intellectual man interposed its veto.

Do we see here a subtle manifestation of the envy I described as part of dogmatic equality? Just as in welfare charity the social worker does not want to see the beneficiary rioting in pleasure, so in intellectual charity the unavowed feeling seems to be: 'Why should he

---

*The philanthropic view of man, which is indeed productive of good when it spurs the individual to show the traits that others generously assume to be present, works in reverse and *against* talent when it sets up an ideal that no actual talent can match. Consider a typical description of the qualities one expert looked for in the young students to be selected for acceleration in school and college: ' . . . emotional maturity should be the main criterion and . . . the following personality attributes [are] the most reliable indices of readiness to move ahead: independence; power of reflective thinking; adventurous outlook and zest for living, deep interpersonal relationships; ability to plan ahead; flexibility.' (*General Education in School and College,* ed. A. Blackmer, Cambridge, 1952, 113.) By this set of specifications, Newton would certainly have failed, and indeed any great mind we have a record of, for their early ability almost always shows itself as a *leaning*—therefore a lack of balance—toward a particular interest, often with disturbed emotions and an unprepossessing appearance. The well-rounded man may be the ideal companion, but he is not the genius or great talent these absurd 'profiles' envision.

revel in the joys of research and writing—superior and independent—while the rest of us carry on this important but unrefreshing paper work?' We do not, it is true, begrudge youth that same freedom, and as we shall see, freeing a man for a mission occurs every day. But the Fulbright student or scholar is an 'ambassador,' so that he is not indulging himself in the pure luxury of doing only what he most wants to do, uncommitted, unclassified, unlectured at.

What strengthens the suspicion that these emotions exist and affect the giver's judgment of the petitioner is the delight that all keepers of money evidence when they are asked to pay, not for a man working, but for equipment, clerical help, microfilm, travel to research centers, and incidental expenses. When such things are required in order to pursue intellectual work, what relief, what joy! We are being virtuous and sensible too. The bill will be large. We are spending *enough* money and not frittering it away piecemeal on intellectuals. It is this yearned-for security that has given first place in foundation fancy to the conference.

The conference has the advantage of maximizing at once high purposes and down-to-earth costs. One hundred learned men brought to one spot for a stated cause are known to produce a foundation effect directly proportional to the square of the distance traveled, multiplied by the cube of the mimeographed matter given off. And for these *exciting* results nothing is paid but railroad fares and hotel bills, taxi drivers and stenotypists. This is not caricature: I have myself been offered a quarter of a million dollars without formality—over the counter, so to speak—to organize a world conference on a particular topic which at the time was thought momentous. All I had to do was to give up everything I was doing and start inviting notables from all over—I would know who they were and the magic of the subject plus an offer of expenses would draw them like a magnet. My intellectual contribution was to divide the subject and assign congenial topics and hotel rooms. When I declined and proposed a more lasting use of the money, for a related purpose yet not one furthering any ends of my own, I was told that the suggestion would be taken under advisement.

For the participants, the conference has become a principal form of intellectual togetherness. Though it makes a heavy drain on intellectual energies—or rather on the energies of intellectuals—a conference is always welcome: it is gregarious, egalitarian, and inclusive. Come confer with us and we will exchange ideas until it takes a really unco-operative mind to tell which was whose. It should be added for the sake of future historians that a panel, a round table, or a forum is simply an embryo conference. The principle, the attraction, and the results are the same.

That conferences can be useful is not to be denied, nor should we imagine that they are imposed by foundations upon the conferees. To suggest this would be to fail in gratitude toward those who make conferences possible not only financially but also physically, through their advice and organizing ability. A conference could be, indeed, a temporary materialization of the House of Intellect. What is regrettable is that, despite our ample means and best wits, the conference has become rather a tribal rite and the possible House of Intellect a nomad's tent. The ritual is even growing more complex: the biggest and best conferences, it is now believed, require a pre-conference conference.

The composition of these meetings threatens the work of Intellect very directly. The haunters of conferences are brought there, upon invitation, by the fame of their secluded work. But as habitual conferees they have less and less time or strength to bring fresh thoughts to the gatherings. One sign of this is that the 'papers' to be read and discussed are almost never ready in time to be perused by the appointed critics: they are thrown together at the last minute. As some scholars awaken to the danger of sterile agitation and fend off invitations, the group comes to include as many 'intellectuals by position' as intellectuals by achievement; so that while the leaders repeat themselves and rediscover 'the contemporary chaos,' the listeners and discussers do little more than give the approved rejoinder to the familiar gambit. The level of discourse allows them to wade comfortably across any difficulty, and the atmosphere—to say nothing of the food and drink—is conducive to their mental repose. Yet propinquity, some new faces, and the change of scene, act sufficiently on the nerves to make everyone in chorus declare the occasion 'stimulating.'

In effect, the conference has become, the world over, a substitute for work. That is its appeal. Take at any instant a census of the great talents of the world and you will find a large proportion preparing, attending, or recovering from a conference. When you add to the burden of the physical event itself the mass of ancillary paperwork required, from the preparatory letter-writing to the transcripts of discussions that nobody reads (except to correct his own stammerings before publication), you may conclude that here make-believe reaches its apogee.

One reason why my counterproposal was never heard of again was that it violated—as I knew in advance—the chief tenet of foundation lore: instead of being a new creation, my idea only buttressed an existing enterprise; and instead of being observation, a study of others' work, it would directly aid those already working. The principle of compulsory newness is an offshoot of school creativity and utopianism. I have heard an official call his foundation's grants the 'venture capital of social change.' He was devout in the belief that his chosen projects were helping remake the country and the world; the recipients of funds were evangelists, though being scientific they were without a gospel, and the foundation had only the dogma of rationalized habit. Like other foundations this one represented its projects as original in conception, pioneering in purpose, and epoch-making in promise. Applicants hampered by sober ideas must impart to them an apocalyptic glow, and men engaged in recognizable activities need not apply. In truth, most foundations decided from the start that whatever schools, colleges, and universities were already doing was of no interest. This purely academic work would go on in its old-fashioned way and be paid for out of old-fashioned endowments. No one engaged in the central duties of a going concern could be foundation fodder; but obviously, any such person should be encouraged to take a look at his performance, in the expectation that when he saw it as it really was he would do something else.*

In this we see the vestiges of sound instinct. Nearly everything is susceptible of improvement, and money should certainly be offered for things never before done. But the instinct is polluted by creative pride and secretly stirred by the ancestral repugnance to schoolwork. That the result denies the value of tradition and experience in human affairs, particularly the affairs of Intellect, does not bother men whose patterns of thought tend to be formed by analogy, not so much with science, as with scientific research, that is, the external preparations for science. The studies subsidized imply, for example, that a college does not know by inspection when it needs more books or teachers. This must be 'studied' and 'found out' by comparison and exchange of ideas. Here is part of the preamble of an actual proposal by an experienced projector who was really interested in raising money for a community arts center, but who knew that to ask for this outright on its own merits was futile. He therefore proposed first a *study* of arts centers: 'As a frame of reference for all planning of Arts Centers, there should be first of all a penetrating study, in both scope and depth, of the philosophy behind a program for the coordination of the arts. A clear analysis of the aims and purposes—civic, cultural, pedagogical—is an absolute necessity before any reasoned planning can be done. What is to be achieved must be defined before considering questions of method.'

The talk of 'method' and 'objectives,' and the air that the proposal, though fresh and new, is uncommonly mature for one so young, belong to the solemnities that nineteenth-century science used to affect. It is now for all 'studies' an earnest of the rigor and depth to come, just as the insertion of the disjointed notes of consultants and 'resource persons' into the committee's 'philosophy' is

---

*This assumption is no doubt what led to the suggestion made a few years ago by a university president, but never acted on, that ten universities raise $10,000 each and award the sum to a leading foundation for a self-study.

the sign of positive results, another brick in the foundations' great monument to incoherence and inconclusiveness.

This is not to say that all studies sponsored by foundations have been of small use. But when useful, the utility has been confined almost entirely to those making the study. Neither the institutions of learning nor the intellectual public could possibly assimilate as much 'knowledge' as they are offered in this form; first, because our channels of intelligence are clogged or broken down, and second, because despite their aping of science, the reports of studies are almost always too large and too vague.

By contrast, the effect of foundation grants on our seats of learning has been simple and may be shortly stated: inflation and strain. By pouring money into projects, studies, and institutes—all new and superimposed on existing purposes—the foundations have steadily added to the financial and administrative burdens of universities, while creating on the rim of the central structure vested interests whose allegiance is to the outside source of funds, not to the institution they happen to belong to. The unity and sense of loyalty of large companies of scholars have thus been undermined. Again, by encouraging individuals with a knack for project-making, the foundations have entrenched the idea that the prestige of a grant, free funds, and the comforts of adequate equipment and a private secretary come only to the intellectual promoter. Oh, to be the director of a project and lead an airport existence! To stay on the spot and teach or meditate is the sign of the unenterprising if not the mediocre.

As by temporarily enriching scholars they have weakened the intellectual and perhaps the moral fiber of men and institutions, so by baited gifts the foundations have insidiously impoverished university teaching and all nonprojectable research. The 'matching grant' which calls for an outlay by the institution equal to the gift being offered, has meant starving the whole to get the money for one part. The five-year grant has meant mortgaging future income to support permanent additions which the donor has expensively set up.* Moreover, all grants for a defined purpose have levied a hidden tax, owing to the foundations' refusal to recognize overhead costs. Space, personnel, utilities have been accounted as nothing in the erecting of institutes, programs, and 'centers,' which immediately become parasitic on the general resources of the main body. This policy is so far from an oversight that with many large gifts—say, for the endowment of a research chair—it is stipulated that the funds must *in no way* relieve the general budget of the institution. The institution must bear all the costs of naming and housing the incumbent, reorganizing programs, and finding replacements for him if he happens to be a member of its own staff. And these costs, in our complex arrangements, are not small.

Businessmen would not of course tolerate the same treatment in private or public contracts. Whether as trustees of charitable funds they impose these iron compulsions knowingly, because charity and cruelty are close kin; or whether ignorantly, because they are as little aware as their executives of the nature and conditions of intellectual work, is a question I find it hard to settle. Certainly, some of the actions taken after much conferring and deliberating suggest the reign of ignorance. Within the last four or five years, for example, both private and public funds have been given to institutions that wanted ostensibly to improve or expand their facilities in view of the coming flood of students. The grants for this purpose reverse the former 'holy negatives' against money for teaching, and they make up in size for their lateness in coming. Everyone is happy that, in places hitherto deficient in certain subject matters, the means of bringing teachers now exist. But what has been the practice, ratified if not required by the donors? To buy prestige, by luring to the institution a scholar of renown from another, better-supplied university. We have seen in another connection how this is effected: the lure is not money alone, but an offer of what must be called regulated inac-

---

*One university president has computed that a foundation grant of $34,000 to his institution cost it about half a million dollars—and endless bickering—in the ensuing twelve years.

tivity—a high salary, plenty of money for research, the right to take a leave of absence at will, and no specified duties while in residence. The man may teach a course if he insists. This cloistering of the most learned teachers goes on apace, decimating departments at the older universities and patently subtracting from, rather than adding to, the 'facilities' of the country. One is reminded of the eighteenth-century monarchs who thought they were furthering the arts and sciences by causing the notable performers to move from one capital to another.

Indeed one finds in the modern habits of patronage much the same restlessness, the same belief in the superiority of what is remote and unknown, the same intellectual imperialism. Most large foundations take pride in having a foreign-aid program, whether or not it is required by their charter. To bring to this country foreign students, scientists, and scholars is laudable. It is also expensive and uncertain in its results. From the special delight in these programs, the great busy-ness which attends the foray for candidates in alien territory and which suspends all the executive's home activities for weeks, from this official bustle, one suspects that the chief attraction of the program is that once again it is enchantingly peripheral; whatever it entails, it is not plain hard work at the main task: it is Borrioboola-Gha. For the products of modern schools the diversion is normal and natural, the full-blown form of their earlier classroom 'activity' and educational make-believe. In a word, it is 'exciting.'

As for the trip in the reverse direction—the 'mission' or Fulbright or attachéship—its character is well described by the name it has acquired among its devotees. It is a junket, and our leading men have quickly learned the taste for it. Pleasure and prestige alike depend on being away as often and as long as possible.* The agencies of despatch

---

*Already seventy years ago, Matthew Arnold noticed the frenzy of 'exchange,' limited though it then was to Western Europe and the Eastern United States: 'The friends of civilization, instead of hopping backwards and forwards over the Atlantic, should stay at home a while, and do their best to make the administration, the tribunals, the theatre, the arts ... become visible ideals to raise, purge, and ennoble the public sentiment.' *Civilization in the United States*, Boston, 1888, 106.

are innumerable, the State Department and the large foundations naturally leading in their instigation of travel. You have just been appointed to a new and important post; should you not like to leave it and see how others go at the same task? Or, alternatively, do you wish to lecture in Rome, to observe the educational system of Baluchistan, to confer with a select group of your peers in Karachi, to learn new methods of wool-gathering in New Zealand? All you need is a modest reputation and a little persistence. To be sure, you must have faith in your ability to accomplish something in three days or three weeks, or else an intense desire to interrupt for three years whatever you are accomplishing where you are. In either case, the opportunities of release by 'exchange' are today nearly as good as in a war.

The consequences are important for the substance of thought as well as for the persons involved. Intellectual co-operation, so called, was invented after the First World War to help prevent its recurrence by establishing bonds between the leading minds of Europe. Meetings face to face were to add the warmth of friendship. But it was clear from the start that the inevitably official character of the meetings reduced their intellectual contents to platitude; and the friendships that sprang up did not stop a second war. In the present or Unesco period of the same futilities, the stress has shifted from unspecified Intellect to art and science. The scientific congresses are, of course, older than the two wars, and when genuine and well planned they produce on balance more good than harm, as they did in the nineteenth century. It is the contemporary treatment of art at government and foundation expense that is new and suggestive. Art is now an instrument of national policy in the ideological war. Though the Russians launched a durable satellite before us, we retaliated with the pianistic prowess of Mr. Van Cliburn. When South America is disaffected, we send Mr. Lincoln Kirstein's (North) American Ballet to quiet public feeling. Mr. Benny Goodman, who goes everywhere, is described as an 'ambassador of the clarinet,' and one reads that the Latin-American tour of the New York Philharmonic Orchestra in 1958 was 'a momentous journey,' one of its concerts being 'history-making.' The authors of this 'exchange' hyperbole and those whom it represents as national heroes are so sure of their virtue that they do not balk at the language of charlatanism.

In contrary motion, the Old Vic Theatre and ballet come to convince us that England is still great; the Comédie française and M. Jean Vilar imply that France still lives, and the visits of Mr. Oistrakh or the Bolshoi Ballet prove that Russia is (as the phrase goes) people. The artists innocently enjoy this acclaim and that is unquestionably the best part of the whole affair. But the hardening error in the minds of the public and the administrators of exchange is deplorable. The assumptions are: that if this art for export is applauded, our country is great; that if the foreign audience applauds, it loves us; that if we are loved we shall not be attacked; and finally, that if art can achieve this when treaties and alliances fail, it is the greatest force in the world, and *therefore* deserves our support. A leaflet before me, soliciting funds to encourage music, states as if it were a truism: 'The importance of music in the world today must be heavily underscored, for it is the most universal language we have for creating understanding and friendship among peoples and nations, and in consequence of this fact it is one of the powerful influences for world peace, as was brought out during the recent United Nations Day.'[2]

Unfortunately, I see also that the People-to-People Sports Committee argues that sports are an obvious 'influence for goodwill in a troubled world,'[3] and it must be granted that the language of sports is even more inarticulate and universal than that of music—unless it be the language of square-dancing, which Mr. Rickey Holden declares 'cuts through the language barrier, almost through cultural barriers, and communicates directly from people to people and from heart to heart.'[4] The descent from world conferences through subsidized art to the wordless communion of hockey and dancing suggests the next step, which is sexual congress. It is not new and needs no subsidy, but it shows—since it is an ancient people-to-people device—that world peace is not to be attained even by ecstatic effusions of good will. One might accept that failure if in the meantime the motives for travel and correspondence with foreign scholars, for seeing a play or a ballet, for supporting an orchestra or sending a student abroad, had not all been denatured by bad reasoning. When in the realm of the voluntary everything is done for the wrong reason, with irrelevant motives and illusory hopes, none of the ordinary benefits can accrue, and none of the extraordinary ones either.

That this grand misprision should stem from the anti-intellectualism of philanthropy is not to be wondered at, for the fault in both is sentimentality, that is, the failure to sustain a feeling by its appropriate idea. A foundation only expresses with large means the charitable urge of private persons. And they, lacking the support of a tradition for intellectual giving, follow such habits as they have acquired in other occupations. They give to what they love or approve, and would be quite surprised to be told that this is as wrong as the nepotism they would scorn to commit. They are 'for' peace or 'for' science, or they 'believe in' foreign exchanges or the small liberal arts college or mass psychiatry, and so they indulge these illicit passions when they ought to be considering what it is that the country (or the art, the institution, the person) requires of them—of their thought and of their purse.

This is not to cast blame on these amateur givers as individuals but only to point out what effects follow a culture's losing all knowledge of the nature and conditions of intellectual life. The conditions are even more important to know than the nature of the innumerable arts and sciences that make up the whole. A society that understood the conditions and maintained them could reap the products without worrying about what took place in between. Our mania for fiddling with processes and qualifications and neglecting plain prerequisites is seen in the attempt to produce art by mass procurement—establishing a program at an institution, or offering fellowships to applicants, with the hope that 'in a ten-year period' some works shall be produced.* All this generates is paper work, commit-

*The contract for one such piece of procurement, which incidentally turned out very successful, stipulated that the party of the second part, or recipient of the regional award, 'produce an opera in at least two acts and of the level and quality that prevails at the Metropolitan Opera of New York.'

tees, and quantities of respectably unimportant work. There are only two ways in which to go about adding to the stock of great art: make an outright gift to a proved master, young or old, without project-forging and reference-hunting; or free an already active artistic center from commercial necessity, again without strings, promises, *or hopes*.

These two ways, unfortunately, require excellence of judgment and the willingness to use it. We are betrayed by our cultivated inability to know and choose men and ideas at a glance, the way the jewel expert knows a diamond. Such men exist—the teachers or colleagues of those from whom we may expect good work. It follows that we could reduce enormously the waste of time and effort by giving, not a fellowship or grant directly to the applicant, but to an instructor or sponsor the privilege of awarding it. The list of awarders' names, changing from year to year, would not be hard to compile. The best men would most frequently receive the right to nominate, would draw the best students, would know in any year who among them deserved the prize. The objection to this can be foreseen: the scheme would make for partiality and jealousy. Quite so. But that partiality, of one fine mind for another, is what is meant by an intellectual tradition. As for jealousy, it is a regrettable fault, but we cannot abolish it by tactfulness, and we shall never have excellence unless we are willing to distinguish it in public from mediocrity.

Instead of this direct judgment, fallible but apt, we rely on what we like to think is a more democratic choice, because it is made by a committee from among unlimited applications. In fact, democracy is foiled by the inevitable 'preliminary screening,' done by some trusted assistant, who necessarily works by rule of thumb upon the external appearances of the record. In a short time, every alert applicant knows the 'line' to take for success in the first stage as well as for the later interview. By this as by other roads, our young intellect is brought to see his career as a subdivision of public relations. One might indeed generalize and say that wherever the style and procedure cost large sums, Intellect is submerged and judgment warped to advertisers' standards.

The money of philanthropy should smell of its object, not its origin; which does not mean being Puritanical about its use. The intellectual life is expensive and it deserves solid comfort, but if due relations obtained, foundation offices would not look like the headquarters of a billion-dollar trust where the student's overcoat and hat seem a blemish, and where the long meditations of young executives are guarded by murmuring vestals trained to be kind to scholars. If minds were concentrated on the work, there would be fewer releases and reports, illustrated newsletters, and syrupy expositions of educational problems. The note of sensual competition would be absent, as would the tone of the middleman who, with a little co-operation from all parties, will make anything as pleasant and plausible as anything else—this month, next year, for you, for me, for basic research, for applied research, strongly with the current, sweetly provocative, a conservative man, a pioneer armed with precedents, emancipated in spirit, respectful of the *status quo,* against sin.

Philanthropy, in sum, is manipulation for the general good, anxiously contrived, timidly eager for approval, and therefore seeking love and publicity. The fact that by now every agency of Intellect without exception must praise itself in print in order to survive is no sign of commercialism in its leaders or in culture; greed is not the motive; the motive is fear of isolation through privilege, and especially fear of the appearance of privilege, coupled with profound distrust of its own judgment.

VIII

❧

Philanthropic Businessmen
and Bureaucrats

The latest class of givers of money, the business corporations, *
are naturally inured to the modes of advertising and deductible
expense. The soberness of Intellect is foreign to their ways, and the
present intellectual world with which these patrons are in touch has
done nothing to make any different style prevail, having none of its
own. The one clear gain has been, at long last, the recognition of
overhead costs. Otherwise, the closer contact between business and
seats of learning has not changed the fundamental predicament in
which Intellect has stood in its dealings with the foundations. It is
the predicament of having to ask, when the giver does not understand the reason and has not even enough mind to have faith.

The result is not only that every gift from business comes mixed

---

*How new these recruits are is fixed in my memory by a conversation I had
with a famous corporation lawyer on V-J Day. To my arguments showing
the logic and necessity of corporation gifts to educational, artistic, and scientific establishments, he opposed the law, the outcry of stockholders, and
the jealousies of directors with diverse allegiances. He predicted that capitalism would have to be overthrown before such gifts could be authorized.
This was less than fifteen years ago. Now all the largest corporations make
regular gifts for the general welfare.

with pity and envy, but also that the giver unconsciously tries to obtain something in exchange. He does not really give, he buys. On the surface there is in this nothing very wicked, it is 'very human.' Still, it is contrary to the right conditions of Intellect. Sometimes the giver wants the childish satisfaction of publicity—a name, a notice, another illustrated booklet. More often, he wants the pleasure of handing out the dole, of fussing around the beneficiaries, of appointing the holder of the chair, and even of rebaptizing subject matter. If the money is for fellowships, there must be many meetings with university officials, week-end interviews with the candidates and their wives, conferrings and telephonings and lunchings over every step, all this annually repeated. The students chosen, moreover, must be coddled separately from the rest, enjoy a special program of lectures, have a meeting room to themselves, and be progress-reported to the hilt. These requirements are not conscious criticisms of the institution's normal course; they are expressions of the maternal instinct, well known in philanthropists, and now becoming common in corporations. The tendency may also permit a retired man of business to do what he has always wanted and never had time for—mix with scholars and, while disclaiming any acquaintance with their work, tell them how it should be managed. It is diverting at any age to play school.

The influence of business philanthropy, coming at a time when large increases in college enrollments are expected, has coincided with the vogue of one or two new practices which have caught on so quickly that they and their 'philosophy' are now taken as part of the accepted system. One is borrowing to pay for one's education and the doctrine of need; another is crowding the premises and the doctrine of 'plant use'; a third is cost accounting and the doctrine of 'charge what education costs.' These are logical extensions of foundation practice and they fit the conditions of Intellect no better and no worse. The notion of borrowing to 'invest' in one's education because it is sure to bring a return is the individual form of 'venture capital for social change'; that is, it holds true for the man who wants to rise socially and financially with the aid of a college or pro-

fessional degree.* But for the teacher, scholar, or scientist the investment to be made, if any, is properly society's, not his. Society needs
and wants to exploit his talent and this, if business analogies are in
order, is part of the country's natural resources. He will never be
paid in proportion to what he contributes; why should he saddle his
younger years with a debt which, when the estimated full cost of
education becomes the rule, will be in the neighborhood of forty
thousand dollars? Let him rather become a tennis star and find himself sought out by patrons who know how to value and pay for
uncommon ability.

With the generalizing of the loan policy has come the degradation of scholarships and fellowships to the level of another remedy
for poverty. The idea of an honor and prize awarded to merit is dis-
appearing, blanketed by the monumental forms to be filled in order
to prove need. For college students, the Parents' Confidential Statements[1] searches into the last recesses of family life and puts the
hoped-for award unmistakably in the category of relief. Superficially,
the device seems fair: parents who want to help their children will
not hesitate to grasp the opportunity, and all are treated alike by the
judicious reviewers of these pecuniary autobiographies. But the
requirements of Intellect, if indeed they are in anybody's mind, differ from the plan at innumerable points. If we remember, for example, how frequently talent is born into families with developed
intellectual interests, it is at once obvious that the children of such
families should be given a preference. Their 'need' is of a different
order from that of the ordinary good student. Besides, such families
are doubtless more prosperous than the average, they have more
expensive tastes, and they will want to send not one, but all their
children to college. And it should be to one of the best colleges.

Now, the head of a county hospital, or a full professor in a liberal

---

*The Census Bureau has compiled figures showing that whereas the lifetime
salary of a high school graduate is $165,000, that of a college graduate is
$268,000. Three years of college bring only $190,000, which suggests that
the value of the diploma by itself is $15,000. Dr. Paul C. Glick, quoted in
Money Manager, Union Central Life Insurance Company, April, 1958, 3.

arts college, or a museum curator, may have an income which on paper looks like munificence when compared with that of the clerk or artisan; it may even seem large to the young men who in our leading universities scan the applications for scholarships. A passable academic record being enough to satisfy these censors, what they are looking for is this average ability coupled with the impossibility of attending college without help. They too are sentimentalists and love to give the poor boy a chance without looking farther. Their philosophy will help swell the number of graduates fated in this vale of tears to earn $268,000, but it will do little to increase the quantity and quality of intellectual talent in the nation. It makes harder than it should be the path of the brilliant student whose father unluckily has a salary of ten thousand dollars.* The son is forced to waste his time on odd jobs for self-support which he ought to spend in study. This may be good practice for the time when, as a teacher, he will have to take the equivalent of a second full-time post in order to decently survive, but it is a poor economy for the country which at every commencement exercise pays him so many empty compliments. Meanwhile, the young man's family is restricted for a term of years in the wild indulgence of its intellectual tastes—it gives up buying books and records, attending the theater or traveling abroad—all this so that the sons and daughters can prepare for a profession in which they may earn ten thousand dollars at the end of twenty years. During those years, of course, they repay the large debt incurred to get there—their so-called 'investment.'

There is more to say about teachers' salaries and I shall return to them later. Here it is the confusions of the business outlook that I

---

*Academic families are by no means the only intellectual ones in the land, but they form a large group from which talent can be expected to spring. The salaries of the most prosperous among them are therefore indicative of the situation sketched above. According to the Higher Education Association, half of the college and university teachers in the country in 1957–58 received less than $6,015 a year, but full professors showed a median of $8,072, which means that the upper ranks of the profession, including its administrators, earned salaries automatically disqualifying them from scholarship aid.

want to pursue. England is a business civilization, the first industrial power and once the world's greatest banker; yet despite its diminished financial strength its subsidy of learning is through a council of professionals not responsible to bureaucrats, and none of this nonsense about 'investment' goes on. All students deemed of superior ability are put through the university at government expense. Scholarships are an honor and a full release from irrelevant drudgery. So clearly is it held an honor, that recently a well-known man of business who holds an important post in the Cabinet was deeply disappointed that his son failed to obtain an Oxford fellowship at the public (i.e., private) school he was attending. Had the award been made, the money would have been returned and the honor kept, an important milestone in the youth's nascent career. The three things—the award, the declining of the stipend, and the significance of the title—result from a tradition which means what it says when it praises Intellect.

It may be replied, 'The class system is behind it.' True, but the classes did not spring ready-made from the brain of Jove and sharing his ideas on scholarships. There was a time when the classes of Britain were savages who painted their chests blue, since when they have learned to understand the necessities of civilization, including those of intellectual work. The same can be done in this country, whose grand philanthropic ideas originated in the intellectual minds of Franklin, Jefferson, Hamilton, John Jay, and the Adamses. At the present time the business treatment of mind in this country is ridden by two notions detrimental to its own object: one is the common idea of charity, hospital and social work rehabilitation—what has come to be called welfare. By its light one very properly seeks out always the poorest, weakest, and worst. Hence the continual struggle of men of talent, who cannot help being the strongest and best. The second error comes from a misunderstanding of the term 'nonprofit.' Many directors of corporate foundations and some university trustees handle money for research and education not as if they were engaged in a nonprofit enterprise, but as if they were engaged in an enterprise that was failing to make a profit.

In other words, they do not see where the actual profit lies. It being intellectual, and they not, it is to them invisible. To be sure, they have begun, with the touching superstition of a primitive, to accept the necessity of fundamental research in science: it may lead to curing cancer as it did to atomic energy; but the large indirect and invisible benefits of maintaining intellectual activity these worthy men do not as yet recognize. When owing to a recent scarcity teachers' salaries began to go up, school boards and trustees groaned. They should have said 'At last!' proud of this vindication as they are of the American workman's high standard of living. When the expected flooding of the colleges with students was announced, they should have rejoiced again, seeing the chance to choose and fully support the finest intelligences in that bountiful supply. Instead, their worry seems to be that of the warden of a prison: 'Where'll we put them?'

In looking for an answer, the first thought that occurred to many was that we must have more 'facilities'—let us build colleges, and do it near home to reduce costs; let us use TV sets 'featuring master teachers.' Who could be found to do this teaching, either in the flesh or screened down to pygmy size, and what quality of work would result from this mass processing were tertiary questions. The industrial analogy of 'plant and personnel' overrode all other ideas, and it led to the further principle of 'efficient plant use,' that is, filling classrooms day and night, summer and winter, as if they housed machinery that could be tended in shifts. It is not so. Apart from laboratories, teaching premises are just roofs and windows, and quite useless without *particular* students and teachers, willing and able to work, fresh in disposition and calm in spirit. No atmosphere more fatal to teaching and learning can be conceived than the bustle of crowds coming in to occupy the warm seats of those going out. We have already had the dismal experience of the two-session high schools and of the late evening courses, the twelve-week summer sessions, and other assembly-line arrangements, including the quarter system. I favor acceleration, I am all for an end to dawdling and playing, but acceleration in matters of the mind must be internal, not physical; the aim must be intensity not speed. A college plant cannot be worked; it is the human animal wandering inside who must be. And to learn anything permanently he needs periods of intellectual loafing. Speed will come of its own accord if we have teachers good enough to teach the best students something in such a way that it stays taught. And these we cannot have if we continually dilute the quality by cheapening the conditions of work. If education were milk we should never imagine that we could increase the supply by adding water indefinitely.

It ought perhaps to be said again that the intrusion of business or industrial principles into educational problems is not an evil consciously plotted by the men in charge of foundation and corporate funds. Their latest ideas are, on the contrary, painstaking attempts to fill the void left vacant by the absence of an intellectual tradition. This tradition being weak or absent from the centers of learning themselves, there has been no proper indoctrination of the holders of money and consequently there can be no 'charge' leveled against them, no melodrama in which the philanthropic villain takes advantage of the innocent man of learning. And since the people at large share the same unspoken assumptions as businessmen, it is not surprising that when the national government comes to deal with intellectual matters it enforces with absolute confidence the judgments that any voter, lawyer, or factory owner would spontaneously make.

The government's great interest in thought and education dates from the last war and affects chiefly one branch: in 1957–58, the federal government's outlay for academic research was nearly half a billion dollars, of which 95 per cent went to science. But the relation between the state and Intellect is of course older and more complex than the doings of the last fifteen years, as is shown by the practices of tax exemption and tax deduction upon which the country now depends for the support of some indispensable institutions. At other points too, government impinges on Intellect, and a complete review of its conscious and reflex actions would include such things as post office rates for books and manuscripts, the laws of patent and copyright, the interpretation of all the income tax laws, the administration of the Selective Service Act, the distribution of all public moneys for education and research at home and intellectual propaganda abroad, the activities of all the departments of education, state and federal, and finally the fate of the attempts to establish a federal agency for the arts and other nonscientific works of the mind. Canada undertook such a review of its intellectual and artistic management some years ago,[2] and it makes two large volumes which I have not the means or competence to emulate. But I may be able to point out the relation of a few public facts about these matters to the domestic difficulties of Intellect.

The principle of federal support to institutions of learning and research has been that of procurement by contract. The existence of overhead costs was recognized for the first time, which is to the credit of the legislators, but in such a discriminatory way as to bring out the rooted popular conviction that intellectual beings eat less, want less, need less than down-to-earth mortals: shadowy creatures doing nebulous things, their overhead is in the clouds. This discrimination is measurable: overhead rates allowed by the government to universities, medical schools, and research centers range from 8 per cent to 65 per cent and form an average of 45 per cent. The overhead charged government by industry averages 124 per cent. The overhead charged by one government agency to another is 100 per cent. In one important series of contract negotiations, the government lawyer who was arguing the munificence of a 15 per cent overhead charge kept referring to it as 'your profit,' evidently convinced that the sum was a bonus that the institution would never have to spend. The scholars and scientists were already in being and their minds would be working *anyway*. The near-invisibility of the intellectual task and its product once again made it seem as if some sleight-of-hand were being practiced.

Though it is clearly impossible, the government expects to buy research and ideas in the same way as it buys soap and chairs. In this it shows ignorance of the respective ways in which men and money work. I have heard a legislator of great ability affirm that if we spent as much on medical research as we did on the atom bomb, we could 'lick cancer.' Yet all the money lavished on certain rockets did not make them go, and men are even more difficult to set off than rockets. They can be stimulated by rewards, but also paralyzed. They can be aided or hindered by conditions of work not related to material expense—aided, for example, by a clustering of talents like their own. But in the end, success comes only out of a happy conjunction of circumstances; it cannot be bought because they cannot be specified. Still, the procurement routine goes on, which means that at some point the object paid for must be shown to accord with the specifications. How this testing fits the products of mind is easily guessed: the paper work is enormous and its vocabulary remarkable. Since a government research grant is easiest to obtain when the project seems related to some practical aim already approved by an agency, the first requisite of a scientific project is 'relatedness.' 'X went to Washington but he didn't have relatedness, so they turned him down.' After a time, when the grantee has by his reports shown his honesty as a scientist, if not as a petitioner, the grant is continued though relatedness is allowed to lapse. Nothing could make plainer the original distrust, which is removed by better acquaintance with the person rather than the subject.

Duplicities of this sort are not new in government subsidizing. It is said that for decades, in states noted for their mosquitoes, the pure science of entomology has profited from annual grants for mosquito control. Subterfuge is perhaps inseparable from representative government. As Shaw pointed out, if the ordinary citizen knew that the Greenwich Observatory was being maintained out of his tax money, he would want it torn down. Modern peoples are beginning to learn that an observatory is useful for looking up into space, where they want to roam; but this leaves a great area beneath, where all sorts of desirable work goes on, of which the public will never see the relatedness.

The indifference of those who have no interest or opportunity to come close to the conditions of Intellect is of no moment if other men, better situated, have been educated out of their primitive responses. College graduates now fill our legislatures and civil service; if they act toward the national Intellect without recognizing that it is a subject as technical as treaty-making, they are betraying their trust. So far, this recognition has been sparse. It took twelve years of unhappy experience and of hard persuasion by a group of our leading scientists to get the appropriate bureau of the federal government to accept a set of reasonable principles for the drawing up of research contracts. Hardly had a Congressional Committee ratified the agreement when the same bureau changed its mind apropos of new appropriations, introduced unilateral changes in the bluebook (as it is called), and tried to saddle the scientific institutions with modes of cost accounting which would not only be ruinously expensive to attempt, but which would be meaningless if achieved. For example, measuring the space used in research as distinct from that used in teaching is an absurdity when one knows that researchers teach in their own laboratories, and that no self-respecting university accepts contract work that is useless for teaching. Seats of learning have their relatedness too. So one might as well ask for cost accounting by a tally of lobes of the brain used by their men in each of their activities.

Moreover, the production of new and important ideas is synonymous with the development of new talents, of new men. This means a necessary 'waste,' open-eyed and deliberately protracted. One must, for instance, give fellowships to a dozen men of first-rate ability, only one of whom will make a discovery and win the Nobel Prize. If the procurement were of chairs, it would be evident far sooner which should be disposed of. But the able men whom fortune does not favor have not on that account squandered the public funds; they are part of the apparatus of Intellect from which the discovery does in fact come. And not only as intellectual but as moral risks, they are at least on a par with the government suppliers of clothing or canned soups, whose traditional ways are gratuitously substituted for the ways of Intellect.*

That what is lacking is a tradition and not merely an explanation,

---

*Apropos of risks, one cannot wonder at the government's mismanagement of scientific and other talents, when one discovers the grounds on which patriotism and character are judged in certain agencies. Thus it has been held one of three main reasons for doubting a man's loyalty and emotional stability that when in college he took a course in anthropology.

appears from the unending difficulty of making clear the points at issue. They are simple enough, but desperately unfamiliar, since the doubter's experience contains nothing complementary to convince him from within. Just as one can give a foundation executive fifty descriptions and a thousand examples of humanistic research without making a crease in his cerebellum, so one can distinguish fundamental science from technology with hairline precision and leave government or corporation officials impressed but unaffected. The moment the air has ceased to vibrate their minds turn back toward familiar ideas like homing pigeons.

It is only fair to add that this lack of conceptual power, so palpable in dealings with the purveyors of earmarked money, is more and more a characteristic of the expert in any branch. It is as if specialization could not be proved genuine unless linked with an incapacity to understand things outside itself. The result for the whole realm of mind is that even in the presence of money, brains, and good will every departure from common ruts is extraordinarily difficult. When by luck and dint of pushing, someone manages to set in train a small innovation, everyone cries out at the bold, brave, heroic deed. The emotion, it would seem, is nowhere appropriate to the idea. And the exception to this generality that immediately occurs proves the rule. In one department, that of medical research, the ability of our lawgivers to imagine disease and death stimulates their conceptual powers and leads them to give with a free hand and without questions. Though it knows nothing of cardiology or bacterial genetics, year after year, Congress appropriates handsome sums for the best-publicized ills. In a recent budget, it allotted for medical research $21 million more than the Department of Health had asked for.[3] The headlines announced: 'Senators Falter in Economy Drive,' after which it seemed superfluous on their part to recommend 'increased attention to the evaluation of tranquilizers.' For the only disturbed parties in this transaction were the deans of medical schools, who could not find enough takers for the millions pressed into their hands, or enough laboratory space for the expensive decimation of rats.

This lavishness is not more agreeable to behold than the miserly suspicion and rationalized parsimony that prevail elsewhere in the philanthropic world. The senatorial generosity betrays the vulgar emotion of wanting to save one's skin at somebody else's cost. Yet in the absence of systematic criticism our legislators should not be blamed. Their education, being the same as other people's, never gave them the sense that one may lose one's life in trying to save it, and their constituents do not number any groups embattled for Intellect in the way other groups are militant for morality. Yet a lobby in behalf of Intellect is not so ridiculous as it sounds. It would not merely draw attention to disparities in appropriations for research; it would not merely assist in the drafting of such bills as the National Defense Education Act (Public Law 85-864), which means so well and is so unbelievably difficult to bend to its own intention. A lobby would set out to improve all the permanent relations between intellectual work and fiscal policy, beginning with the rules of the income tax bureau. There, if anywhere, is the image of our nonintellectuality. With only a few exceptions all the rules of accounting and deduction applied by the tax inspectors are framed to suit the man of business. If he buys a dictionary to help his stenographer to spell, that is part of his office expense; but if, say, the historian of the Navy, Samuel Eliot Morison, buys a work of scholarship or reference, that is idle luxury, nondeductible except by an absurd guess at the annual depreciation of all his books. If the businessman goes to a convention, it is obviously to do business and the double martinis are deductible; if Mr. Morison attends the austere gatherings of the American Historical Association, he does so out of riotous self-indulgence and before he can deduct his outlay he must prove that failure to attend would mean dismissal by his company, Harvard University.

Before permission was given by the income tax bureau to spread book royalties over three years, long parleys took place between the Authors' Guild and the Treasury Department. And even now the application of the principle is beset with harassment: persons have been asked to produce notes showing that they actually began writing a textbook three years before it appeared, instead of three weeks as the tax inspector preferred to think.

It is said that in Rydal Mount, where Wordsworth lived, the peasants speculated among themselves whether the poet's son would carry on the business of poetry when the old man died. That is the natural assumption of the farmer, trader, or manufacturer. Every one of them toils with the hope of leaving his heirs a morsel of substance—everyone but the man of intellect. Even when he is successful and his products are in demand, the community limits him and his heirs in the fruition. The framers of the Constitution believed themselves enlightened when they granted Congress power in Article I, Section 8 'To promote the Progress of Science and useful Arts, by securing for limited times to Authors and Inventors the exclusive Right to their respective Writings and Discoveries.' And it is true that industrial technology treats the modern inventor fairly well. Large machines have made thievish entrepreneurs obsolete. But the authors of 'science,' by which the Founding Fathers meant all knowledge, continue to be taken advantage of by the uncaring public. Copyright with us extends some fifty years from the date of first publication, which means that it may lapse within the author's lifetime. Even on his last works it extends no great distance into the lives of his descendants. If Herman Melville had had a grandson, the rediscovery and glorification of the grandfather's works, in print and on the screen, during the last thirty years would not have brought the descendant one penny.

By way of compensation, we writers take comfort in the thought that printers, binders, and papermakers have been fully protected. Until very recently, works by American authors were denied international copyright because this country required books in the English language to be manufactured in this country before it granted American copyright. We thus harmed British authors and were indifferent to our own. After all, one book is much like another—we may not say this, but that is how we act, slaves to our habit and our secret wish.

· · ·

So subtle and so strong is that secret wish, the wish to disown Intellect and have it out of the way, that one can detect the feeling in intellectuals themselves. Certainly theirs is the strongest resistance to concerted action for their intellectual interests. It is as if they longed to be anything but what they are. In the many negotiations to revise the Copyright Act, academic men and librarians—that is, the very trustees of intellectual work—were often more hostile to professional writers than were the lawyers and politicians. It would be foolish to expect unanimity from any group, yet it might be thought that certain public events would present such a clear and present danger to the pocketbook that only one opinion could prevail, in which case a huddle of sheep could for once make a noise like a pride of lions. One such act is the suppression of books for other causes than obscenity, obscenity being a legal and moral issue of great intricacy and which cannot be settled in the abstract. But when some months ago *Huckleberry Finn* was dropped from library lists by the New York board of education as likely to aggravate race prejudice, only two letters of protest appeared in the *Times*. The great hive of intellect which is New York buzzed on without notice. This was criminal negligence. A blacklist of books, especially one that interprets liberal feeling so stupidly, should cause such an uproar that the board of education would remember it anxiously for a period of years.

The second type of public occurrence which the friends and practitioners of the intellectual life should take note of is that in which their kind of work is judged by implication and in practical terms, as when a foundation's annual report comes out, showing millions given for science and social science and thousands for the humanities. Instead of bewailing their Cinderella state and trying to prove that they too, like the physical and social sciences, are curative and remedial—music bringing world peace and Sanskrit rounding off the well-rounded man—the humanists should use their wits to show that they exist to make life livable on a rugged planet by satisfying desires implanted in the hearts of the majority of men, though cultivable in relatively few: the impulse to art and religion, the love of color and shape, song and storytelling, the curiosity about whence we come and why we are here. This established, it should be easy to show how the academic humanities serve the arts, philosophy, and religion by bringing order into the heritage of civilization.

One barrier to such collective demonstrations is the timidity of those whose duty it should be to organize them. They are critics on the hearth but not on the marketplace. It took virtual starvation and collapse by overwork before the teachers in the lower schools banded together, here and there, to remind the community that they lived in the same economy of soaring prices and needed the same amounts of rest and recreation. And such protests for immediate needs do not go far toward initiating even a beginning of change in the public view of money for Intellect. Only one man, to my knowledge, has addressed himself to an actual fragment of the question. This is Mr. Beardsley Ruml, who in a speech entitled 'Pay and the Professor,' made at the Bank Street College of Education on February 1, 1957, discussed the use of money in higher education, saying much in a few sharp words. One could disagree with him because what he said was crystal-clear, and alike free of jargon and unctuousness. Starting from a comparative survey of wages and professions, he first assumed that the average salaries of college teachers should amount to fifteen thousand dollars a year and the top salaries to thirty thousand. He then asserted that we waste what we do spend by being miserly: to recruit enough teachers of high quality is 'completely out of the question at present pay scales or at anything like them.' This means that we recruit largely from the unfit. As in eighteenth-century Spain, bad schools in large numbers produce an intellectual proletariat which becomes the teaching profession. The exceptions cannot form the basis of a nationwide system. Other observers have noted that among us the most energetic minds nowadays are attracted by the paying professions—law, medicine, engineering—both because future material rewards are greater and because their intellectual discipline still remains more strenuous.

The high salaries Mr. Ruml proposed, he went on to say, should be given for merit—not seniority or other forms of endurance; and with a sure touch he defined merit in pedagogy as 'talent and effort applied in the arts and skills of liberal reading, writing, and instruction.' While behaving as a perfect guest within a college of education, Mr. Ruml managed to flash his torch on the worst cracks of the scholastic edifice. He spoke of re-creating, with the aid of a new salary scale, 'a faculty with a common purpose, dedicated to re-establishing a curriculum whose central purpose is the advancement and diffusion of knowledge and understanding in the liberal arts.' The money for this revigorated faculty would come from tuition fees, all of which would be spent on salaries. To make the pay adequate without enormously increasing tuition, he would raise the teacher-student ratio from the present one to ten to one to twenty, make use of the best lecturers to instruct large groups, and teach the rest in discussion classes of fifteen to twenty.

His observation is that colleges offer too many courses; the departments pull each its own way, wanting to act as small universities, destroying themselves financially together with the unity of the knowledge they once imparted. Mr. Ruml is right, and I would add that the tradition of Intellect is lost in the country in part because it no longer exists in the college. So long as we think it respectable in a college man or woman to say: 'I don't care for mathematics (or English, or philosophy),' so long will we have the cafeteria curriculum and a nonintellectual undergraduate body. But Mr. Ruml's reform will have to begin in the minds of a faculty determined to make the freshman year a systematic putting away of childish things.

Perhaps the new plans for admitting high school juniors into college or advancing seniors rapidly will help the transition to a new order. But it will need the additional push which can come only from the intellectual use of scholarship money. The total subsidy of the science student who is needed by his country suggests the need for a total subsidy of the intending teacher, whom his country needs no less. And there must be a brake on the competitive bidding for both students and teachers. In either guise the young scientist (and now the linguist, economist, sociologist) sits waiting for the most attractive offer and develops the unfortunate outlook of the project promoter. Moving talent about does not increase its amount, nor do the rival bids improve the salary scale; it only introduces the star system with its usual evils. It is characteristically in a time of academic penury that we see the most lavish expenditures being made for pure prestige.*

The countries of the free world that are struggling with the difficulties of mass education and of a superior technical and intellectual education may find that they cannot support both a faculty and an ivied tower. The truly economic course would then be, not a cheaper faculty, but physical austerity; not turning the place into an all-night hotel with the feeling that this justifies keeping the place heated and lit, but returning to a modern form of the medieval university. The choice is not likely to be made, but we might nevertheless consider whether colleges and universities ought to continue providing students with expensive 'services' of a social kind. Academic advisers and rooms for conversation, yes; but why social and religious and medical advisers, why organized games and parties and extracurricular activities? These are excellent things in themselves, but why are they part of the responsibility of an institution Mr. Ruml rightly calls bankrupt and wants to put under a Receivership Committee?

Most citizens and most faculties are not ready to give an answer, which shows again how much adrift we all are about the seemingly simple act of spending money. But Mr. Ruml has an excellent remedy for this indecision: he says of his own proposals: 'Of course we will not call it a Receivership Committee. We will call it a Joint Committee on Educational Policy and Administration. And we will get a few thousand dollars from some foundation whether we need it or not, just to sanctify its work. This is strictly ethical since it does the foundation as much good as it does the liberal arts college, and it provides at once a responsible outside audience to which the

*For an exact survey and lively discussion of the present dislocation, see *The Academic Marketplace* by Theodore Caplow and Reece J. Magee, New York, 1958.

reports of the Committee, neatly typed and bound, can be addressed.'

It is evident how well qualified Mr. Ruml is to speak about money and the world of learning. His one difference from a regular insider and paid-up member of the guild is that he uses common words to express his original ideas. He gives the impression of having kept his mind's eye on the object of his thought and to be more interested in communicating that vision than in justifying his existence by ritual displays or pledges of virtue. In short we miss in him that touch of pedantry which in this century is the true people-to-people bond. Since it is also a by-product of learning, our next and last descriptive chapter must try to define and isolate this canker of contemporary thought.

IX

❧

The Language of Learning
and of Pedantry

The web of intellectual activities in modern civilization has its center in the enterprise of learning. Whoever engages in journalism or broadcasting, whoever buys or promotes art, whoever sells or publishes books, whoever works for the informative branches of business, industry, labor, or government, is a client, direct or indirect, of learning. The library and the university have become public institutions to which thousands have recourse who in earlier days could have carried on their work without facts, figures, or the latest conclusions of research. This new bookishness explains why so many of the deficiencies of Intellect have led us to inquire into the minds of scholars and the ways of universities, and also why the language of the learned matters as never before: it is no longer spoken only by its adepts but by anyone who takes it into his head to borrow and adapt it for his own use. In this ultimate opportunity to make all things work in all ways, the substance of knowledge is implicated and a common temper is produced which is both cause and effect in the discomfiture of Intellect I have retraced.

What is needed to complete the description, therefore, is a generalized notion of how we think, how we speak and write, how we go to work, when our purpose is to impart or discover knowledge. Let it be clear once more that our concern is not with intelligence but with Intellect, which is the form intelligence takes in the artificial products we call learning. As knowledge is to intelligence, so learning is to Intellect. Now if in the passage from intelligence to Intellect the faculty of thought is spoiled by some radical vice of form, it follows that the tradition of learning—a continuity of principles, habits, and beliefs—is also radically distorted. Having spoken of the intellectual weakness of our public opinion, of the intellectual evasions of our manners, of the intellectual failure of our educational practice, of the intellectual misuse of educational and research funds, I now turn to the weakness, the failure, the evasions, the misuse of the mind in intellectual work.

All those earlier shortcomings lend themselves to satire and often incite to laughter. Not so learning, because its decay cannot help being the sign of the decay of institutions; it marks the end of the culture. It is not the end of civilization, for if civilization has risen from the Stone Age, it can rise again from the Wastepaper Age; it is always a mistake to equate one's culture with culture itself. But one is entitled to private regrets; one can be selfish and resent seeing only the last frayed edge of the great tapestry. And it can be emotionally wearing to live at the tail end of the Middle Ages, vaguely hoping that some Renaissance men are in the womb of Time.

The simile is deliberate: we live in a kind of fifteenth century, rife with national wars and infatuated with the Dance of Death. And contemporary learning is passing through a period akin to the prolix scholasticism which for so long (and so unjustly) gave a bad name to medieval thought. Very likely, the joy the Renaissance humanists took in the classics of Greece and Rome was not—as is commonly taught—because the old texts satisfied a desire for pagan sensuality after an excess of Christian saintliness; it was probably something much simpler, namely, the relief at finding experience recorded with clarity after a long course of obscure and affected nonsense; it was sense regaining its rights over pedantry.

To define pedantry is not an easy thing to do. The meaning assigned should be neutral and fixed. But pedantry is relative to occasion. When it was forbidden as pedantic to quote Greek in the House of Commons, it was not forbidden to quote Latin. Today Latin would be as pedantic as Greek, though in a classics seminar both languages must be quoted, and can be, without taint of pedantry. The idea by which to test pedantry, then, is fitness—and fitness not only as regards time and place, but also as regards degree, quality, amount, or kind. Aristotle was warding off one sort of pedantry when he said that no subject should be treated with more precision than the purpose required. Should one want to know the average number of children in each American family, it would be pedantry to carry the count to five decimal places. The teller of an anecdote who interrupts himself to ascertain whether the event took place on the Tuesday or the Wednesday is a pedant—unless the day matters for an understanding of the point. In other words, it is intellectually right *not* to try to know or tell more than a subject contains of significance; or in still other words, knowledge is not an absolute homogeneous good, of which there cannot be enough. Beyond the last flutter of actual or possible significance, pedantry begins. Now think of the huge yearly mass of scholarly research and apply the tests of fitness and significance: clearly pedantry predominates; it is the sea around us.

Men having found, thanks to the efforts of scientists to discover and of historians to preserve or organize, that inquiry yields useful knowledge, search (or, as it is often truly called, *re*search) has become an institution, one of the most massive constituents of Intellect. The name of research has changed from a simple description to a term of honor, and the occupation itself has acquired an inherent sanctity; the quality of the work and its results are secondary. This is shown by the fantastic estimate placed upon research in our seats of learning. To do research is deemed nobler than to teach; the men whose names bring prestige to a university are those whose research has impressed others of equal 'research potential.'

For, I repeat, it is not deemed necessary to discover if only one 'produces,' production being defined as publication. To bring new and valuable knowledge by lecturing before fifty or a hundred students a year is not research, for it is not publication, except in the legal sense. But to print this knowledge in a periodical where only a few will peer at it with skepticism or dismay—that is to enlarge human horizons, to make the university shine with a new glory, and to justify an early promotion.

Since this reward and those linked with research grants (travel, secretarial help, and freedom from teaching) combine lucre with glory, it is not surprising that inside the university and on its industrial and other fringes the practice or pretense of research should have become a compulsion. Thousands of young men are at work on little papers; thousands more are racking their brains to think of an experiment or study. Most of them worry more about the acceptability of the subject in academic eyes than about their chances of doing and saying something useful, that is, few care about the fitness of the matter and none about the readability of the results. 'Communication' occurs by good luck, while everybody groans ritually at the bad writing, excessive length, and prevailing insignificance of what the journals print. In a word, this army of researchers by conviction or impressment are technically pedants.

But let us be careful. These men may also include the scholars and scientists whose results are original and great, and who add to knowledge while assuring its continuity and discipline. It is the cult and the needless stimulation of research that are pedantic and blamable, whether judged intellectually or economically. And indeed socially, the constraint to do research is blamable as an infringement on the free exercise of one's talents, which may be genuine though not allied to the temperament of the writer of monographs. It seems odd that a profession whose exercise requires the making of fine distinctions should fail to make one between significant knowledge and insignificant scribbling, while insisting pedantically on one restricted means of imparting newfound truth.

'Significance' itself requires apt and not pedantic interpretation. It does not mean that a searcher after truth should discard all findings for which he cannot at once see the use and meaning. Many discoveries have come from a later study of data amassed without a thesis. A great example is that of Tycho Brahe's observations of the planets, which enabled Kepler to enunciate the laws of orbital motion. Observation may precede hypothesis and be justified. Pedantry results rather from intellectual activity which lacks any intrinsic interest and cannot serve another's; which does not merely postpone, but disregards meaning, understanding, interpretation. The pedant is really not looking at the object, but going through the motions or technique he has learned. At bottom he is thinking about himself and the relation of his results to himself—'What a good boy am I!' Pedantry is affectation and pretense. The pedant uses knowledge to fashion himself a poultice against the world, to show off virtuosity, to remind himself and others of his industry and skill, and to ogle the reward for sitting in libraries when he might have been sitting in bars.

The general form of contemporary pedantry derives from natural science. It was about a hundred years ago that scientists began to wage war on philosophers and theologians with the aid of two words which were in fact claims to an exclusive righteousness. Those two words are: 'patient' and 'careful.' When science had justly risen to high estate, the idea that none but scientists exercised patience and care defined the pose of the man of learning. From equating science with the patient accumulation and careful verification of facts, we have come to believe that these props of scientific method suffice for attaining all desired knowledge. Fact-gathering is the one industry that knows no recession, and the stance and speech of science are everywhere imitated. Its serious, numerical look inspires worship and causes despair. Whenever subject matter precludes number, a special language, marked by abstraction and heroic detachment, must be devised to prove oneself justified in spirit and one's words worthy of credence.

Perhaps the most striking examples of this solemn imposture occur in the domain supposedly at the other extreme from science, the fine arts. Historically, painters' and sculptors' minds have most often been of a virginal innocence toward ideas. The ability to construct by hand visually expressive artifacts often goes with inarticulateness, or at least the power to body forth makes words unnecessary. What do we find today? That inspired by the general pedantry, modern painters compose around their work statements which they believe to be impressive and explanatory. In New York three years ago, an exhibition was held entitled 'Twelve Americans.' Here is one of the creeds printed in the catalogue: 'For me the challenge of painting lies implicit within the act—to penetrate inherited conceptual deposits and attempt the possible impingement of spirit, the personal image remains the enduring command of conscience.'[1]

Hardly science, you say. True, but full of the air of science. Note the geological flavor of 'deposits,' the pseudo-experimental suggestiveness of 'penetrate,' 'possible impingement,' and the psychological profundity of 'personal image.' Another of the twelve informs us that 'The very matter of painting—its pigment and spaces—is so resistant to the will, so disinclined to assert its plane and remain still [that] Painting seems like an impossibility, with only a sign now and then of its own light, which must be because of the narrow passage from a diagramming to that other state—a corporeality.'[2] Painting, we are to think, is an arduous technology. To conclude this small sampling, let us hear a sculptor's words: 'Forms that have a catalytic force growing from an ambiguous but strongly felt fountainhead in nature, frequently with double meanings and feelings, have a hold on me. This play of double meanings in sculpture is the plastic metaphor in operation. . . . Metaphors with varied suggestiveness pulling in several directions keep the experience open. The visceral excitement of suspense evidently forced me to seek formal organizations suggesting "process" as a never-ending mystery, a never-closing experience.'[3] This is making the best of both worlds of creation—science and poetry.

Of the Twelve Americans, only one—a woman—says anything intelligible. Perhaps the majority all have their tongues in their cheeks: it is hard to tell. But however this may be, it does not affect the evidence that the sophisticated public which pays a dollar to read these pronouncements comes to believe that this is the way to think importantly about art. Hence it would be a mistake to dismiss these lucubrations as negligible by saying that they are, after all, 'only a catalogue,' 'only a means to self-advertisement,' 'only a piece of propaganda.' Pictorial pidgin is a worldwide idiom, firmly established in all the capitals of art.

Just as character is gradually undone by every little fault of sloth, so Intellect deteriorates after every surrender to folly: unless we consciously resist, the nonsense does not pass by us but into us. Of this nearly every spoken word and morsel of print affords proof, for they reveal the clear determination of Western men to translate simple thought into supposedly science-born language. A single word gives us away, as when President Eisenhower said: 'Marshal Zhukov and I *operated* together very closely.'[4] Not *worked*—'operated.' Why 'operated'? Because it is loftier, more abstract, more suggestive of complex doings, more praiseworthy because more pretentious—one senses the patient and careful effort that goes into operating closely together. And when a plain, straightforward army man falls unknowingly into pretentiousness, one can gauge how powerful the cultural pressure is to be a pedant. More needs saying about the state of the common tongue; what follows is but the sequel to the demonstration of pedantry in the arts.

Musicians naturally differ as much among themselves as painters; but in musical 'explanations' as in pictorial, pedantic self-regard prevails. The fashion, indeed, was set by the Western world's leading musician, Stravinsky, who in his utterances since 1920 has projected the image of himself as an austere seeker, patient and careful, agroan at the exhausting task of finding the certified musical germ. Of his duo concertant, his boast was not: it is fine, it is beautiful, but: 'It is extremely thoroughly worked out.'* Stravinsky's juniors have fol-

---

* *'C'est extrêmement travaillé.'* Quoted in Joseph Szigeti's *With Strings Attached*, New York, 1947, 124–5.

lowed suit in pointing out through their program notes that their works are intricate and learned, replete with technique, foreseen and weighed in every detail, like successful suicide. The older composers, one infers, just threw black notes into a coffee grinder and turned the crank.

But it is perhaps in literature and literary criticism that we see pedantry most powerful and complacent. The coming of literature into the curriculum seventy-five years ago established the belief that poetry and fiction are for study. And not for study once, but again and again without limits. The purposes vary, though all aim at proving a result in the manner of science. Considering the recent history of literature, one is bound to admit that modern writers and their critics could scarcely avoid their bias toward pedantry. Coming at the end of a century of great originality, they were forced into habits of reminiscence. Everything had been said; it only remained to be 'worked out.' Echo and allusion assumed a new importance as symbol or wit and gave a new fillip to reading, now indistinguishable from research—except when poet or critic explained the allusions, as is now usual. From *The Wasteland* on we have had a tradition of footnote poetry and since *Ulysses* one of ciphers, *Finnegans Wake* being the longest and best-keyed example. That this is only one aspect of these works does not change the intellectual bent given to the minds of the beholders: no longer readers of literature but specialists in it, decoders, exegetes, *Gelehrte*—so close to pedants that only by being one of them can the imputation be avoided.

Nor does one have to fly high to encounter this atmosphere. The semi-intellectual genre of detective fiction, which also takes its rise from the interest in science, was not long in putting on trumpery ornaments drawn from scholarship. Those who recall the vogue of the novels of S. S. Van Dine in the thirties will remember the pseudo-erudition couched in footnotes with which he 'enlivened' his books. The author, a decently educated art critic, had rightly judged the contemporary mind: renitent to the solid food of apt information it will readily swallow anything false. Since Willard

Huntington Wright (alias Van Dine), we have had the tough school of detection; and there, too, pedantry flourishes in the minute description of clothing and furniture, in the verbal sparring by allusion, in the inserting of musical or other aesthetic dissertations into the rapid flow of alcohol and gore.

What have the critics been doing meanwhile? They have saved their place by catching the infection. Of all the critical schools, none has been more violently opposed to science and industry than the men known as the New Critics. Yet what is their 'method' but a verbal counterpart of scientific description and analysis? A New Critic considers a work of art a self-contained object which he means to dissect and appraise by reference to its structure. Though a trifle pompous in its suggestion of rubber gloves and sterile instruments, this is a tenable attitude for the critic provided he adopts it as needed, without system, and provided also that his talk about structure retains the character of an analogy: remove a structural member from a bridge, and the bridge will collapse; but important parts of poems, plays, and novels can be cut and still leave something to read—spoiled and fragmentary, no doubt, but still intelligible and interesting. Every stage production of Shakespeare and Wagner testifies to this. Far from recording this experience accurately, the New Critic draws out his metaphor about structure and arrives at judgments purely mechanical. He requires, for example, that every poet shall be a consecutive thinker, an ideologue in imagery, and shall rivet the parts of his vision together like a truss. This is known as 'systematization of imagery.'[5] By this standard it turns out that Shakespeare was a pretty poor engineer: his metaphors 'do not work out.' In consequence the critic cannot understand the hitherto intelligible speech from *Macbeth* which begins 'Tomorrow and tomorrow and tomorrow.' 'The connections between part and part in this speech are psychological, and looser than logical, though psychological will always include logical, and indeed, act as their matrix. And the point is that mere psychological connections are very good for dramatic, but not for metaphysical effects. Dramatically, this speech may be both natural and powerful; so I am told. Metaphysically it is nothing.'*[6]

From this we know how the critic's own image of himself works out: he is testing, applying a method (the phrase no longer shocks us) in order to find out what intuition and reflection fail to disclose. Once again, judgment is abandoned or disguised in favor of an objective gimmick. The point here has of course nothing to do with whether Shakespeare is approved or disapproved. The critical literature of approval is just as contrived.†

Antedating and sustaining all the 'scientific' schools of criticism, another makes it a business to tabulate and classify images, track down hidden themes, and discover myths and symbols. 'Patient and careful!' it seems to say, 'patient and careful does it. You always thought, mere reader, that *Moby Dick* was about a whale; that Melville was a sailor, fond and fearful of the sea and curious about whaling, who happened on a sea legend suggestive enough to re-express an ancient generality about man's will and man's fate. That is not so. Melville concealed his purpose from you and indeed from himself. For this we have found: *Moby* stands for Melville—an infant approximation of his own name when a child with childish fears. *Dick* in German means "thick"; he wanted to build a thick wall between the universe and himself. The whale is both the universe

---

*The critic is aware of the competition he is trying to meet with his 'systematization': the poetry, he says, which we 'dispose of . . . as romantic . . . does not pursue its object with much zeal and . . . it involves in a general disrepute all poets, the innocent as well as the guilty, by comparison with those importunate pursuers, the scientists . . . ' John Crowe Ransom, *The World's Body*, New York, 1938, 279.

†'To read this [Polixenes' first speech, *Winter's Tale*, I, ii] as no more than a conventional expression of royal gratitude is largely to miss the point of the whole utterance. The elaboration of the sentiment, such as it is, is of the same kind as that already discussed in Camillo's prose speech. It is perfectly deliberate, the result of a conscious poetic purpose engaged in creating a style suited to the ends it has proposed to itself. This style calls for a deliberate complexity, overlying the ease and freedom of the rhythmic structure, as a means of arriving at the elaborate pattern of interwoven images which imposes upon the action its subsistent unity.' Derek Traversi, *Shakespeare: The Last Phase*, New York, 1955, 109.

and the wall—wall-whale—and also wail, the cry of the frightened child-man, white with terror; hence white whale, that is, the projection of Melville's great fear, as we see again in *Whitejacket*, which for all its lightness is a self-portrait.'

This parody, for brevity, is still too concrete. The true affectation makes more out of less, as does science, legitimately, with *its* symbols, arbitrary assumptions, and constructs. A paper recently submitted to a literary quarterly but unpublished because too long, exemplifies the true scientific distance from fact. It tried to say—or rather, it attempted to demonstrate—that the central character in Faulkner's novels was Time. The people in the novels either came to terms with Time and thus were permitted to bloom as truly human types; or they refused to 'realize Time in their own persons' and after agonizing struggles Time destroyed them. This was declared to happen independently of Faulkner's will. Once the author had chosen Time as his central character, the lives of all the others conformed by logical necessity. Whoever denied or ignored this discovery was debarred from a knowledge of Faulkner. And if indeed criticism is a science the exclusion must be right.

The doubter's question, which applies as well to the painters' explanations of their work, is What do we know afterward that we did not know before? And how does it fit into the knowledge we carry about for use? It often seems as if in the critic's mind the operation, and his own part in it, mattered more than any namable result. A cry which still rings in my ears sums up the case. Discussing criticism with friends and some brilliant young men, the subject of D. H. Lawrence's *Studies in Classic American Literature* came up. Two of us praised the book and were met by violent objections, in so solemn a task as criticism, to the use of colloquialisms, snatches of verse, and apostrophes to the reader. We replied and won some grudging admissions; Lawrence was granted to be a sort of critic— and then came the cry from the youngest of the young men: 'But no *method*, don't you see, no *method*!'

• • •

The sway of 'method' did not overcome literature all at once. It filtered into it through the textual and historical criticism to which nineteenth-century science gave a strong impetus. But text and history, as twentieth-century critics complained, could not reach the heart of literature. Method finally reached it by way of the new psychology and social sciences, which now form with belles-lettres an indissoluble amalgam. The methods sometimes act modest and call themselves 'approaches'; actually, anthropology, psychoanalysis, and sociology miscegenate with criticism and with creation until at times the point of a given essay is as hard to discover as the meaning of particular sentences in it. There is accordingly no need for any transition from letters to the 'ologies'; one steps across the continuous crust of pedantry, aware that in the social sciences one will find appearances still more closely modeled on science.

The distinctive sign is, as everybody knows, the manufactured vocabulary. The history of the physical sciences shows that until the elements of experience are rightly conceived and distinctly named and defined, they cannot be truly measured and related. Hence the technical terms forged by each branch of science to isolate the unit, or substance, or function, or species, from those loosely named long ago in the vernacular. Air, earth, water, and fire give place to 'elements' which are clearer because simpler. The four humors vanish, once they are seen to be composed of subtler, yet stabler biological or chemical particles; and the mysterious qualities of objects are reduced to exact relations expressed in as few words and as many symbols as possible.

Of this superb work of the Intellect, scientism tries to carry over as much as it can into other subject matters. It begins bravely with technical words. Only call a common event by a new and abstract name and the work of Patient and Careful has begun. It prospers when you can abbreviate, symbolize, or assign numbers, and it reaches its goal when a generality can be framed. But how are the words of would-be science defined and applied? Here are the titles of published papers arranged in pairs to show how the language of natural science generates the language of social science by rhythmic correspondence; in each case the words of natural science come first:

1. Reaction of Aldehydes with Monosubstituted Malonic Acids
1*a*. Hostile Drive, Conflict, and the Recall of Hostile Material

2. Ultrasonic Propagation in Liquid Ammonia and in Liquid Ammonia Solutions of Sodium, Lithium, Sodium Bromide, and Sodium Iodide
2*a*. Environmental and Personality Determinants of Adolescent Boys' Evaluations of Rewarding, Neutral, and Punishing Power Figures

3. Ion-forming Equilibria of Triarylmethyl Chlorides in Liquid Sulfur Dioxide
3*a*. Conclusion-Drawing, Communicator-Credibility, and Anxiety as Factors in Opinion Change

Unless the layman has a fine ear he thinks one song is as good as the other. He accepts the equivalence between 'Liquid Ammonia Solutions' and 'Punishing Power Figures,' or between 'Ion-forming Equilibria' and 'Communicator-Credibility' or again between 'Aldehydes' and 'Hostile Drive.' The misfortune is that terms such as 'Hostile Drive' have a vaguer, not a more precise, meaning than the common names of the experiences to which they refer.*

---

*To particularize: is Hostile Drive an aggressive impulse at large, without clear purpose or selected victim; or is it a deliberate desire for revenge against a particular person, whether rightly or wrongly seen as an enemy? Is it sudden and spontaneous or brooded over? Or is it perhaps violence directed against another for an end to be gained, rather than to cause hurt? And how is Hostile Drive measured—by intensity or by effect, both necessarily expressed in words and defying the touch of number?

Passing in this way from one kind of name to another not only encourages the verbalist in his hopes of achieving science, but by virtue of tables, graphs, and abstract prose in the conclusion, he is also confirmed in the belief that the vague entity to which he gave a generic name does exist as a thing. Soon he sees all of life—all persons and their doings—at once vaguely and generically. In the end, by diffusion through newspapers and other print, the air of common day is colored and thickened by the presence of these supposed entities. The common man soon acquires a vocabulary in excess of his needs, thanks to which he is never at a loss for the wrong word. But meantime he has lost the habit of testing words and ideas by experience and is content to combine them like terms in algebra, without reference to the actual. To adhere to my rule and take only examples of the best, I quote, not simply in illustration but also in support of my views, passages from a still unpublished document which embodies the thought of several leaders of social science, men whose integrity and intelligence are above question. Their words are especially apposite because written to explain and justify the use of a 'laboratory of social science.' One passage describes 'social diagnosis':

'Case material was available on families who had been investigated prior to the depression. The students were asked to predict how these families would react to the economic and social emergencies of the depression. Actually, material was also available as to what happened to the families after 1930. The confrontation of diagnosis with actual data was especially instructive; it is somewhat similar to the use of autopsies in medical training. Obviously such material can be provided in many fields. Good use was made, for example, of case studies where the political history of individuals was well-documented; a diagnosis was made as to how they would behave in the next election and again the diagnosis was confronted with actual information originally withheld from the student. Precisely because this permits a subsequent review and comparison of expectation with actuality, it serves to sharpen the interpretive skills of students. These trial-analyses of sets of data may yield a valuable research design at the very time that they are being used as a means for instruction.'

The questions to be asked about even so small a part of the enterprise are many and not easy to compress. But take the analogy with medical autopsies. The comparison is dubious because in social affairs 'what happened to the families after 1930' and what was predicted about their 'reactions to depression' are both extremely vague notions, quite unlike a diagnosis of cirrhosis of the liver based upon the unmistakable appearance of that organ. That we have here a bare approximation is virtually admitted by the writers when they say that these 'experiments' serve 'to sharpen the interpretive skills of students.' A method that *was* a method would not call for the caution also voiced in this document that 'perceptiveness or ingenuity is a precious asset for the field worker.' Nor would this professional, suddenly in the same boat as the mere 'insightful observer,' have to be warned in these terms: 'To an increasing degree, social scientists have come to recognize that, whatever their merits and their indispensability for obtaining data about large numbers of people, the standardized quantitative procedures (involving questionnaires, interview schedules, etc.) have become too nearly the exclusive resource of the social science field worker. It is widely felt that these procedures need to be supplemented and extended . . . by a program which aims to develop skills in the less formalized procedures for collecting qualitative field data. . . . The student is brought to see that behind each significant statement . . . there lies a problem, more often implied than stated.'

This discovery comes a little late, when enormous harm has been done by heedless scientism to language, first, and through it to everyone's mind. And though the writers themselves declare that their purpose is to *'curb the inadvertent tendency for a new barbarism in social science,'** their sentences seem framed as if to show the fault they have in mind. Consider this statement purporting to

---

*Italics in the original.

express one connection of thought to reality: 'The actual workaday experience of professional practitioners of social research in government, business, industry, labor, and welfare organizations provides a storehouse of raw materials which can be drawn upon for the preparation of training documents.' Superficially, nothing is wrong. But Intellect is by habit analytic, so let us analyze: workaday experience, we are told, 'provides a storehouse'—one does not quite see how the flux of life can be an organized depot; it is a 'storehouse of raw materials'—materials in what sense? And why 'raw,' if we are to take experience and storehouses as implying organization? These materials can then be drawn on 'for the preparation of training documents.' But to an historian the sense of document is destroyed by the idea of preparation, and by now the relation between whatever is thus made to the original 'workaday experience' by way of the storehouse seems remote indeed. The meaning probably is: 'In teaching students we take cases from life.' But then what has become of our precious aura of science?

A little farther on one reads that the social scientist must 'know how to apply procedures for discriminating between valid causal relations and spurious causal relations.' What is meant of course is 'discriminating between relations that are causal and those that are not.' But how can one trust a scientific worker who allows himself to speak of 'spurious causal relations'? In his science no fundamental laws or mathematical formulas exist to set him straight: the success of his effort depends *wholly* on his ability to name things accurately and to sort his thoughts with precision.

Remember also that he is debarred from physical experiment and that his 'raw materials' are the unstudied answers of ordinary people to questions probably worded in his habitual idiom. These answers will be similarly loose, as a result of contagion from the newspaper or of individual creativity on the same pattern. The science thus works by palimpsest—layer upon layer of jargon, offered and taken in different senses and rarely examined. By dint of referring to 'punishing power figures' for both the infant's image of the father and the grown man's dyspeptic office manager; to 'the interpersonal resentment factor' for both an old grudge and the trivial friction of daily life, we have taught people the art of—let us be pedantic too—*reifying and obnubilating*: making objects out of the intangible and using words to becloud the real.*

At several places in these chapters, I have suggested that language was both a symptom and a cause in the present debility of Intellect. This goes against the current inclination to suppose that 'mere words' should not distract the thoughtful from their contemplation of art or science, whose true essence will surely in the end speak for itself. The example of social science shows how fallacious is this belief that protracted, co-ordinated thought—Intellect—can subsist without a clear medium, whether verbal, numerical, or (as in the arts) material. The practical work of words in politics, diplomacy, and the law is enough to remind anyone that words are not simply the casual containers and carriers of thoughts and feelings, but their incarnation. Change the words and you change the law. But words by their choice and disposition also exert a subtler influence directly upon the mind, as we acknowledge in the respect we pay to poetry and fiction. And this being so, it cannot but follow that the state of the language, its direction toward or away from art, science, religion, or Intellect, changes the very feel and taste of life.

A study of language that would relate the types of expression favored at a given time to prevailing emotions and habits of mind

---

*Occasionally a man of affairs cuts through the cloud. Testifying in an appeal by the Union Pacific Railroad on the issue of corporate gifts, Mr. Roland Harriman was asked: 'Was there, postwar, in your thinking, a degradation in the individual concept of responsibility toward charitable or educational or public welfare contributions?

'A. A "degradation," did you say?

'Q. Yes.

'A. In other words, did individuals give less?'

(Superior Court of Utah, No. 8762, August, 1958.)

would tell us as much about a people as its architecture and pot-sherds. The difficulty is that these emotional nuances can only be caught or conjectured by the contemporaries, which would perhaps justify the present small-scale attempt, even if it were not required by the central place of language in the work of Intellect.

The observer's first impression of modern speech in any Western language is that never has the urge been so strong to magnify trivial events through terminology. The taxi driver says that he is behind time because 'the filling-up process was slow.' The shop-keeper explains that he stays open late because five to seven is 'a major belt of selling hours.' The dentist does not enjoin the patient to brush his teeth regularly but tries to 'enlist him in a clean-mouth program.' Now the motive of this grandiloquence is wrapped up in its effect, which is: depersonalization, the sub-merging of the individual by his own wish to be important vicari-ously and not in himself—which would be undemocratic. This 'major belt of selling hours' acquires the potency which used to reside in the merchant and his wares. The negligible relation of Tom the taxi driver to Joe the garageman is transfigured in the impersonal majesty of the filling-up process; while the pedantic abstraction of the clean-mouth program absolves the dentist from being authoritarian.

But there is more. These phrases and the thousands with which workaday affairs go on in every department of life have the two properties of being static and inclusive. They deny the doer and replace him by an activity, a process (a favorite word), which is there-fore unchanging, eternal, and which also gives the user the sense of being 'scientific' through 'covering' the events by abstraction. Thus 'process' and 'program' in the examples above include numerous small acts which 'getting gas' and 'brushing teeth' seem to leave out. In each a verb is dropped and a noun substituted, as in the strik-ing instance visible on post office storage boxes: 'Not for deposit of mail.'

This small shift from one part of speech to another has important consequences for thought. First, the language is overrun by a plague of nouns, most of them ending in 'ion,' with the result that formal writing (reports, public speaking, scholarship, even fiction) becomes a string of nouns weakly tied together by prepositions and connective phrases of the type 'as far as . . . is concerned' and 'in terms of.' This sort of writing, easy to write and dull to read, is the surest protection against the critical analysis of thought. It sounds as if its meaning were not only lucid but important, for example: 'This is undertaken in the context of comprehensive patient care and includes theory and supervised practice related to the assumption of a leadership role.' Who is doing what? No one; nothing. This part of a nurse's training has been lifted from the world of bedpans and wrinkled sheets to the abode where the eternal abstractions are.

A curious by-product of this deep desire to escape triviality and criticism at the same time is the disappearance of 'the.' In English, the omission of the definite article betokens generality ('Man is a featherless biped'). The article is now being omitted in places where it idiomatically belongs to show (the) relation of parts: 'Not for [the] deposit of mail'—as if all prose should resemble signs and captions—and also where the idea calls for the mark of definiteness. Thus: 'Appointment of Mr. Jones was announced last night'; or, after (the) re-emergence of two British diplomats in Moscow: 'Appearance of the two men was first, etc.'; and even: 'Board member declared at a press conference. . . . ' It is no clear intellectual or other purpose that is present in the writers' minds, but certainly a sense of generality, a brisk dismissal of the idea that anything can be unique and non-repeating, in short, the indirect suggestion of one more 'process.'

The same tendency produces the familiar noun-cluster in which, through loss of articulation, no distinction of persons and acts remains; whatever happens gets itself done, anonymously—a kind of intellectual automation: 'Since page make-up for press lock-up is now in process, further additions increasing lineage are not possible now, entirely aside from the obvious necessity of screening *Who's Who* with national reference applicability in mind, and as well the fact that every inch conserved—without affecting its coverage of data of national interest—is a gain in our efforts to keep the size of *Who's Who* within reference-shelf limitations.' The writer relented only once, at the place where he could have coagulated his still articulate thought into: 'national interest data coverage.' But the rest succeeds in giving an impression of breathless haste amid irresistible forces which earlier styles of business English could not attain.

That this *is* business English can be easily verified by reading one's unsealed mail.* Its likeness to academic and scientific pedantry will at once appear, and the thought may arise that what we find is not a style but a fault of style, commonly called jargon. This is inexact. Jargon is the special vocabulary of a trade or art. The terms are fixed and they exist because none other will do. The language which modern pedantry devises is an imitation of jargon, a pseudo-jargon, in which the terms are not fixed and not necessary. It is this very latitude which is wanted in order to achieve the mixed, in fact the contradictory, purposes in view. The promoter's effort is to make his idea appear fresh and young, and also wise and rooted in physical things; the democrat's desire is to dignify and yet stay unobjectionable. These quasi-technical noun-clusters serve all these purposes while imparting an air of intellectual hospitality tempered by delicacy, a genteel worldliness. And if pseudo-jargon were not easy to improvise and distort, it would fail to convey the last pair of opposite feelings we detect in it, those of speciality combined with mass approval: 'For full modern home living enjoyment let us accessorize you expertly from cellar to garret, as hundreds of our customers have approvedly done.'

---

*From a firm of Design Associates: 'Capable operations personnel are done an injustice when expected to compromise operational requirements to planning, design, or development criterion [*sic*].'

At this point the consumer of these hints may decide to ascribe pseudo-jargon to the creativity of advertising, as he was tempted to do before in reading the painters' creeds and confessions. Advertising is a good scapegoat, and it is true that it helped to popularize the strain. But this truth leaves several puzzles: why was the style adopted, for other uses than the selling of goods, by intellectuals generally hostile to commerce? Nowadays, preachers *and* politicians, educators *and* industrialists use this language in their conversation, business correspondence, daily work, and—for all I know—in their love letters.

The desire to be free of fixed meanings occurs in other forms, and again for purposes unrelated to advertising or politics. Advertisers' copy is generally written by talented people who do not flout grammar and misuse words. It is the educated citizen, the journalist, the teacher, the housewife with a college degree, who nowadays distort the meaning of words, common and uncommon, in a manner that makes Mrs. Malaprop seem one of them. This is not hyperbole. An attentive ear will collect abundant evidence of usages that are neither slips of the tongue nor isolated personal peculiarities, but the result, rather, of a new kind of self-indulgence, half ignorant, half willful. A distinguished sociologist speaks in public of his current work and asserts that it will lead to an 'actionable statement.' Some in his audience already visualize him in the dock and paying damages when it appears from his later remarks that all he means is a statement which will specify suitable action. Daily in newspapers and literary journals one finds 'cohort' used to mean partner or companion, the original member of the pair being, one supposes, the hort. A leader among linguists writes that it is 'presumptive' for anyone to publish a grammar 'in total disregard of modern linguistic study.' And an instructor in radio and television at a large university refers to his colleagues, the commentators, as appealing to the public 'directly, personally, and repetitiously.' Indeed, it is rare these days to read or hear three sentences together without a gross impropriety of terms.* When sense cannot be twisted, form is. One reads of self-indulge*ment*, of element*al* instruction, of a panel discuss*ant*; of a prim*al* dwelling-place—denoting not a cave or a hut, but simply the first house in which a restaurateur established himself.

The license extends to idiom, sometimes with serious confusion, since idioms are often closer in form than in meaning. 'Agree to' differs from 'agree with,' just as 'differ with' differs from 'differ from'—and thus for dozens of similar pairs whose forms are set like a proverb's. The bishop who remarked that 'they will be forced to eat humble crow,'[7] may have said, 'They will be forced to eat humble pie' and been misquoted; but the journalist, who dimly remembered 'eating crow' and thought it not humiliating enough, would probably argue that words belong to everybody and that for most purposes their 'drift' suffices. As in art, communion is sought, rather than a clear message. Explicitness is resented as small-minded and rigor as an affectation of superiority. By this twist in cultural standards it is the plain speaker, the man who wants the shortest and easiest way to his own and others' meaning, who appears as pedantic, while the users of pretentious mouth-filling phrases esteem themselves the friends of democratic light and simplicity. It was not long ago that an anxious correspondence was published in

---

*For example: From the wife of a publisher: *mixgivings*. From a college girl: 'I am in the *throngs* of packing.' From the editor of a musical journal: 'After 8.30 they began to *strangle in* [repeated twice].' From the director of an arts center: 'You can't get them to step up on the *roster*.' From a physician: 'Sports are not *indigenous* to my life.' From the Congressional hearings of Mr. Bernard Golfine upon his gifts to Mr. Sherman Adams: 'Counsel is trying to *delineate* between those that might have been used for the purposes that are admitted here and . . . ' From an editorial in the *Journal of the American Medical Association* (November 18, 1950): ' . . . the medical profession stands with the rest of the nation to play its *inseparable* role in helping to guide one's country's destiny.' From the *New York Times*: 'Some students are *repulsed* by the thought of going into debt . . . Five thefts in 121 years do not make for *vulnerability*, after all.' From a novel published by a firm which is proud of its stylebook and copy editing: 'He now writhed in a positive *plethora* of confusion. . . . A good point on the face of it but not *infallible*.'

the *New York Times* about the need to invent a new word to signify one-third of a year. A San Francisco businessman started the inquiry, a librarian took it up, then schoolteachers, doctors, and the unprofessional citizenry. Half a dozen learned vocables were made up and proposed, of which the favorite was *quadrimester*.[8] No one thought of saying simply 'a third' as we say 'a quarter': 'In the first third, prices rose.' This would have been too obvious, patently untechnical, and especially not long enough.* Idiomatic uses of common words smack of the street, not the study, and to learn or recognize them gives one no sense of distinction. There is, besides, a vague suspicion that idioms are the mark of the uneducated. For example, apropos of a boxing referee, a newspaper enlightens its readers: 'Long ago Harry embalmed the time honored "May the best man win." With him it's "May the arm of the worthier partici- pant be elevated in token of victory." Harry drew favorable com- ments from English purists who commended his short form "May the better boxer emerge victorious." This is superior, they said, to the usual, but ungrammatical "May the best man win."'[9] We need an O. Henry or a Ring Lardner to write for us 'The Pedant of Madison Square Garden.'

Reflecting on these typical facts, not by themselves but as a part of the culture of industrial democracy, one is led to conclude that

---

*Note the announcement in trains: 'Luncheon is being served. Please take your transportation with you.' This absurd injunction perfectly illustrates the literalism, that is, pedantry, of the modern mind. 'Transportation' is made to 'cover' the several possibilities—some passengers will have tickets, others tabs or checks replacing their original tickets; some will have passes, and a few will have only cash. Therefore, thinks the pedant, if we say: 'Take your ticket with you,' somebody may think 'I have no ticket,' and will be unable to interpret and carry out the instruction.

This reasoning, now nearly automatic, accounts for the proliferating of terms such as 'residual supply' meaning 'the rest,' which business and government invent daily to make us more exact and profound. We may no longer write 'Book Rate' on a package: the contents might not be pre- cisely a book, though entitled to the rate. We must spell out: 'Educational materials,' which will cover everything from a lantern slide to a stuffed snake.

the free disregard of customary rules of speech gives routinized men satisfaction by being the easiest form of originality; once literacy has been achieved, each violation re-enacts a small declaration of independence. Real novelty is rare, difficult, mysterious. But everyone can play with words, is exposed to verbal instability, and has been encouraged from childhood to be creative. Our favorite children's books, Lear's and Lewis Carroll's, also play with words, divide, unite, and invent them, and their nonsense is taken seriously by critics of literature; the maker of patented products not only may but must misspell and hybridize common names to form a trademark; and much of the poetry and prose that is 'advanced' achieves its effects by ambiguity and puns. Add to this the mixing of peoples which has laced the language with foreign turns and misconceptions and you can gauge the combined strength of the destructive tendencies.

Nor is this all. The same vanity which is fed by pseudo-jargon also relishes abbreviations, or more exactly acronymia, the making of words out of the initials of other words. The maker enjoys a little triumph when he has produced a pronounceable one, behind which stands a series of pompous words that 'cover' the 'activity.' It is by now astonishing when any group, say, the trackers of certain unusual radio noises call themselves simply 'Whistlers East' and 'Whistlers West.' Can they really be scientific? Unintelligible words and signs do not merely abridge; they have the force of magic and secrecy, and I suspect that in the growing habit of using initials for names and works in literary scholarship it is the spell of science that is being invoked. The preface to a new edition of Goethe's *Faust* a year or two ago was written entirely in this strain: 'The text was first scrutinized by R-MSH, with HR and WFT discussing R-MSH's proposals and making their own. . . . Thereafter WFT kept the books on text revisions with proposals coming from R-MSH and HR and WFT.' Note, in this attempt to make editing resemble chemistry, the 'scrutinized,' the permutations, and the ostentatious reference to keeping the books on the experiment.* One is intended to see in all this something more than three men working together, as men were wont to do. Indeed we are told that they did no such simple thing: they 'participated actively in every phase of the work . . . submitted sketch outlines of the desirable material . . . a mimeographed work version was prepared. Vigorous and voluminous discussions followed. . . . '[10] One might add: 'A process was in progress.'

The hope of magic is tied to both art and science, and because both are analogical as well as creative, the ordinary speaker's wish expresses itself through excess of metaphor. Not only are the fine arts dealt with in tropes, as we saw, but the worst errors of the common judgment are memorialized in a species of bad poetry. In war we speak of the 'rape' of a country; in revolution, the insurgents who are killed are not called heroes, but martyrs; in education, the part that is discovery has been represented as the 'cutting edge of learning'; in the new technology of digital computers, everyone feels a compulsion to call the machine a 'brain' and its mechanical acts 'memory' and 'learning';† when Alexis Carrel devised a certain apparatus for circulating liquids, the press at once named it a 'heart'; and when we launch an ephemeral box into space, with our signa-

---

*Other instances are: the *Encyclopedia Britannica*, which in the work of Mr. Herman Kogan has become *The Great EB*; the literature about the James family, which ever since R. B. Perry has reduced them to WJ_1 and WJ_2, HJ_1 and HJ_2, like so many isotopes. In the New Arden Shakespeare, the notes refer exclusively to H-IV-I, KR III, and so on through the chance initials of the plays and poems, leaving the works of other writers and the trivialities of ballad mongers their full titles. Again, Ernest Newman in his latest articles had begun to refer to famous musical scenes by initials. Berlioz's 'Royal Hunt and Storm' became RHS, as 'Good Friday Spell' would be GFS. The possibility of a critical algebra seems near.

†Many articles have appeared on machines that will 'translate.' This is the most foolish of the bad metaphors, since the task of the machine is and can be no more than that of responding to conventional signs, which must first be prepared as a 'dictionary' covering the bare bones of a narrow language, such as the scientific. On this subject, see A. D. Booth, 'The History and Recent Progress of Machine Translation' in *Aspects of Translation*, Communication Research Centre, University College, London, 1958.

ture in it in the form of a dead dog, no one questions the impertinence of naming it a 'moon.'

The duty of Intellect being to analyze and keep distinct, its failure in the face of so much nonsense and confusion argues dwindling forces of resistance. The judgment that would make one refuse to accept a lead coin or grasp a red-hot poker seems tranquilized and inert. The condition is progressive: loose language first makes analysis difficult, then absence of thought is hidden by technical discourse, as if the words were doing the analyzing. Think of the innumerable articles that begin: 'The term delinquency is a broad one; it covers every kind of infraction of rules, from . . . ' You know at once that the chances are poor of finding an idea among the tautologies. Yet this strain is able to elicit respect, concern, and even admiration. This bland speech evacuates the mind and in the end makes it incapable of retaining anything solid. After a steady course of this, students who are asked to read books written by English scholars of the old style cannot follow. The links between ideas are too tight, the skillful use of overtones distracts or is ignored, and the absence of redundancy makes the pace too rapid for untrained minds. Yet the unregulated ease of pseudo-jargon is far from democratic in its effects. It unfits the educated for the precisions of conversation, literature and the law, as well as for the companionship of the happy few who are still conversant with true jargon and palpable necessity—sailors, farmers, old-world artisans.

For the state of the language as we find it in the centers of culture, certain modern linguists bear a grave responsibility. In wanting to prove their studies scientific, they went out of their way to impress the public with a pose and a set of principles that they thought becoming: a true science, they argued, only records, classifies, and notes relations; it never prescribes. Hence the old grammar was sinful and must be harried out of the schools. It was unscientific, dangerous, and—they added irrelevantly—it was impossible to teach it to the majority. The campaign succeeded. The graduate of an elementary school today cannot with certainty be accused of knowing any given subject, but he can be guaranteed to know no grammar. In one generation grammar has been uprooted and pedantic fantasies about teaching the mother tongue have been made to seem liberal and advanced.

The linguists' fallacy has two parts. In one we are asked to acknowledge the difficulty, the virtual impossibility, of teaching standard English to the masses. A few hours of instruction a week cannot outweigh the influence of home and community where substandard English or a foreign tongue prevails. This difficulty is real and would suggest to any responsible teacher the desirability of selecting the best young minds for the intensive training in good English which would open to them the highest opportunities of thought and power, while the less able would have borne in upon them the value of good speech. In the next generation we might reasonably expect a somewhat greater desire to master English, for it would be linked with accomplishment and prestige of every other kind.

Frivolously, the would-be scientists argued the other way, saying that democracy and their science alike called for a policy of 'Hands Off.' As scientists they maintained that the speech of any group is good speech for that group; as democrats and progressives they maintained that the child should not be made to feel inferior (or superior) by changing his speech. 'There can . . . never be in grammar an error that is both very bad and very common.'[11] Thus spoke Charles Carpenter Fries, the theorist who engineered the demise of grammar in the American schools. Yet this doctrine and his crusade were not, as he thought, objective and detached in the spirit of science. Rather, philanthropy and egalitarianism inspired him. To teach one kind of usage, pronunciation, and grammar seemed to him tantamount to reintroducing social distinctions of the most artificial kind. Wanting the opposite gave him his first principle: Accept what comes and in time we shall have a classless speech corresponding to the usage of the most numerous.

The second part of the fallacy combines the affectation of science with the 'progressive' principle of learning by doing, here carried to a ludicrous extreme. The proposal was that children be shown the welter of linguistic facts, be asked to tabulate them and then to draw their own conclusions, that is, write their own grammars. The teachers who were considered unable to teach the standard grammar were suddenly supposed capable of leading their pupils in the difficult task of analyzing a language—their own, which by hypothesis they knew most imperfectly.

In the schools the plan was wrecked by its own folly, but something like it has survived for adults. In advanced circles, instead of the usual grammar book, the learner is faced with what is called the General Form of the foreign tongue. This is a list, from a thousand to fifteen hundred pages long, of all the types of expression—verbal, rhythmical, and tonal—that are common and characteristic in the language. So scientific a description avoids all the old dangers of learning rules that have some exceptions, of profiting from analogies, and of grasping masses of facts from paradigms. In short, the device (which is said to have been adopted by the State Department in its foreign language training) is called General Form because it avoids every form of generality.

The delight of learning each unit by itself, like a parrot, goes with the claim that the new science has replaced 'a body of fixed doctrine' by 'a method of study.' This too is a pose, for the 'democratic' argument against standard English is certainly not a method but a fixed doctrine. And so is the decree that the teaching of English to ten-year-olds must follow the same 'method' as advanced research. The antigrammar swept out the old categories on the ground that they were derived from Latin, and English is not Latin—away with noun, verb, adjective, pronoun, and the half-dozen other parts of speech. In their place, the pupil must memorize four parts of speech, fifteen function words, and nineteen classes of forms, some of them overlapping. And when we ask on what body of English speech this 'experimental' grammar was based, the answer is that it was derived from three thousand letters written to the United States War Department after 1918 and dealing with the single theme of pension money.

Beyond this blinkered view of what English is, a view which the author naturally calls 'realism,' the scientific linguist evades responsibility for his arbitrary act. 'He makes no pretense,' he tells us, 'of knowing better how the English language should be written than those who have written and spoken it effectively, gracefully, powerfully.'[12] That is a handsome admission, but now that standards have been declared unscientific, how do we judge prose to be effective, graceful, and powerful? With the same lack of consecutive thought, the antigrammarian argues from historical examples to show that some modern error is acceptable because it was once correct—for example, Chaucer's use of double negatives. But if we are not allowed to call anything correct today, how could Chaucer? And how long will it be before some of our usages are urged against future generations, who will no longer think them effective and graceful? And finally, why did Professor Carpenter write whole books without a double negative?

To appreciate the extent of the intellectual disaster brought on by the liquidation of grammar and to gauge the fanaticism, the bad reasoning, the incapacity to come to a point, the self-righteousness of the antigrammarians, one should scan the five-hundred-page report of the Commission of the National Council of Teachers of English on what they first called 'The English Curriculum' but later renamed 'The English Language Arts.'* The volume is one long demonstration of the authors' unfitness to tell anybody anything about English. Their great maxim, an act of faith in the teeth of the evidence, is that 'change in language is not corruption but improvement . . . especially in English, [change] is in the direction of simplification and clarification.'[13] If after this 'pro-English' optimism it is

*Published in 1952; the authors promised four more volumes of the same size. In the first volume, see especially 'New methods for describing the structure of English,' pp. 281–300, and 'An overview of the task of the language arts teacher,' pp. 371 ff.

not indelicate to recall a Latin author, I shall quote here the famous words with which Gregory, Bishop of Tours, writing in the sixth century, prefaces his *History of the Franks*: 'Woe to the present age, which has seen the study of letters perish, and in which nobody any longer knows how to preserve for future times the record of events. The liberal arts have fled the land; nobody any longer a master of grammar and rhetoric—everything is in decline, is at the point of death. Therefore I beg that you will excuse my errors of letter or syllable—I have been so badly educated!'

The bishop did not exaggerate: his Latin is generally bad and in parts undecipherable. The change which had been going on before him was not improvement but corruption, just as the change which is overtaking English is not simplification and clarification but obscurity, pretension, and pedantry.

The elaborated language which Intellect works with is not a creation of the remote past. For the modern nations it dates from about four hundred years ago, when a flexible, unambiguous prose style, full of nuances and distinctions, developed—just in time to take over the succession from late medieval Latin. It is this prose style, whether in English, Italian, French, or Spanish, which is now disintegrating. A comparable German prose developed later, in the so-called Classic period which was actually the age of Romanticism, but it soon fell into the hands of an intellectual class lacking in traditions and bedeviled by science—the academics—who spoiled a splendid instrument very much as English and French are being spoiled now. The *Gelehrte* German prose not only hampered its literature, but both the prose and the literature helped ruin German politics and thought.

The weakness of the language as we are remaking it is of the same order: it is not primarily aesthetic (though it is that too) but intellectual. There are excellent poets and prose writers among us, but they segregate their art from what they ordinarily say and write and (therefore) think. Accepting from day to day the invertebrate idea is not only bad for their immediate purposes, it is bad for the cultural institutions in which they profess an interest. Around art, criticism puts a pall of methodical verbiage, and soon art is dragged down from its throne to become an adjunct to the ologies and their kindred, the welfare agencies. Around science, pseudo-jargon keeps alive the superstition of mystery and omnipotence. For anyone to say that physics or mathematics is a simple subject and must remain so to command universal assent sounds like a paradox. Yet the failure to grasp this *linguistic* fact about natural science is what permits the imitations to thrive by means of contrived, vapid, or impenetrable complication, both aggravating the plight of the language at large.

This pseudo-scientific pedantry has obscured the important fact of the willful inexactitude of science, that is, its deliberate refusal to grasp the individual and relate him to its models and systems. Not to know this results, for the whole realm of learning outside natural science, in a superstitious reliance on figures, graphs, and labels. Give a man a rating on a scale, call him a something-or-other, and no amount of direct evidence will erase the suspicion that he is what he has 'scientifically' been called.* Hence the modern abdication of direct, responsible judgment by human beings. Judgment, to be sure, depends on comparison, but rarely on mechanical, point-for-point comparison. Rather, it requires the bringing together into one view of many elements differing in kind, probability, and importance; and this comprehensive, eagle-eyed assessment, the highest and most valuable, cannot be done by an inarticulate mind. Only words in their right order and sense can present to the judgment the manifold reality in which objects, memories, immediate ideas, principles, and future purposes commingle. After this presentment, the intuition of the talented and experienced plays its part to produce

---

*An example of the force of numbers is the demand of the National Science Foundation for a rating by numerical order of all nominees to its fellowships. If within one institution there are, say, five groups of twenty young men from five different sciences, one of the hundred candidates must be called eighty-sixth in merit, so as to 'help' the final committee in making its awards. Whether this candidate is successful or not, that meaningless '86th out of 100' will follow him through life.

the decision which the event declares just or true. To dismiss this as 'subjective' and always to prefer the inexactitude of crude and pretentious measurements is simply to repudiate tailoring and, as in *Gulliver,* have one's clothes made by trigonometry.

This distinction between two modes of judging, which our religiosity about science ignores, is nothing new. Three centuries ago Pascal drew it, in a chapter which significantly links Intellect and Style.[14] There are, said Pascal, two ways of thought, usually found in different minds. The geometric, or scientific, mind works according to principles that are plain and few, but remote from common life. It may be hard to find these principles and grasp them from the very first, but once they are grasped one would have to be mentally deficient to confuse or misapply them. On the contrary, the subtle mind (*esprit de finesse*) works with principles that reside in the midst of life for everybody to see. But one needs a good eye to detect them because they are so numerous and so fine. It is almost impossible that some of them should not escape notice. Now, oversight inevitably leads to error, and hence one must be absolutely clear-eyed, and be a strict reasoner besides, if one does not want to go astray on well-known premises.[15]

Pascal goes on to describe the instantaneous synthesis by which the trained mind of the second category grasps a situation and judges it. I have purposely avoided saying: 'grasps a problem and solves it,' because it is precisely our self-immolation to science which misleads us into making a problem out of every situation. Our poets, painters, and novelists themselves talk of 'solving problems' in their respective arts. This is nonsense. They encounter difficulties, they are perplexed, but they face no problems in the sense of stated requirements which can be completely satisfied. It is not a problem, and there is no solution, when we ask the question, 'Shall we elect Mr. X president?' What is wanted is a judgment, and asking a sampling of citizens in advance of the election will no more supply us with a solution than would a series of medical tests on the body of the candidates. 'When the scientists,' says Pascal, 'want to deal geometrically with these matters of finesse, beginning with definitions and going on to principles, they make themselves ridiculous, for such is not the way to reason in those cases—not because the mind does not proceed by reasons, but because it does this tacitly, naturally, artlessly. The full expression of it is beyond all men and the awareness of it belongs to few.'[16]

Science solves problems and language guides judgment. This is true because language is the work of the *esprit de finesse* and alien to the geometrical mode of thought. Consequently, when language is distorted by the attempt to stuff it with words suggestive of geometry, the product is an instrument which is useless for both *finesse* and geometry and, as Pascal says, ridiculous besides. The handling of words is to the thinker, the historian, the publicist, what dexterity and mathematical ingenuity are to the experimental scientist. Results rarely come except in these embodiments of thought. Style is not everything, certainly, but it is one of the requirements of intellectual technique, a means to accuracy and to invention. More than that, the apt use of words, though less and less necessary in science itself, is as indispensable as ever in the teaching of science. One reason why the young are so ill prepared in mathematics and physics is that they are taught by persons who are not articulate about their subject, who cannot word the difficulty and remove it, guard against misconceptions and leave on the mind of the pupil an imprint of the working of their own. To be sure, it takes two for teaching to go on, and as manual dexterity cannot make up for blunt or skewed instruments, neither can the user of words compensate for the skew and bluntness of his hearers' minds. People who are half articulate cannot properly listen or read; hence lacking early and continuing attention to language, the 'problem of communication' is bound to be chronic. It is notable that in our obsession with the scientific mode, two of the most remarkable uses of language in society are today in small repute; though not entirely neglected, they are at least reduced to the rank of commonplace services such as any able-bodied man could discharge for his fellows. I refer to diplomacy and the law.

Diplomacy, which is now an underpaid and ill-supplied profession, requires more than the ability to put a perpetually good face on ugly facts or evil intentions; it requires an awareness of others' minds which is one of the chief attributes of the prose writer, second only to his capacity for meeting argument with finesse and clear reason. A self-centered diplomat, an incoherent diplomat, are contradictions in terms. Yet one wonders whence the recruits to such a calling will come when it is so ill rewarded, when the study of foreign languages is hampered by the abolition of the native grammar, and when more and more of our university students can barely rank as monoglots.

To overlook the art of diplomacy in the national culture and be insufficiently grateful to its practitioners is understandable: the work is done outside and the publicity is small. But contempt and ingratitude toward the interpreters of law is a grave fault. It shows ignorance of the long, arduous growth and superior merit of an institution to which we owe our ease and privileges as thinking beings. The law is a model of intellectual work, and it is a work of words. It is a profession easy to ridicule by its externals and it is criticizable, like other institutions, for its anachronisms. But as an attempt of the *esprit de finesse* to mold coherent conceptions of the true and the just on the restless multiplicity of human life, it is a triumph of articulateness and exactitude. In the United States in recent years, the failure of local efforts at reforming court procedures and the persistent clamor, shared in by men of law, against the Supreme court, show that the legal Intellect is, for whatever reason, at a disadvantage. Some of its troubles come from the dominance of casualness in our mores, which makes the law seem to the ordinary citizen a series of expensive quibbles: 'What difference does it make what statute you convict him under if you know he's guilty?' A deeper cause is the lowered standard of the linguistic power, which accounts also for the fact that only a few judges no longer living— Holmes, Brandeis, Cardozo—furnish us again and again with the verbal concretions of ideas we should be lost without.

· · ·

In place of an informed reliance on the principles of our law and our other historical disciplines, the frequent and inaccurate use we make of the word 'scientific' to mean 'clear, tested, reliable,' has bred a false security in intellectual matters, paralleling the self-confidence many persons feel in matters of taste when they hear that a hundred thousand people have approved an article of consumption or that a reputable firm is 'behind' it. In fact, life affords no security, much less security from a single source. There is no guarantee in 'research,' which is properly a neutral term and not the honorific it has become. There is no assurance in all the 'findings,' all the knowingness of the psychologist and the advertiser and the educationist, whose verbalisms cover and conceal the gaping holes in their empiric arts. There is no guarantee in language, even when skillfully used, and none in Intellect even when highly developed and firmly based on a tradition. In a word, there is no guarantee.

But there are unending deceptions and threats and invasions against which Intellect, with the aid of language, can make a stand. It can dissolve clotted nonsense and resist superstition, unmask affectation and show up the greatest of the ologies—tautology—for the vain fraud it is. In the large sense, it can make war on pedantry which, as here defined, is the display of intellectual means where they do not fit, for the sake of show or self-conceit. As I suggested earlier, our morbid anxiety about small error, matching the indignation with which each one is seized on, is a sign of pedantry and of secret hostility to knowledge. So is the captiousness of literary and other criticism, which, in looking for El Dorado or the Koh-i-noor overlooks solid merit and misleads the public as to the limited possibilities of each art. What critics and specialists do to one another, with all the certitude that a reference library inspires, seems like upholding the standards of accuracy, but in fact accuracy is only tangentially concerned. For accuracy is of the whole as well as of detail, and the fear of error—as against the zeal for truth—yields only a lesser correctness, desirable no doubt, but insufficient and sometimes negligible. A man of intellect and an educated scholar, the late Albert J. Nock, put this principle with finality in speaking of the

American biographer James Parton and of his captious critic, Francis Hirst. 'There are qualities that outweigh occasional and trivial inaccuracy, and Parton has them, while the other biographers of Mr. Jefferson, as far as I can see, have not; and the worth of his book should be judged accordingly. Indeed, if one were condemning books on the strength of minor inaccuracies, Mr. Hirst himself would get off badly. . . . [A] book should be judged on the scale of its major qualities. . . . "Let us never forget that we are all pedants," said Benjamin Constant to his literary associates; which may be all very well for those who live to read, but hardly for those who read to live.'[17]

There speaks the voice of Intellect which, knowing its place and purpose, and having no desire to usurp the power of other arts of the mind, will not let itself (or them) invert the roles of mind and life.

X

The Summing Up

In one of his short studies, James Anthony Froude imagines himself at the end of the journey, on the day of judgment, and called on to testify to what he has accomplished. He cites his works and is confronted with the witnesses against him: 'They seemed literally to be in millions, and I had eaten them all. I talked of wages. These had been my wages. At this enormous cost had my existence been maintained. A stag spoke for the rest. "We all," he said, "were sacrificed to keep this cormorant in being, and to enable him to produce the miserable bits of paper which are all that he has to show for himself." '[1]

This parable raises the first question we must decide when we consider Intellect not for use or pleasure, but under the aspect of eternity. The moment the animate creatures speak up, the few dead books look pitiful and we are reminded of their cost. At the same time is conjured up the image of a man's own life, transcending in richness and mystery any books or other conceivable traces of Intellect.

Yet no sooner has one made this reflection than one sees that the power thus to estimate life depends on Intellect. Without language, books, and a long tradition of thought, neither Froude nor the reader would be concerned with the question. We should all be animals who had eaten other animals, without conceiving or leaving behind us a notion of the meaning and moral weight of existence.

The great mass of mankind living in Western civilization possesses such a tradition of thought, whether they know and approve of it or not, and many among them know its past well enough to be now disquieted about its future. So at this point the option before us is not that of giving up happy thoughtless ways and newly establishing Intellect as a life-darkening institution, but that of deciding whether its already existing forces should rally to sustain it, with general consent, or allow it to fall by transforming themselves into other forces which seem at the moment more congenial to our culture—the forces of art, philanthropy, scientism, primitive public opinion, casualness. The previous chapters may sometimes have given the impression that they pleaded for the answer 'Yes, let us rally and restore the House of Intellect forthwith.' This is an unavoidable effect of the common forms of exposition. The argument was in fact a choice, and one characteristic of intellectual judgments: if you want *this,* you must have, or do, *that.* The intention of my words was not so much to persuade as to direct attention to incongruity and disease; this book is a pathology of the subject, of which the fundamental principle resides in just this conditional proposition: if ——— then.

Despite popular belief to the contrary, enlightenment and reform by no means always require one to be 'positive,' to have a program and make converts. In the most important matters persuasion is an offense. But addressing the will and showing it the conditions and connections of its object—'if ——— then'—is possibly a service. This seems especially appropriate today, when childishness of will and apathy of mind countenance a blind belief in the *un*conditioned. The physician, having found a drug and calling it good, administers it as if the patient and all his oddities did not exist. The philanthropist, thinking exchanges of ideas and persons good, encourages them as if the agitation did not interrupt other work. The pedant, thinking technical language good, manufactures it ad lib as if the worth of words did not lie in their relative fixity and general acceptance.

The reader can readily apply the same touchstone of cost and condition to every act, habit, situation, and attitude that my rapid survey has tried to present, and to many others equally manifest. The inducement to doing so is that the indulgence of looseness and confusion in the domain of mind and fancy has gone so far that one may apprehend a fierce and no less stupid reaction toward the opposites—rigidity, punctilio, and moral brutality. Schools having gone lax, one now hears of places where beating is again in favor with parents and masters. The pedantry which is still a pastime can easily become a guilty obsession and begin to persecute. All this can happen when men abuse their privilege of ignoring consequences. Not to foresee the irritability of nature, not to expect the recoil of even the best actions, not to halt or shift course before advantage dwindles and turns to drawback, is another form of that groundless faith in the unconditioned with which man unguarded by Intellect tempts retribution.

It can be held, to be sure, that these violent swings are uncontrollable by mere thought, representing as they do the unconscious force of millions of souls, which can unite far more easily through their unworded instincts than through Intellect. This is true but irrelevant to the actions of the thousands among the millions who possess intellectual faculties. *Their* actions cannot recapture the abandon of dumb tropism; they *think,* and more or less gracefully adapt their unconscious energies to their thoughts. Consequently, what they know and what they think makes a difference; and since the greater mass, too, declines to regard itself as a herd of buffaloes in stampede, the ideas emanating from the thinkers affect it, modify its acts, and end by serving them, however feebly, as a borrowed intellect. Never knowing where or in what form its influence will take effect, near and far, Intellect is not entitled to doubt itself and abdicate. It must on the contrary act always as master in its own house and at the top of its powers. For the individual, who has a physical right to think as he pleases, this means that he has a moral duty to think as he ought according to the dictates of fact and logic.

What these compelling powers of the Intellect are has been indicated by generality and example throughout these pages, though no more than indicated; for to attempt more would be to undertake anew and on a modern scale the eighteenth-century *Encyclopédie*. Here all that can be done is to summarize the critical and co-ordinating functions of Intellect by repeating Newman's remarks on ratiocination: it is, says Newman, 'the great principle of order in thinking; it reduces a chaos into harmony; it catalogues the accumulations of knowledge; it maps out for us the relations of its separate departments; it puts us in the way to correct its own mistakes. It enables the independent intellects of many, acting and reacting on each other, to bring their collective force to bear upon one and the same subject matter, or the same question. If language is an inestimable gift to man, the logical faculty prepares it for our use. Though it does not go so far as to ascertain truth, still it teaches us the direction in which truth lies, and how propositions lie toward each other. Nor is it a slight benefit to know what is probable and what is not so, what is needed for the proof of a point, what is wanting in a theory, how a theory hangs together, and what will follow if it be admitted. Though it does not itself discover the unknown, it is one principal way by which discoveries are made.'[2]

Assuming that discovery and the collective participation of many in the search for truth still interest Western man, the question next in order is how to restore the tradition of Intellect? The most obvious answer is 'reform the schools.' At this instant many are uneasy about the actual lack of instruction and the future minds of the great horde of youth now upon us. Let us, the reformers conclude, reverse all the assumptions on which our schools have worked; let us at least teach the gifted in ways opposite to the present *reductio ad absurdum* of education, and perhaps in fifteen or twenty years we may see improvement. It is natural to want reform such as this, *in aliena republica* rather than at home; it is easier to delegate it than to carry it out. But even if schools and teachers were thrown into reverse gear by magic, they would accomplish little without a corresponding change in the conditions of the intellectual life.

To effect these changes is not a superhuman task if the firmness and rigor that are being preached to the schools exist also in our individual souls. The discipline of hard work in reading, writing, and counting must be matched at home by attention to speech, manners, and thought. In the outer world the change must take the form of more starch in the leaders and purveyors of public opinion. If each waits, trembling, upon the whim of the other, in the vain hope of undercutting him in point of popularity, the public mind will continue to drift, and to drag with it whatever of private mind the home and the school manage to nurture between them.

All private and public affairs, moreover, must have unremittingly applied to them the criterion of work. The business of learning must above all others be represented in its true guise as difficult, as demanding effort. If television is to be used for teaching, there must be no more coaxing and wheedling—not: 'Come with me as we explore the land of numbers,' but 'Ladies and gentlemen, this is arithmetic which, like many another branch of learning, is full of difficulty, danger, and pleasure.' Outside teaching and learning, every new proposal and habitual device must be interrogated: is it going to be talk, travel, writing, publication for nothing? For nobody? Or has it an end, an effect that will *take* effect on someone or something?* This is the great moment for the American mind to show itself pragmatist as it has never been,

*As Mr. Faulkner once wrote when he was chairman of a committee: 'I think there is no need in calling a meeting until we are agreed on what we are going to do in it.'

never having understood that the doctrine is primarily that of the conservation of Intellect. To apply the pragmatic test one might even begin by asking, 'Is the proposed undertaking going to be difficult—or merely fatiguing?' The difference between work and wearisome futility lies in that distinction, now buried in our tired minds, or sluggishly trying to reach them through the fog of useless words.

The desirability of work is more than a canon of Intellect; it is commanded by emotional needs that our civilization represses. Unlike the Greeks whom we so admire, with our lips, for their taste and their reason, we make no provision in society for the bacchanalian part of being. We do not know how to laugh or revel. We are serious thinkers or serious alcoholics. Like the late Wolcott Gibbs, we live 'with a hard ball of panic in our stomachs.'[3] We read Freud's *Civilization and Its Discontents* and approve but do not heed. The Middle Ages, for all their fits of puritanism and supposed fears of eternal punishment, knew how to wash away panic in laughter and make room in civilization for the dionysiac as well as for its sublimation in work. We have lost all three forms of release and can only look for 'relaxation,' wondering why we are timid and tired, afraid of power and looking for shelter in little huts—art, the home, the religions of the East—like sufferers from agoraphobia.

The relation of work to passion suggests another relation, that of Intellect to sex, which I neglected to discuss, as it would take a volume apart and much additional inquiry. It can nonetheless be said that a chief hindrance to the development of Intellect in the young is the incoherence of our sexual morality. It bedevils them by enjoining prolonged continence, yet subjects them also to guilt by tolerating inelegant substitutes and furtive infractions, attaching always, and enforcing at times, dire penalties to the crime of being found out—in a word, we show the young in every way that on this subject mental chaos rules. Science itself, allied to advertising and cultural snobbery, has complicated the fulfillment of the sexual instinct by the pedantry of 'technique,' only to find this destructive of the pleasure it was meant to enhance; so that after a quarter-century of profitable pontificating and book-selling at the expense of mortified couples, the new wisdom advises a burning of the books.

All this implies a failure to turn the full light of Intellect upon a subject generally conceded to be important. The impression prevails that the twentieth century is liberated from Victorian absurdities about sex, and that science—meaning some physicians, the psychiatrists, and the late Alfred C. Kinsey—has here also achieved its goal of knowledge for control over nature. This is obviously not true, and dumb misery amid the books is rather the rule, especially among the intellectual young.

To begin with, the connection between sex and Intellect has never been established as a generality. The connection is of course not definable with the last precision, but its existence is known—by introspection as well as by 'science'—and the knowledge of it is in itself an aid to life. If Intellect is in some way an expression of sexual appetite, then man is not simply driven, but may gain power over impulse by directing it. He then has the right both to repress and to express his sexual urges, and he acquires as it were a varied and extended vocabulary for doing so. About any manifestation, direct or sublimated, he puts to himself as a question the intellectual 'if ——— then' and makes a choice. Immediately, the character of the hunted beast seeking dark corners is banished and something like a civilized attitude toward the root passion appears. The atmosphere of catastrophe which now invests it is dissipated, at least for the individual, who takes the risks of legal or illegal gratification knowing what he is doing and on what terms he serves his senses and his mind.

But this internal clarity is only the beginning. For there remains the need to reform the mores of the society. Its 'views' hardly matter as long as its behavior is in its present state of self-contradiction. The very use of the words relating to sex, love, chastity, decency, and marriage is corrupt: it is impossible to square the state of our language and literature, of our public entertainment and professed science, with the social and legal rules that do in fact govern sexual behavior.

One would suppose that under our laws, it would be punishable to incite the innocent passerby to sexual thoughts. But that is, of course, what industry and business do without cease through advertising. So do our motion pictures, cheap fiction, modes of dress, and table talk: it is, as Mr. Geoffrey Wagner has said, 'a parade of pleasure.' Is this substitute gratification? Hardly: it is for the eye alone, and a deep deception goes with it. Like our idealization of youth, our visual lust is a magic mirror: it protects us by a false reflection. From the public imagery one would infer that the modern world is a kind of South Sea Island as the eighteenth century conceived it—simple, healthy, and free in the expression of natural impulse. Unremitting sexual suggestiveness gives the illusion of a primitive happy world, an anticivilization of loveliness and sensuality. Living up to part of that vision, we go about naked in the sun and resistant to clear ideas, lip servants of the great myth of casual ease, though sight-bound by skin and sex: it is a child's paradise.

In keeping with this, custom decrees coeducation, precocious courtship and engagements, and marriage on the threshold of conscious life. And, inevitably, the intellectual failure to order our thoughts on sex creates conditions prejudicial to Intellect: young men and women marry during college or graduate study. The men, burdened by new cares, make their intellectual training secondary to domestic duties. To marry these men, the women generally give up college for paid employment and help support the home where the men are housekeepers. The woman's education, an undertaking that shortly before was deemed of great moment, is now thrown away half-used, quite as if it cost nothing to parents, teachers, and the institution. Yet no adult has the courage to hint that higher education is a privilege the acceptance of which binds the taker; or to say, with even more daring, that the marriage of unfinished minds of equal age stands a poor chance of being permanent.

In contemplating these many choices presented by the existence of Intellect in civilization, the distinction once made by the German social historian, Max Weber, may strike the observer as offering an alternative to the hard task of thinking and judging, which the majority of the educated today cannot or will not nerve themselves to perform. The true intellectual, said Weber, lives *for* ideas; the ordinary professional man lives *by* them. The implication seems to be that the second choice gives the latitude of living by very few. The implication is false, like the distinction itself. Every mind capable of ideas must live for them as well as by them. Living exclusively for ideas does not define an intellectual but an emotional type. The man of this type is not necessarily a genius and he may be a fanatic. Even if it were desirable to have such men produced or nurtured by our institutions, we should not know how to go about it. And there can be no rational desire, certainly, for their appearance on the political scene of a free country. For although men and events move fast under the fanatic's propulsion, the inevitable retreat is slow, the action and reaction costly in blood and treasure, and the decimation of the new crops of intellect steady and sure. The scourge may come nevertheless and later men be the better for it, as Burke foresaw, but it cannot be rationally desired. To provide for one's blind chastisement would be as absurd as it is in these days to work for agreements that will take the unexpected out of surprise attacks.

And although Weber did not intend it to do so, his notion of living 'for' ideas easily leads to the worst errors of democratic utopianism—the aspiration to the highest without regard to intermediate steps, and the resulting impatience with barriers and categories. These seem to the rebels like vestiges of an old regime of Intellect, in which ideas and things had altogether different purposes, resembling those of social class; whereas we have abolished all that and found that everything—animate or inanimate—is nearly the same as everything else. Like the 'bad poetry' I spoke of, which uses metaphor to save thought, the careless finding of identities produces comfort, a sudden warmth and easing of the stretch of mind by which things are kept apart. 'It seems to me,' says an able writer, 'that our three basic needs, for food and security and love, are so mixed and mingled and entwined that we cannot straightly think of one without the others. So it happens that when I write of hunger, I am really writing about love and the hunger for it, and warmth and the love of it and the hunger for it . . . and then the warmth and richness and fine reality of hunger satisfied . . . and it is all one.'*[4] This may be the philosophy of the young kangaroo in its mother's pouch, but it is not that of Intellect, even though it is quite able to perceive similarities between hunger and love and their respective satisfactions. The pleasure of perceiving what is alike depends on perceiving what is unlike. It is not 'all one.'

Nor is it all one when, in the effort to dignify and ennoble and avoid invidious degrees of success, the democratic striving toward ideas, say in school, skips or ignores the rudiments, scorns mechanics, and looks only for brilliance. The teacher may be right to begin by saying, 'Never mind spelling, write eagerly and quickly'; but he goes on saying it so long that in the end orthography is an offense in the nostrils of the 'gifted.' The youth thinks he is writing essays like T. S. Eliot's, yet he cannot write a report like a well-trained policeman. The social man assumes he is displaying ease and informality, though he lacks the most rudimentary manners and does not suspect that ease and informality depend on discipline and convention. The would-be artist repeats the slogan: performance equals creation: 'The conductor is also a creator,'[5] though he may indifferently understand what he performs or understand it so well that he is inspired to tamper with it, lacking once again humility and discipline. The newspaper or magazine wants to pass from its tested vul-

*Suspension dots in the original.

garities to high intellectual matters, though its reporters are devoid of respect for learning and for those who amass it. Envy, not admiration, is at work here, desire without consent. Intellect disowns all these and their ideas; it demands what belongs to each role in the life of the mind and to each stage in its products, from rudiments to formulated thought; it wants competence, which is attainable and can be taught, and is wise enough to let genius and subtlety and ease and creativity take care of themselves.

'Creative' may be (or may have been, rather, before its abuse) a blood-stirring word; but all men, including the genius, live by others' ideas, and it is for the continuance of these ideas—of their form even more than their contents—that the House of Intellect exists. The fresh intelligence which nature so plentifully supplies in each generation, has a right to be endowed with Intellect, while the unintelligent must for everybody's sake be tinctured with it—enough to know its ways, recognize its claims by rote, approve out of civic pride its purposes. When this is done, both groups acquire the necessary sense of knowing much *in common*. It is the want of this knowledge that makes the modern intellectual apprehensive, touchy, shop-ridden, and ready for all the pedantries. The anguish of cohabiting with his own uncertain mind is allayed by absorbing and regurgitating little drops of fact, and following like a hypochondriac the prescription of method. On the contrary, the possession of a common property would permit liberation, the luxury of free judgment and magnanimity. If even a few men so circumstanced were to take part in the distribution of money for learning, their knowledge and the way they wore it would not only banish the unpleasant odor of charity which now makes the scholar think of a hospital when he enters a foundation; but the confidence in something greater than they, of which they were inalienable stockholders, would also increase the frequency of their right judgments and thus doubly serve Intellect.

Must we then sacrifice equality and democracy to an elite gifted with these powers, natively and by design? One should not have to answer that shopworn question; Intellect has nothing to do with equality except to respect it as a sublime convention. Equality *assumes* that all men are equal; it does so in order to eliminate disputes of precedence and privilege, to stop inquiry into the infinite differences on which privilege could be based. Age, birth, merit, strength, color of skin, are adventitious details of the person, which can establish no rational ranking; for the strong man may be of the wrong age for authority, the old man stupid or born in the wrong place. No scheme of inequality can be defended as corresponding to natural fact. And natural fact itself is elusive. Superior or inferior can be determined only with respect to a single quality for a single purpose. Nor can a man's qualities be added together and averaged to give a final score of merit. In short, men are incommensurable and must be deemed equal. As for Omniscience, in its eyes our petty merits are no matter. On both planes, then, equality commends itself to Intellect, which is but one of man's qualities and among the most dispensable.

Militant democrats might therefore begin to take equality for granted, instead of nervously trying to measure it hourly in self-defense. Identity of function and status is impossible, but equivalence we can have. In any case, if the complaint of inequality is to be heard in connection with these high questions, it could most justifiably come from those who work with their minds. They have been left behind economically, which makes their new social eminence artificial and painful; and their conditions of work are for the most part abject and unregulated. Though they toil longer hours than any other group, the time left by modern society for their genuine work is far less than that enjoyed by their nineteenth-century counterparts, and their permanent output is proportionately less.* One lack that hampers them more than most, since their work is domestic and not capable of mechanization, is: servants. It may make edifying reading in the biography of a Justice of the Supreme Court that he

---

*According to the Bureau of the Census, professional men and managers work from 42.6 to 50.8 hours a week. Only farmers work longer hours. The rest of the working force works from 29.2 to 42.1 hours a week.

generally cooks breakfast for the whole family,[6] but the condition of self-help of which this is a symbol is regrettable—as regrettable for the college student as for the justice. Not that manual labor is degrading or 'beneath' anyone; but that life is short and the moments of the talented are precious. When society says that he has no right to squander them, it is presumably not to squander them itself. No solution of the paradox is in sight. The tragedy of a culture is that it is as it is and not otherwise.

These considerations make only more imperative the safeguard of the master virtues of Intellect. They are, once again: concentration, continuity, articulate precision, and self-awareness. Intellect needs the congregation of talents spurring one another to higher achievements by the right degree of proximity and intercourse; it needs the language and the conversation that maintain its unity like a beneficent air; it needs precision to dispel the blinding fogs of folly or stupidity; it needs self-awareness to enjoy its own sport and keep itself from vainglory.

In watching its sport or its work, let us not forget that Intellect is mankind's intelligence caught and compounded. Intelligence is the superior in adaptability and scope, but Intellect proves itself in steadiness and speed. Intelligence comes first and does painfully and at length what Intellect, the second-born, does easily and at once. This gives Intellect, in high civilizations, a special responsibility. If it condemns sentimental education, if it is impatient with the defeatism of intellectuals in the marketplace, if it deplores the ignorant waste of the money reserved for its uses, if it shows universal pedantry as the premises of mental enslavement, it is because its chief business is cultural criticism. It exists to perpetuate itself and to wage battle when attacked, whether the attack be external and violent or insidious and as it were self-inflicted. Intellect watches particularly over language because language is so far the only device for keeping ideas clear and emotions memorable. And language is liable to abuse and decay; it can be ruined as quickly by its guardians, the linguists, or its workmen, the critics and artists, as by the indifferent—the scientists and the democrats.

Intellect, as I have said more than once before, is a great thing and a small one. It is in peril, though not yet in mortal danger. But being what it is—the power which out of man's intermittent flashes of genius fused the clear crystal of alphabet and number—it will survive even if it die.

Objective Tests

An Additional Note to Chapter V
(By courtesy of Professor Banesh Hoffmann)

What of the questions in the two booklets [Scholastic Aptitude Test and *Science*]? I am officially informed that they were selected from actual tests, most of them being copied verbatim and the rest with small editorial changes. Such a process of successive filtering should have eliminated serious blemishes. That the surviving questions are not always clear-cut is implied by the following passage on page 18 of *Scholastic Aptitude Test*:

'As you read through the explanations of the verbal section, you may disagree with what we think to be the correct answer to one or two questions. You may think we are quibbling in making certain distinctions between answer choices. It is true that you will find some close distinctions and just as true that in making close distinctions reasonable people do disagree. Whether or not you disagree on a few questions is not terribly important, however, for the value of the test as a whole is that people who are likely to succeed in college agree in the main on most of the correct answers. It is this that gives the [*Scholastic Aptitude Test*] its predictive power.

'For this very reason, when you find it hard to make or recognize a distinction between answer choices, it is better not to spend much time on that question. It is the whole [*Scholastic Aptitude Test*] rather than any single question in it that makes the test a good indicator of college ability.'

The advice in the last paragraph quoted above has serious implications. Consider it in the light of the mutually exclusive propositions: (a) the test contains genuinely difficult questions that are free from ambiguity but call for reflection and cannot be properly analyzed in a short time; and (b) the test is devoid of such questions. If (b) is true, the advice is reasonable, but the test is unworthy of the highly gifted student, since it gives him little if any chance to display his superiority over his merely clever rivals. If (a) is true, the advice defeats the purpose for which the genuinely difficult questions were included, and is tantamount to a plea for superficiality.

What the two paragraphs just quoted seem together to imply, then, is that the difficult questions are difficult not because they have depth but because they involve close distinctions about which there is room for legitimate doubt.

The above quotations refer to questions that are meant to test verbal aptitude; we shall return to [them]. . . .

It is time to turn our attention once more to the booklet *Scholastic Aptitude Test,* from which we have already taken one example. From now on all examples will be taken from this booklet.

Here is a sentence-completion question:

22. If we cannot make the wind blow when and where we wish it to blow, we can at least make use of its ———.
(A) source (B) heat (C) direction
(D) force (E) atmosphere

Most of the people to whom I show this question immediately realize that (C) and (D) are possible answers. On reflection they realize that (B) is also a possible answer. If they are of a literary turn of mind, they at first see little merit in answer (A); but when I point out that to scientists the phrase 'the source of the wind' implies the combination of the heat of the sun and the rotation of the earth, they look on (A) with renewed interest and often agree that it may well be the best answer. Answer (E) seems impossible: we do not usually talk of the wind's atmosphere. Yet with a little poetical license we might, and then (E) would be a doughty contender. Let us not become poetical, though. These questions are hard enough when we remain prosaic. Even without (E) there are four promising candidates.

The examiner happens to want answer (D), but unfortunately he gives no reasons for his choice. I wonder whether he noticed that the presence of the word 'where' suggests (C) rather than (D) even though force has both magnitude and direction; or that it is possible to see in the phrase 'at least' a further suggestion that (C) is preferable to (D), and this despite the fact that we cannot use the wind's 'direction' without to some extent using its 'force.'

The presence of the phrase 'at least' raises many problems. The sentence would have a sharper focus were 'at least' deleted, especially if the first word were changed from 'If' to 'Although'; and I think the sense of the sentence would not be substantially affected by the change. Why, then, was 'at least' inserted? Was it intended as a clue? If so, it is an obscure one, for the precise significance of 'at least' in the sentence is tantalizingly elusive. Does it imply some sort of a minimum, for instance? I am not convinced that it must; but if it does, precisely what sort? Again, is 'at least' meant to modify no more than 'we can . . . make use of,' or is some of its effect meant to spill over on to the 'its ———'? If the latter, are we supposed to use it in ranking the various answers? And if the former, would not the whole situation have been much improved had the examiner avoided ambiguity by giving the sentence the logical ending '—we can at least make use of it'? To be sure, this would have destroyed the question, but under the circumstances that could hardly be classed as a calamity. . . .

I submit that there is here substantial *prima facie* evidence for the proposition that the College Board tests should be viewed with concern, but that if this concern is justified in the case of products of the Educational Testing Service, which is acknowledged to be outstanding in its field, then one can tentatively assume that similar tests made by other organizations should also be viewed with concern. . . .

[The question] is not whether some of my arguments are bad but whether the questions are good. Therefore, to bring this point into sharp focus, I place on the test makers the affirmative responsibility of showing that the questions here criticized are not defective. Merely picking a few holes in my arguments without showing that the questions are substantially free of defects will not properly meet the situation. Nor will an assertion that intelligent people usually have little trouble picking the wanted answers, for I have tested these questions on my colleagues and have found this assertion not to be true. . . .

I urge the reader to copy the test questions considered above onto individual cards and to discuss them with various intelligent people. He will find the results well worth the small effort involved, for he will discover an unexpected and surprising variety in the responses that the questions elicit, and will thus gain, among other things, a vivid appreciation of a basic defect of multiple choice tests: that they call for choices but not for reasons for choices. Difficulties that seem formidable to some people seem non-existent to others. Defective test questions tend to turn multiple choice tests into lotteries. . . .

Can the tests be defended against the present type of criticism on the ground that they are geared to the abilities of younger people who will not notice fine points that may disturb older persons? Such a defense was made to me, in correspondence, by a prominent test expert. Yet I do not think it can justify poor workmanship, ambiguity, incorrectness of wanted answers, and multiplicity of valid answers. Nor do I think it shows a proper respect for the abilities of our students. Among the most gifted there must surely be some students with, say, a quarter of the mental acuity of a young Bertrand Russell; if not, America is in a bad way indeed. Some of these gifted students will become eminent jurists, and brilliant cross-examiners—even Supreme Court Justices; some who are sensitive to the sounds and auras of words will become poets; some will become subtle philosophers and logicians; some will win Nobel prizes. Will not these and many others notice fine points that disturb older persons? . . .

There are deeper objections to multiple choice tests than the technical blemishes that I have principally stressed in this article. Even if the tests were constructed with impeccable draftsmanship and were free from all ambiguities and errors, they would, in my opinion, still have serious defects as testing instruments, especially when applied to creative persons and to some of those people who, despite impressive gifts, do not shine at parlor games. For multiple choice tests, by their very nature, tend to favor the pickers of choices over the doers, and the superficially brilliant over the creatively profound. And the use of these tests has a baleful influence on teachers and teaching.

Reference Notes

Chapter I   The Three Enemies of Intellect

1. *Dod's Peerage*, London, 1955, 340.
2. *New York Times*, September 17 and 20, 1957.
3. Leaflet from the New York Zoological Society, 1957.
4. Eric Baines, *The Listener*, May 16, 1957.
5. Lewis Mumford in *Toynbee and History*, ed. M. F. Ashley Montagu, Boston, 1956, 145.
6. Edward Steichen, *op. cit.*, 4–5.
7. *Ibid*.

Chapter II   The Public Mind and Its Caterers

1. Obituary of Richard Weil, Jr., *New York Times*, May 12, 1958.
2. *Time*, March 17, 1958, 34.
3. Cf. *New York Times*, August 1, 1957; February 13, 1958.
4. *New York Times*, September 13, 1955.
5. *New York Times*, May 17, 1958.
6. Theodore M. Bernstein, *Watch Your Language*, New York, 1958, 91.
7. William D. Jacobs, in *The CEA Critic*, February, 1957, 6.
8. Henry F. T. Rhodes, *Alphonse Bertillon, Father of Scientific Detection*, New York, 1956.

9. *New York Times*, November 24, 1957.
10. *New York Times*, July 2, 1958.
11. Walter F. Kerr in *New York Herald Tribune*, July 8, 1956.
12. James Reston in *New York Times*, June 13, 1958.
13. See the *New York Times, passim*, between June 25 and September 30, 1957.
14. 'Strikers' Lawyer: Louis Waldman,' *New York Times*, December 13, 1957.
15. The Georgetown University Forum: brochure detailing awards and programs, Washington, D.C., 1957.

Chapter III   Conversation, Manners, and the Home

1. David Riesman, 'Political Communication and Social Structure in the United States.' *The Public Opinion Quarterly*, xx, 1, 1956, 70–71.
2. R. D., *'Was heisst schon Konversation,'* *Die Zeit*, 1957, Nr. 5, 5.
3. Tocqueville, *Democracy in America*, ed. P. Bradley, New York, 1945, 2 vols., I, 263.
4. W. B. Yeats, *Autobiography*, New York, 1953, 139–40.
5. William James, *The Principles of Psychology*, New York, 1904, 2 vols., II, 370–71.
6. *Ibid.*, 371.
7. John St. John, ed., 'The Station Master' in *Britain's Railways Today*, London, 1954, 164.
8. Leslie A. Fiedler, 'On Becoming a Dirty Writer,' *The New Leader*, December 16, 1957.
9. Rebecca West, *The Court and the Castle*, New Haven, 1957, 68–71, 223, 304–305.
10. The reference is to the Metropolitan Opera production of the winter of 1957.

Chapter IV   Education Without Instruction

1. William H. Kilpatrick, 'How Should Teachers Be Educated?,' *The Educational Forum*, March, 1956, 287–91.
2. Edward L. Bernays, 'Public Relations for Higher Education,' An Address to the American College Public Relations Association, Omaha, June 24, 1957, 5 and ff.
3. W. H. Kilpatrick, *loc. cit.*

4. W. H. Kilpatrick, *op. cit.*, 287–88.

5. 'Contact: a Focus for Guidance,' *The Dalton Bulletin* (New York), May, 1957, 3–8.

6. *Ibid.*

7. *Jim Farley's Story: The Roosevelt Years*, New York, 1948, 2.

8. *New York Times*, March 15, 1947.

9. See *The Saturday Evening Post*, March 29, 1958, 10, and *Time*, March 31, 1958, 44.

Chapter V Instruction Without Authority

1. Report of the Dean of the School of Law, Columbia University, 1955, 5.

2. Alex Atkinson, 'How I Done My Research,' *Punch*, October 12, 1955, 416.

3. Dean's Report, Harvard Law School, 1954–1955, 12–13.

4. *New York Times*, March 8, 1958.

5. *The Economist*, March 1, 1958, 734.

6. 'Boy Who Couldn't Graduate Becomes $20,000-a-Year Sales Executive at 18,' *New York Times*, June 8, 1958.

7. *New York Times*, September 2, 1957.

8. *E.T.S. Developments*, September, 1957, 1.

9. *Examiner's Manual*, Cooperative School and College Ability Tests, Second Supplement, 1956, 3.

10. Sir Alfred Zimmern, Fourth Honors Day Address, Brooklyn College, October 15, 1947.

Chapter VI The Case Against Intellect

1. 'Letters on the French Coup d'Etat,' III, in *Literary Studies* (Everyman), I, 295, 297, 299, 301, 302.

2. *Ibid.*, 307.

3. *Democracy in America*, ed. P. Bradley, New York, 1945, vol. I, 264.

4. Quoted by G.D.H. Cole in 'Karl Marx,' *Encyclopedia Britannica*, 14th ed., 1928, XIV, 995.

5. *New York Times*, February 20, 1955.

6. *On The Rocks* (Constable), London, 1934, 183.

7. *The Hungarian Revolution*, ed. M. J. Lasky, New York, 1957, 35.

8. *The Broken Mirror*, ed. Pawel Mayewski, New York, 1958.

9. *Ibid.*, 160.

10. *Ibid.*, 161–62.
11. Quoted by George Gamow in *One Two Three . . . Infinity*, New York, 1947, 24.
12. *The Natural History of Intellect* (lectures of 1850, 1870–71), in *Complete Works*, ed. J. E. Cabot, Boston, 1893, XII, 7.

Chapter VII   The Folklore of Philanthropy

1. The incident happened at Aix. See C. E. DuBoulay (Bulaeus), *Historia Universitatis Parisiensis*, Paris, 6 vols., 1665–73, I, 101.
2. Association for the Advancement of Musicians, Weston, Mass., November 1, 1958.
3. *New York Times*, September 23, 1958.
4. *New York Times*, August 9, 1958.

Chapter VIII   Philanthropic Businessmen and Bureaucrats

1. The College Scholarship Service, 'an activity of the College Entrance Examination Board . . . operated for the Board by the Educational Testing Service.'
2. *Report, Royal Commission on National Development in the Arts, Letters and Sciences, 1949–1951*, Ottawa, 1951. Royal Commission Studies, *Essays . . . on National Development in the Arts, Letters, and Sciences.* See also the outcome in the legislation first proposed in February, 1957 (*New York Times*, February 10, 1957).
3. *New York Times*, June 13, 1957.

Chapter IX   The Language of Learning and of Pedantry

1. *12 Americans*, ed. Dorothy C. Miller, The Museum of Modern Art (Distributed by Simon and Schuster), New York, 1956, 6.
2. *Ibid.*, 36.
3. *Ibid.*, 72.
4. *New York Times*, July 18, 1957.
5. E.g., the critics discussing poetry in *The American Scholar*, 1942, 60.
6. John Crowe Ransom, 'Shakespeare at Sonnets,' *The World's Body*, New York, 1938, 301–302.
7. *New York Times*, July 16, 1958.
8. *New York Times*, September 22–October 9, 1956.

9. *New York Times*, July 18, 1957.

10. *Goethe's Faust Part 1*, ed. by R-M.S. Heffner, Helmut Rehder, and W. F. Twaddell, Boston, 1954.

11. C. C. Fries, *The Teaching of the English Language*, New York, 1927, 33.

12. Thomas Pyles, 'Linguistics and Pedagogy,' *College English*, April, 1949, 395.

13. 'Basic Concepts Evolved by Linguists,' in *English Language Arts*, New York, 1952, 283.

14. Pascal, *Pensées sur l'Esprit et sur le Style, article 1er*.

15. *Ibid*.

16. *Ibid*.

17. A. J. Nock, *Jefferson*, Washington, D.C., 1926, 333–34.

Chapter X   The Summing Up

1. 'A Siding at a Railway Station' in *Short Studies on Great Subjects*, New York, 1883, IV, 368–69.

2. *A Grammar of Assent*, New York, 1870, Chapter 8, 273–74.

3. 'Wolcott Gibbs,' *The New Yorker*, August 30, 1958, 83.

4. M. F. K. Fisher, *The Art of Eating*, Cleveland and New York, 1954, 353.

5. *The International Musician*, September, 1958, 10.

6. John P. Frank, *Mr. Justice Black*, New York, 1949, 133–34.

Jacques Barzun

About the Author

Born in France in 1907, Jacques Barzun came to the United States in 1920. After graduating from Columbia College, he joined the faculty of the university, becoming Seth Low Professor of History and, for a decade, Dean of Faculties and Provost. The author of some thirty books, he received the Gold Medal for Criticism from the American Academy of Arts and Letters, of which he was twice president.

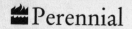 Perennial Quill

Books by Jacques Barzun:

FROM DAWN TO DECADENCE
1500 to the Present: 500 Years of Western Cultural Life
ISBN 0-06-092883-2 (paperback) • ISBN 0-694-52548-0 (audio)

A National Book Award finalist and *New York Times* bestseller, this is Barzun's account of what Western man has wrought from the Renaissance and Reformation down to the present in the double light of its own time and our modern concerns.

"Will go down in history as one of the great one-man shows of Western letters, a triumph of maverick erudition." —*Newsweek*

A JACQUES BARZUN READER: *Selections from His Works*
ISBN 0-06-621019-4 (hardcover) • ISBN 0-06-093542-1 (paperback)

"A sampler of Barzun's writings . . . demonstrating again the depth and breadth of his learning, the originality of his thinking, and his commitment to speak to the general reader in engaging, intelligent prose. . . . Each essay yields unexpected insights, and the volume as a whole makes clear why Barzun is probably our best-known public intellectual. Challenging, satisfying, elegant."—*Kirkus Reviews*

SIMPLE & DIRECT: *A Rhetoric for Writers*
ISBN 0-06-093723-8 (paperback)

Jacques Barzun distills from a lifetime of writing and teaching his thoughts about the basic choices every writer makes in his craft.

"The student of the craft of writing needs the company of others who know the way. Barzun in his instruction and by the example of his own prose is an excellent choice of travelling companion." —*Washington Post*

THE HOUSE OF INTELLECT
ISBN 0-06-010230-6 (Perennial Classics paperback)

Jacques Barzun takes on the whole intellectual (or pseudo-intellectual) world, attacking it for its betrayal of intellect in such areas as public administration, communications, conversation, home life, education, business, and scholarship.

"A stimulating thinker. . . . In 18th century terms he is an enlightened philosopher; in the superlative of our age, a 'genius'." —*The Guardian* (London)